The College History Series

Albany State University

A Centennial History: 1903–2003

The College History Series

ALBANY STATE UNIVERSITY

A CENTENNIAL HISTORY: 1903–2003

TITUS BROWN, PH.D.

ARCADIA
PUBLISHING

ISBN 978-0-7385-1493-2

Published by Arcadia Publishing
Charleston, South Carolina

Printed in the United States of America

Library of Congress Catalog Card Number: Applied for

For all general information contact Arcadia Publishing at:
Telephone 843-853-2070
Fax 843-853-0044
E-mail sales@arcadiapublishing.com
For customer service and orders:
Toll-Free 1-888-313-2665

Visit us on the Internet at www.arcadiapublishing.com

CONTENTS

FOREWORD

When creating a visual chronology of the journey of an institution from its humble beginnings to its beautiful present, one must carefully scrutinize and select the photographs and other important documents that are to be included. It took significantly more effort to describe pictorially the path that Albany State took to become what she is today because three floods took away, with rushing waters, documentation of many of the precious and momentous activities and events that cannot be recaptured.

Quick responses from former administrators provided a safe haven for a good many of Albany State's original documentation. In addition, it was fortunate that some of Albany's wonderful citizens, just passing by, stopped and pulled from the wreckage what they could, dried the documents carefully and returned them to Albany State for safekeeping. Unfortunately, not all was retrieved and thus, could not be examined for inclusion in this book. From the remaining materials, however, Dr. Titus Brown, Albany State University alumnus and historian at Florida Agricultural and Mechanical University (Florida A&M), worked many months to locate more than 200 authentic photographs of the history of our beloved school for this book, *Albany State University: A Centennial History 1903–2003*.

In this unique tribute, Dr. Brown follows Albany State University's progress, focusing on some of the institution's major contributions to the academic success of its students year after year. Dr. Brown wrote to Josephine Holley Jefferson, daughter of Albany State University's founder Dr. Joseph Winthrop Holley, for confirmation of events and for pictures. He spent countless hours conducting research at Albany State University's Pendergrast Memorial Library, following leads, and gathering information from the scores of people he interviewed. The result of Titus Brown's work and dedication is this amazing pictorial history of Albany State University.

Of course, the magnitude of the numbers of photographs had to be difficult to get through and identifying individuals in each photograph created a challenge. And, as you can imagine, photography as it existed 100 years ago compared to recent times made it difficult to document, with clarity, some of the most memorable occasions.

Nevertheless, *Albany State University: A Centennial History: 1903–2003* remains a stunning portrayal of the university's struggle from its roots as a Bible and Manual Training School, to a normal school, to a college, and from there to a university.

From this historical perspective, we find students and faculty serving our institution in many ways. This volume allows readers to recall the good old days and to see the transition of older buildings to the new and renovated structures.

When we see what Dr. Holley achieved with little, we are encouraged to believe that success does not take more than what we have within us. *Albany State University: A Centennial History 1903–2003* validates the foundation Joseph Winthrop Holley laid before us in his reminder, "You can't build a chimney from the top."

Most of all, this book provides evidence of the strong bend toward service and stewardship possessed by faculty, staff, and students many years ago. This same spirit continues today in those who continue to give back to the institution that inspired their development.

The very idea of Albany State University's 100 years of work in southwest Georgia is awesome to contemplate. Through Dr. Titus Brown's dedicated and inspiring work, however, we need not close our eyes to remember the development of Albany State University. We can see it for ourselves. I invite you to experience the enduring legacy of excellence. Enjoy.

—Dr. Portia Holmes Shields

ACKNOWLEDGMENTS

I wish to thank the Albany State University family, especially *The Ram* and *The Student's Voice* staffs throughout the years. I also wish to thank Dr. Portia Holmes Shields, president of Albany State University; Dr. Mollie Brown, interim vice president for Academic Affairs; the Office of Public Information Staff: Cynthia C. Hoke, Marsha Aaron, and Reginald Christian; Desilver Cohen; Clifford Porter, director of the University Foundation; Kenneth Dyer, vice president for Fiscal Affairs; and Josephine Holley-Jefferson, daughter of founder Joseph W. Holley. I am indebted to Mrs. Betty New of the Office of Alumni Affairs; Prince Brown, the former interim vice president for Institutional Advancement; and Reginald Hunter, the former national alumni president. In addition I express deep appreciation for the work completed by Jonathan Allain, graphic specialist with Tallahassee Camera, and Margaret Barlow, who made valuable comments on the text.

No one person can do it alone. I would therefore like to especially thank Mrs. Betty Frazier, instructor in Library Science and acquisition librarian at Albany State University for her assistance. Finally I wish to convey my gratitude to Katie White of Arcadia Publishing.

—Dr. Titus Brown

INTRODUCTION

Albany State University, located in southwest Georgia, is a four-year unit of the University System of Georgia serving 3,403 students. Its five academic schools offer undergraduate and graduate degree programs in more than 40 areas of study.

Founded in the fall of 1903 as the Albany Bible and Manual Training Institution by Joseph Winthrop Holley, the institution provided religious and industrial education for African Americans in southwest Georgia. Holley was inspired first by the example of the renowned educator Dr. Booker T. Washington. Second, and perhaps more influential, was the 1903 publication by Dr. W.E.B. DuBois, *The Souls of Black Folk*, which was directly responsible for Holley's decision to come to Albany, Georgia, to open his school. In 1917, the institution became a state-supported, two-year college with a board of trustees. Known at that time as Georgia Normal and Agricultural College, the school offered programs in agriculture, industrial education, and teacher training. In 1932 the college became a part of the University System of Georgia, under the jurisdiction of the Board of Regents, and in 1943, it became a four-year, teacher-training institution and assumed the name Albany State College. Also at this time, Dr. Holley retired and Dr. Aaron Brown became president. Programs were expanded to offer degrees in three additional areas: secretarial science, elementary education, and home economics. Continuing program expansions added degree offerings in the arts and sciences with majors in humanities and social sciences, followed by programs in science, health and physical education, business, music, mathematics, natural sciences, and nursing.

Albany State College experienced tremendous growth from 1943 to 1996, when the name was changed once again to Albany State University. This growth was initiated and nurtured under the leadership of five dynamic presidents, beginning with Dr. Brown, who served until 1954; Dr. William H. Dennis (1954–1965); Dr. Thomas Miller Jenkins (1965–1969); Dr. Charles L. Hayes (1969–1980); and Dr. Billy C. Black (1980–1996). During the course of these four decades, the university expanded its baccalaureate program and degree offerings as well as introducing several master's degrees. In addition to new initiatives in education, natural sciences, health sciences, and business, the university enhanced its physical plant with the addition of several new buildings and ongoing grounds beautification.

Dr. Portia Holmes Shields, the university's current president, took office in 1996. Following the devastating floods of 1994 and 1998, Dr. Shields has overseen a major campus renovation program, complete with new buildings equipped with state-of-the-art technology. Under Dr. Shields's outstanding leadership, the university's accreditation has been reaffirmed by the Southern Association of Colleges and Schools (SACS) as well as by the National Council for the Accreditation of Teacher Education (NCATE). As the university celebrates its centennial in 2003, every one of its colleges is regionally or nationally accredited.

Albany State University continues to play a major role in educating Georgia's citizens, especially in southwestern Georgia. Having entered the 21st century, the university holds true to the same philosophy upon which it was founded in the first years of the 20th century, a philosophy that develops and enhances shared values. Timeless and time-honored, these values of honesty, dedication, loyalty, courtesy, and helpfulness underlie and support the university's basic operating principles of integrity, accessibility, the effective use of diversity, and a commitment to excellence.

One

Dr. Joseph Winthrop Holley 1903–1943

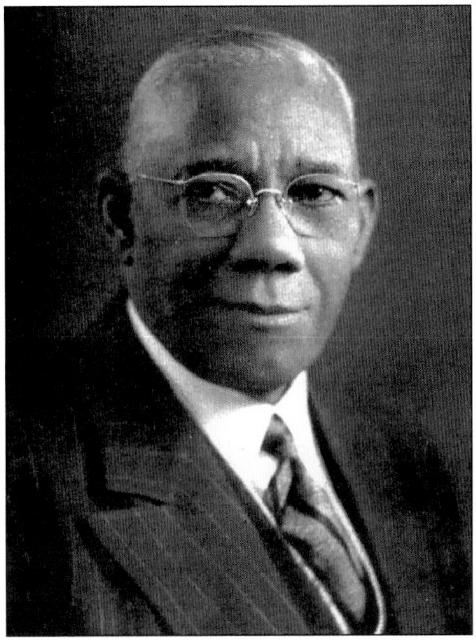

Albany State University, located on the east side of the Flint River, has a "Past to Cherish and a Future to Fulfill." The past is exemplified by the perseverance and endurance of Dr. Joseph W. Holley, a graduate of Lincoln University, and Albany State's founder and President-Emeritus. In 1903, with the financial support of the Hazard family of Rhode Island and local philanthropists, Dr. Holley purchased 100 acres east of the Flint River and organized the Albany Bible and Manual Training Institution. With the services of Prof. H.A. Green, Dr. Holley began the first classes in the Union Baptist Church, providing religious and manual training for the African-American youth of southwest Georgia. Despite severe criticism and economic deprivation, he lived to see the institution undergo several tides of improvement. In 1910, the name of the school was changed to Georgia Normal and Agricultural College. In 1911, the first brick building on the campus was erected under Holley's direction and with the support of R.G. Hazard. Miss Caroline Hazard donated the second building, an administration building dedicated in 1917 and named for its benefactor. In 1917 the school was launched on its second epoch of growth and development when Dr. Holley and H.M. McIntosh, a friend and advisor, decided to ask the state of Georgia to "Take a hand in the education of the Negro." At that time, the name of the institution was officially changed to the Georgia Normal and Agricultural College. The institution offered work on the junior college level in teacher education, agriculture, and home economics. Dr. Holley retired in 1943 after serving for almost 40 years as the school's president. Through his dedication and vision for the future, a new dimension in education began in the state of Georgia.

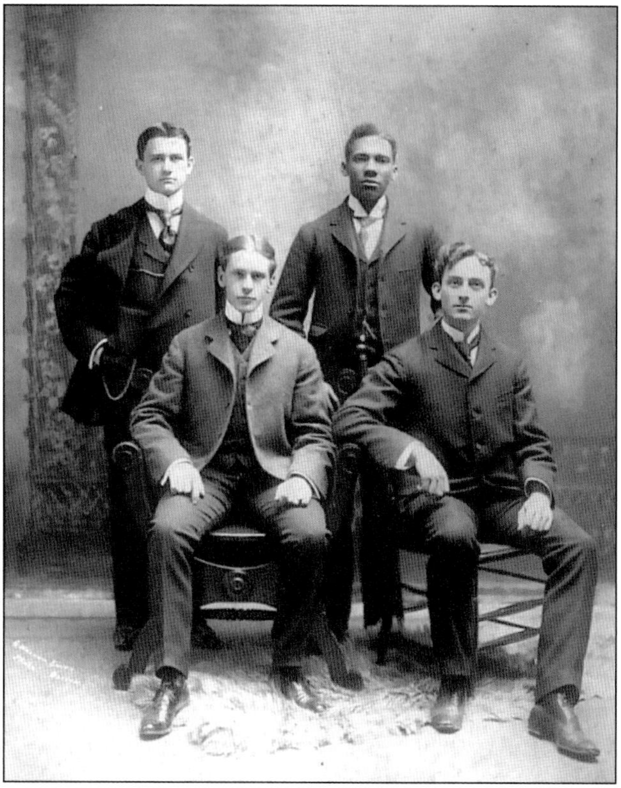

This is the young J.W. Holley as a team member of the Philo-Forum Debaters. Seated from left to right are Z.S. Eldredge and C.L. Kimball. Standing from left to right are W.L. Chamberlain and Holley. Below are members of the Phillips Academy class of 1900. Holley, the only African American in his class, is pictured fourth from the left in the second row from the rear.

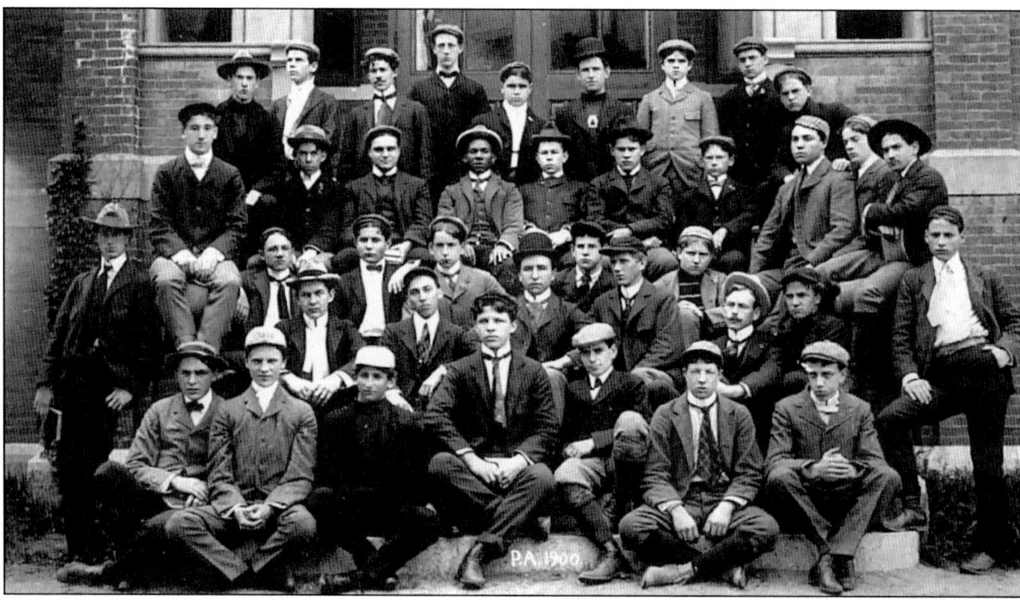

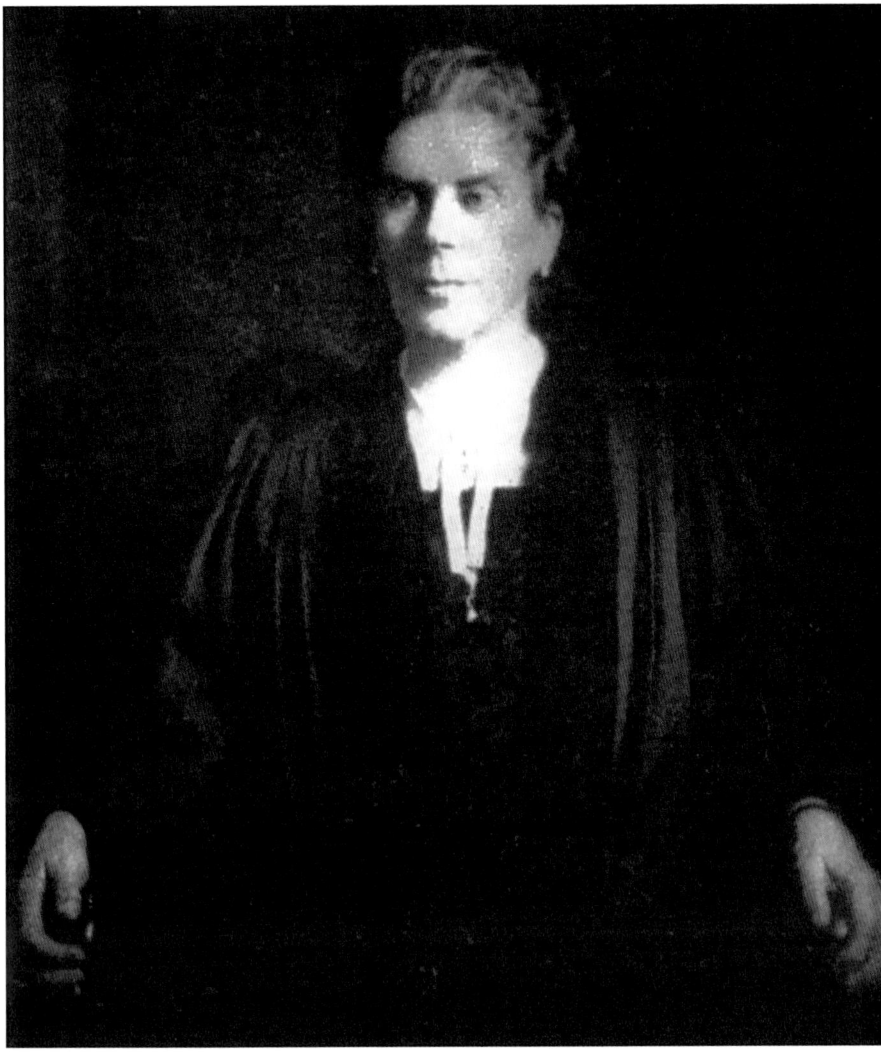

The outstanding benefactor of Albany State College was Miss Caroline Hazard. Miss Hazard was responsible for most of the buildings on the campus, which bear the names of her relatives and even the place of her birth, including Hazard Training School, Gibson Hall, Caroline Hall, Hazard Library, and Peace Hall. Born at Peace Dale, Rhode Island, June 10, 1856, she was the daughter of Rowland and Margaret Anna Rood Hazard. She was educated by her governess, private tutors, and at the Mary A. Shaw's School in Providence. Miss Hazard also had the opportunity to study abroad and she was awarded a number of honorary degrees from outstanding educational institutions. In spite of the fact that Miss Hazard was a member of the outstanding New England Hazard family she was a distinguished person in her own right. Her most significant contribution was made as president of Wellesley College in Massachusetts. She became president in 1889 and served to 1910, during which time a number of advances were made in the education of women in this country. Miss Hazard was an author of note. Among her publications were the following: *From College Gates* (collection of her addresses at Wellesley College, published in 1925); *Some Ideals in the Education of Women*; *A Scallop Shell of Quiet*; *A Brief Pilgrimage in the Holy Land*; *The College Year*; *Thomas Hazard, Son of Robert*; *Song in the Sun*; *The Yosemite and Other Verse*; *Direct Narraganset Ballad and Others*. Miss Hazard died at the age of 88 on March 19, 1945 in Santa Barbara, California. Albany State College can never forget Miss Caroline Hazard.

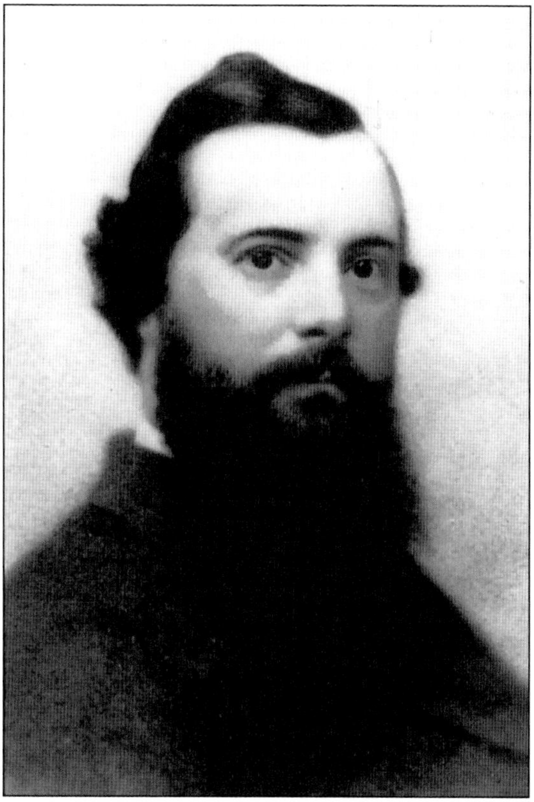

Trustee Rowland G. Hazard was born in Peace Dale, Rhode Island. He was a member of the third consecutive generation of Hazards to carry on the manufacture of woolen goods at Peacedale. He was a symbol of a family long known in New England educational and business circles. He and his father established the Hazard Professorship of Physics at Brown University. Hazard was responsible for the education of the founder of the Albany State College, Dr. J.W. Holley, after Holley impressed Mr. Hazard as a boy working in the Hazard home.

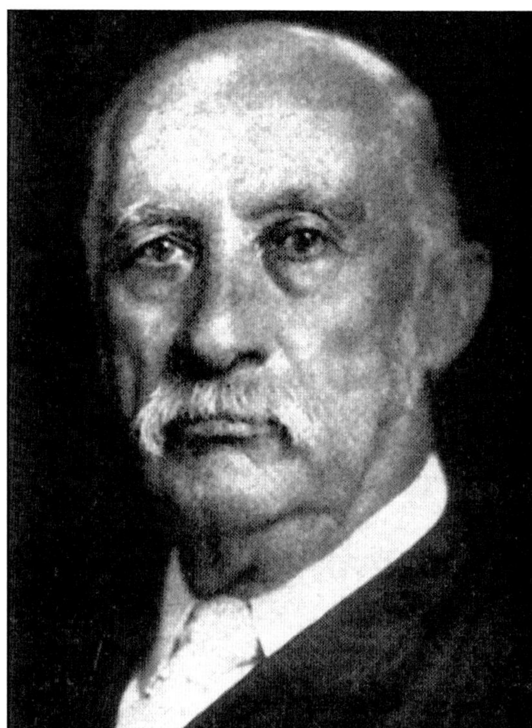

Trustee Capt. John A. Davis was born in Crawfordville, Georgia, June 15, 1832. His father, Rev. Jonathan Davis, was a prominent Baptist preacher, one of the original subscribers of the fund for the establishment of what is now Mercer University. Mr. Davis graduated from Mercer College, then at Penfield, Georgia, and read law. He was admitted to the bar before he was 19 years old. After graduation, Mr. Davis came to Albany and formed a partnership with Judge David A. Vason. He organized the first National Bank of Albany in 1886 and became its president and was a member of the Albany Baptist Church. In 1905 Captain Davis developed heart trouble that in a few days resulted in his death.

Trustee Joseph S. Davis was born in Albany in 1853. After attending local schools he spent three and a half years at the University of Georgia. He became associated with Mr. H.M. McIntosh in the editorship of the *Albany News and Advertiser*, remaining with that paper from 1886 to 1891. He then went with the First National Bank, assuming the office of cashier, a position he held for many years. He was principal organizer and president of the Albany Trust Company. Mr. Davis was a councilman for many years and mayor of Albany in 1902 and 1903. For eight years he was school commissioner for Dougherty County and first devised the plan—now universal in Georgia—of employing teachers by contract. He originated and ably supported many of our notable municipal improvements and reforms. In 1913 Mr. Davis was appointed by President Woodrow Wilson as United States Marshall for the 7th District of Georgia. Mr. Davis was the father of Mr. John A. Davis, who is now managing editor of the *Albany Herald*. He was the second president of the board of trustees of this institution from 1904 to his death on October 10, 1934.

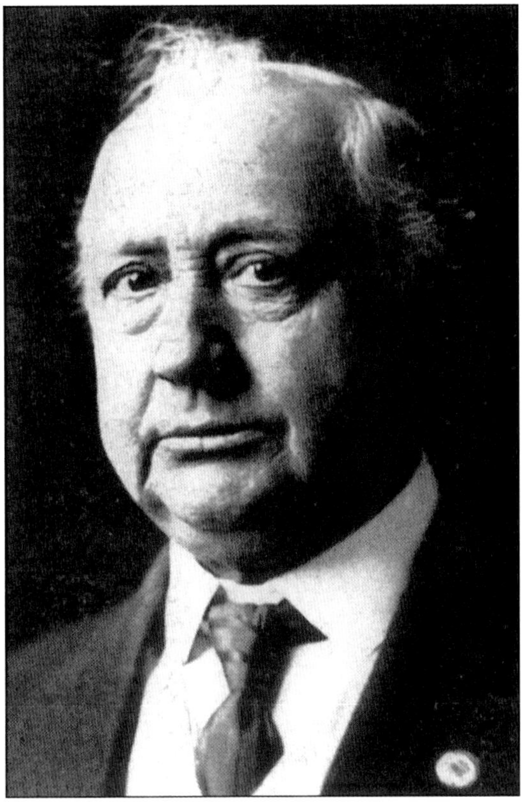

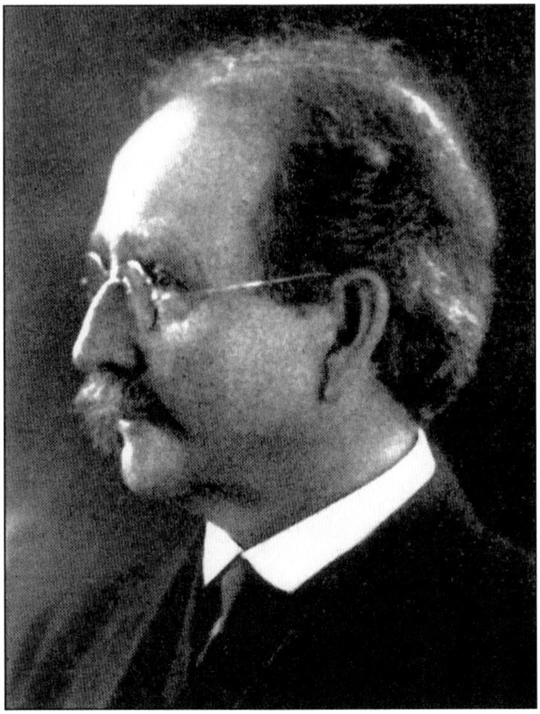

Trustee Henry M. McIntosh, former editor of the *Albany Herald*, was born in Thomas County at the Old Scotch Settlement of Glasgow, January 19, 1852. Mr. McIntosh was once a member of the legislature from Dougherty County. He also served Albany as mayor for one term. For many years he was chairman of the Democratic executive committee of the second Congressional District. He began his journalistic career in 1872, coming to Albany five years later. Through the columns of his paper he exerted much influence over progress, peace, and good order in his city and section. Mr. McIntosh died October 25, 1925. He was third president of the board of trustees of this institution.

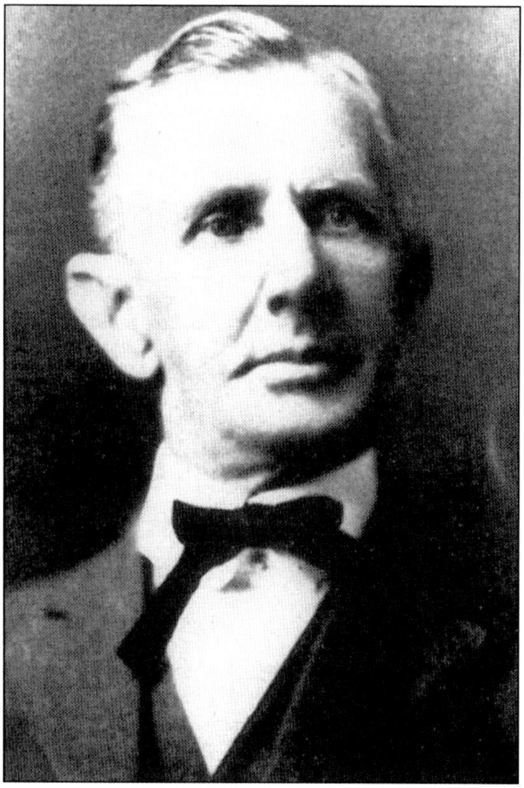

Trustee Augustus W. Muse, born at Lafayette, Alabama in 1849, came to Albany in 1870. Although he engaged in mercantile enterprises for a time, 30 years of his life were spent in the cotton warehouse business. The firm carried the name of A.W. Muse and Company, whose place of business still stands on the northwest corner of Broad and Front Streets, the site where Albany's first building was erected in 1836. Mr. Muse was vice-president of the Exchange Bank and of the Albany National Bank and was interested in various other Albany enterprises. Mr. Muse was superintendent of the Methodist Sunday School for 46 years and acted as Steward for 50 years. He was also helpful to other organizations which carried a religious emphasis, such as the YMCA, the hospital, and the like. He was a trustee of this institution from February 1904 to his death on March 10, 1922.

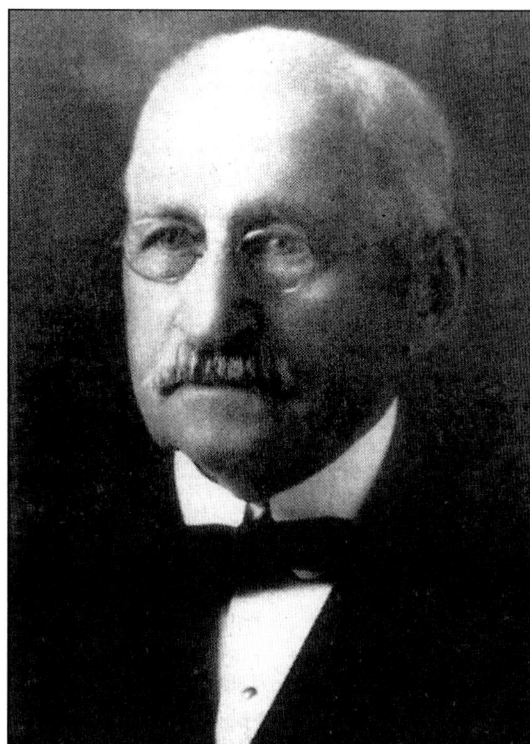

Trustee Judge Francis F. Putney came to Dougherty County in 1865 from Massachusetts. He purchased a small plantation seven miles below Albany on the Thomasville Road. Shortly after his coming he was appointed United States Commissioner, which gave him the title of Judge. He visualized the true value of real estate in southwest Georgia and quietly he began his acquisition until he became the largest taxpayer in the area. In 1908 Judge Putney and associates organized the Georgia National Bank, a strong financial institution. Its liberal management contributions went to the Phoebe Putney Memorial Hospital, amounting to over $40,000 dollars during his life. He also made substantial contributions to the YMCA and to the Albany Presbyterian Church. Judge Putney was a trustee of this institution from 1904 to his death on September 6, 1928.

Trustee Robert Hardwick Warren, son of L.P.D. and Louisa Webb Warren, was born in Albany in 1861. His education was finished at the University of Georgia. Mr. Warren always took a keen interest in educational affairs and in 1906 he was made County School Commissioner, a position he held for 10 years. Previously Mr. Warren was secretary of the Equitable Building and Loan Association. In 1905 he became secretary of the Albany Trust Company of Georgia. In 1921 he severed his connection with this business and opened a general insurance and loan business with his son, and also was superintendent of the Dougherty County schools. Mr. Warren was an ardent book lover and was a founder of the book club, from which grew the Albany Library Association, which was eventually absorbed by the Carnegie Library. These activities, combined with his loyal devotion to Chautauqua, and his long service as chairman of the Park and Tree Commission, identified him as leading factor in the cultural and civic growth of the city. He served two terms as a member of the city council. He was a trustee of this institution from February 1904 to his death on January 5, 1943.

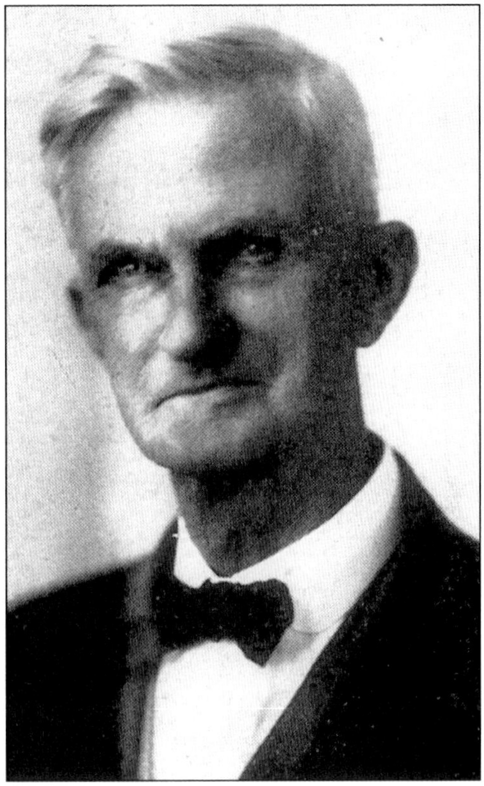

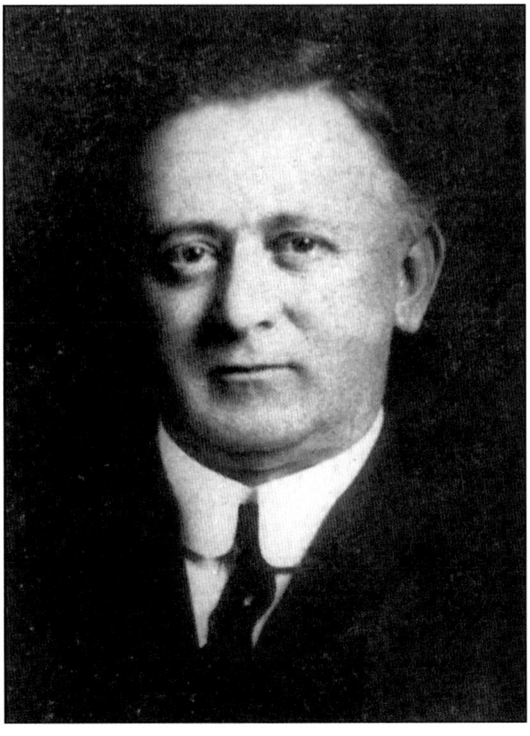

Trustee Morris Weslosky, born in 1861, contributed significant service to the civic and political advancement of Albany. Mr. Weslosky was a graduate of the University of Georgia. He was one of the organizers and Exalted Rulers of the Elks Lodge. Mr. Weslosky served as president of the Third National Bank and was elected an alderman of the city on January 7, 1907 and again on January 4, 1909. He resigned this position on April 13, 1909. Mr. Weslosky was identified with the firm of Wight and Weslosky. He also served as president of the Chamber of Commerce, originally the Business Men's League. He was the oldest of three children and the only boy in the group. One sister survives, Miss Emma Menko, who lives at 107 South Jefferson Street. Mr. Weslosky moved to New York a few years before his passing and died on May 25, 1916, at the age of 55. He served as a trustee of this institution from March 4, 1904, until he moved to New York.

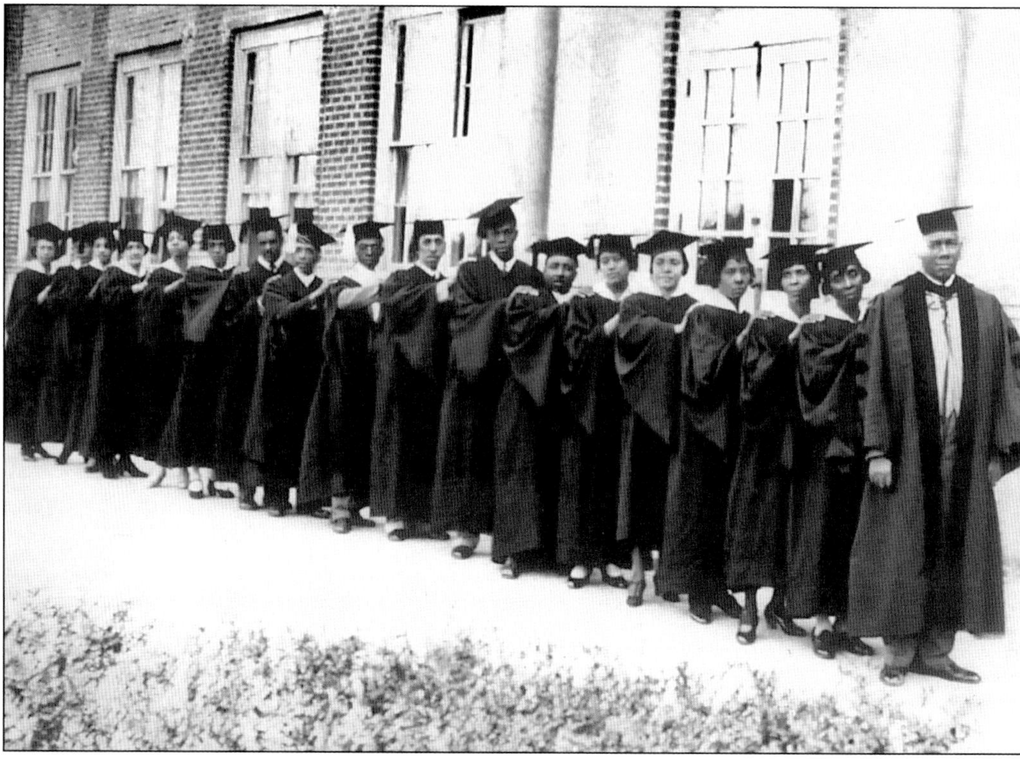

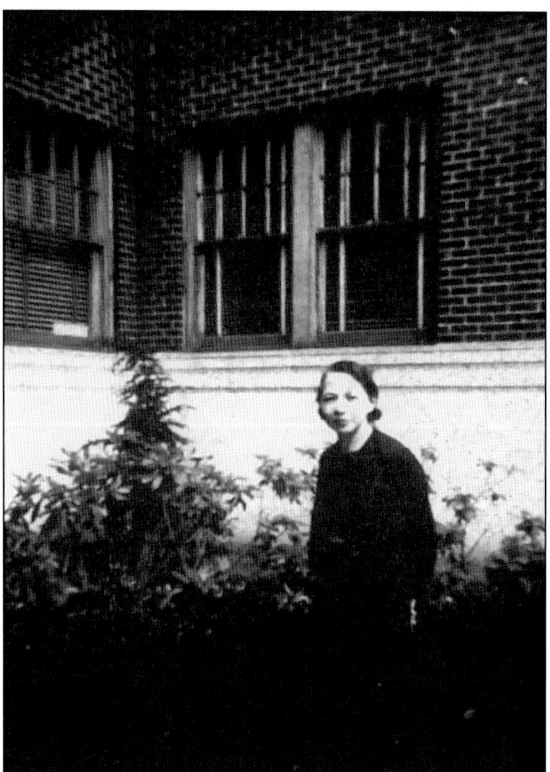

Normal school training had become a primary concern for Dr. Holley and those interested in African-American education throughout the 1920s. The success of an adequate common school system in the state depended on a steady supply of competent black teachers from Georgia Normal and Agricultural College. Students selected a major from the following programs: Junior College; Normal School; Vocational; and Music. By 1928, Georgia Normal enrolled nearly 300 students.

Ruth M. Thomas graduated as the first student of Albany Bible and Manual Training Institute in 1908. After graduation, Thomas became gainfully employed with a telephone company in Newark, New Jersey where she broke racial and gender barriers.

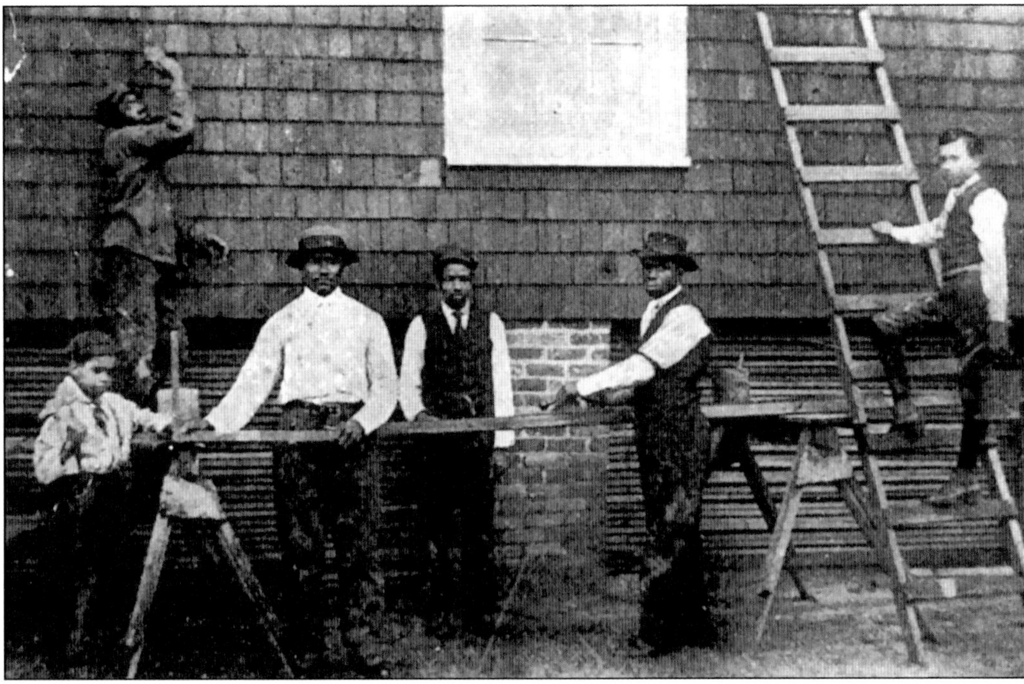

This picture shows male students working in the building trade as carpenters, plasterers, and masons.

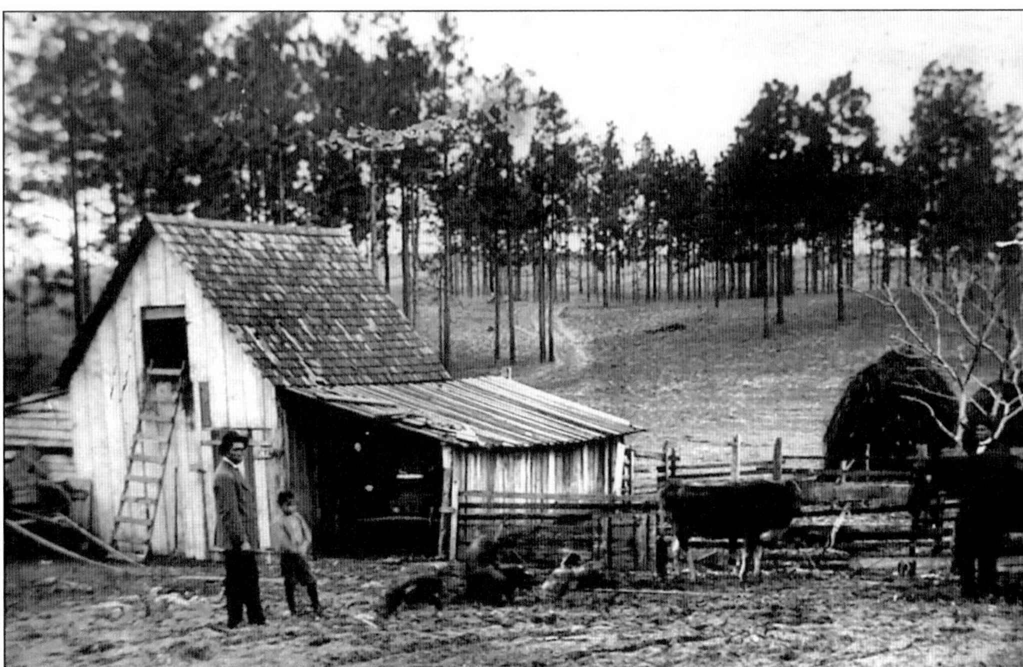

This picture shows a turn-of-the-century shed and barn on campus.

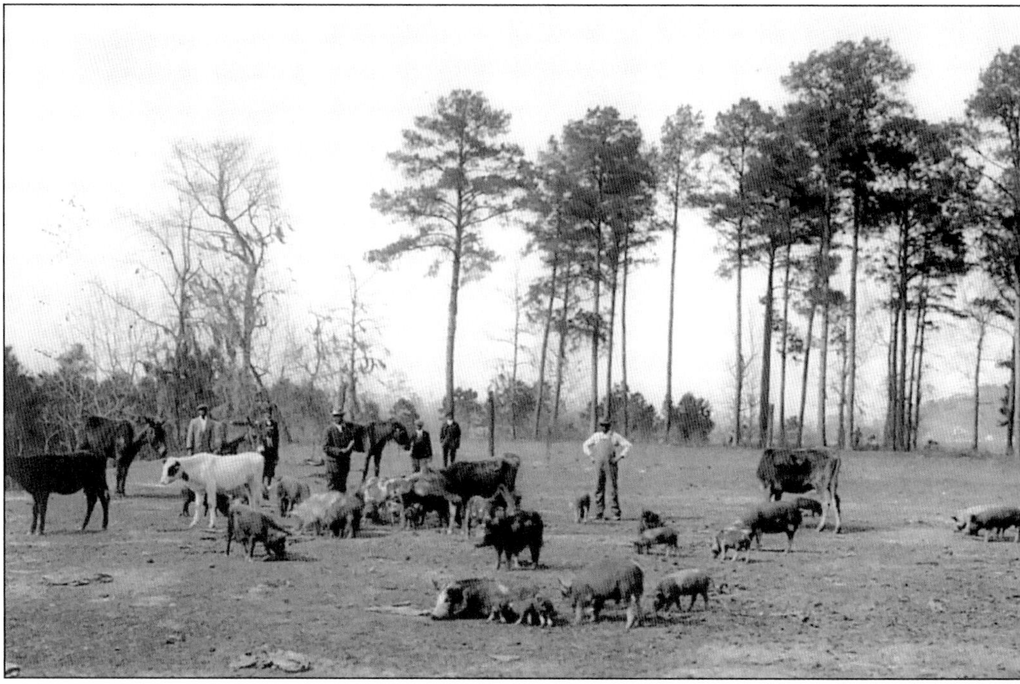

In 1920, President Holly secured a 500-acre farm. Agricultural students now could boldly experiment with crossbreeding plants and animals that would be adaptable to southwest Georgia. The following year the farm produced enough cotton, corn, peanuts, oats, wheat, watermelon, hay, and diary products to earn $14,000.

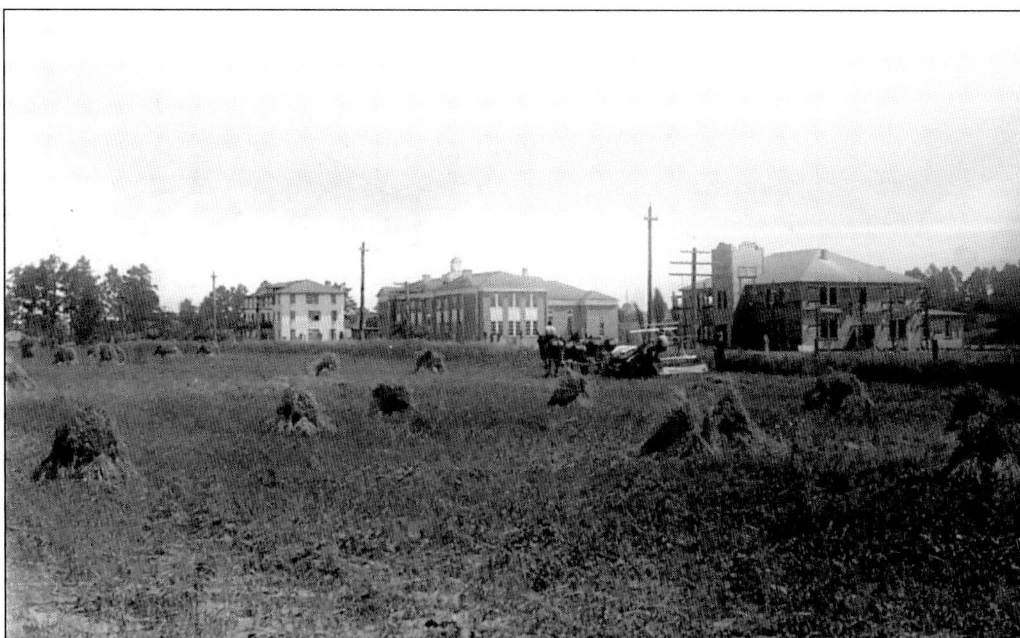

Here rows of cut hay have been left to dry in the field and to be bundled. McCormick's mule-driven reaper deposited cut grain neatly on a platform from which students raked into windrows.

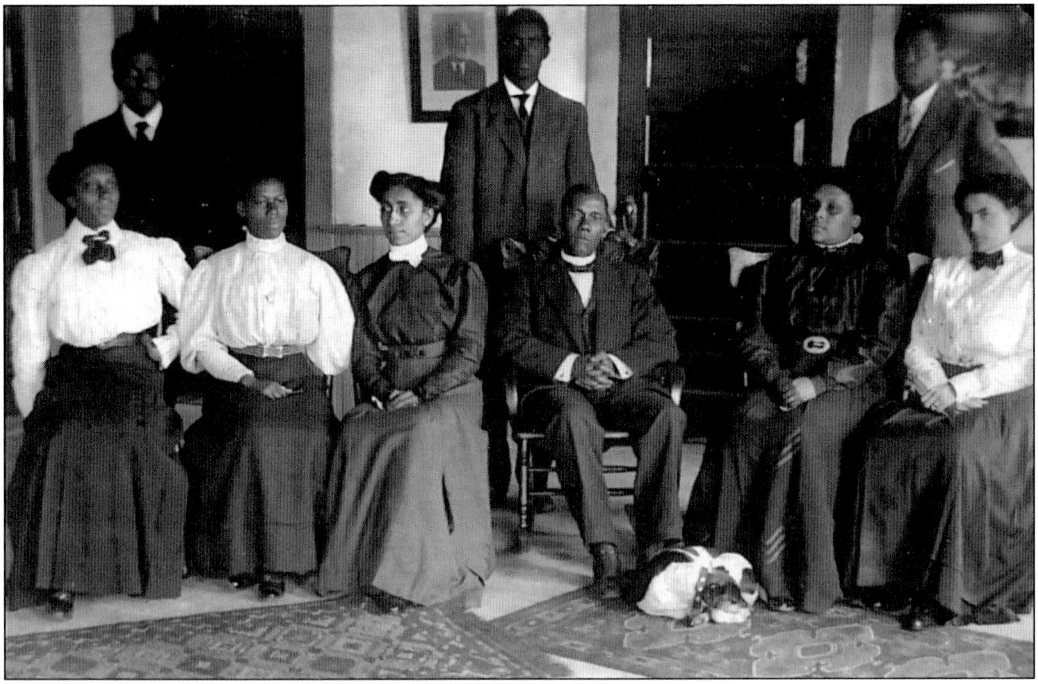

The Albany Bible and Manual Training Institute Faculty is shown here *c.* 1910. Seated from left to right are Sonia Foster, Eula Foster, Carrie Jefferson, Dr. Joseph W. Holley, Mrs. Holley, and Carolyn Whitman. Standing, from left to right, are T.T. Tilden, G.C. Robinson, and Mr. Floyd. The faculty of Georgia Normal was trained along academic rather than industrial lines.

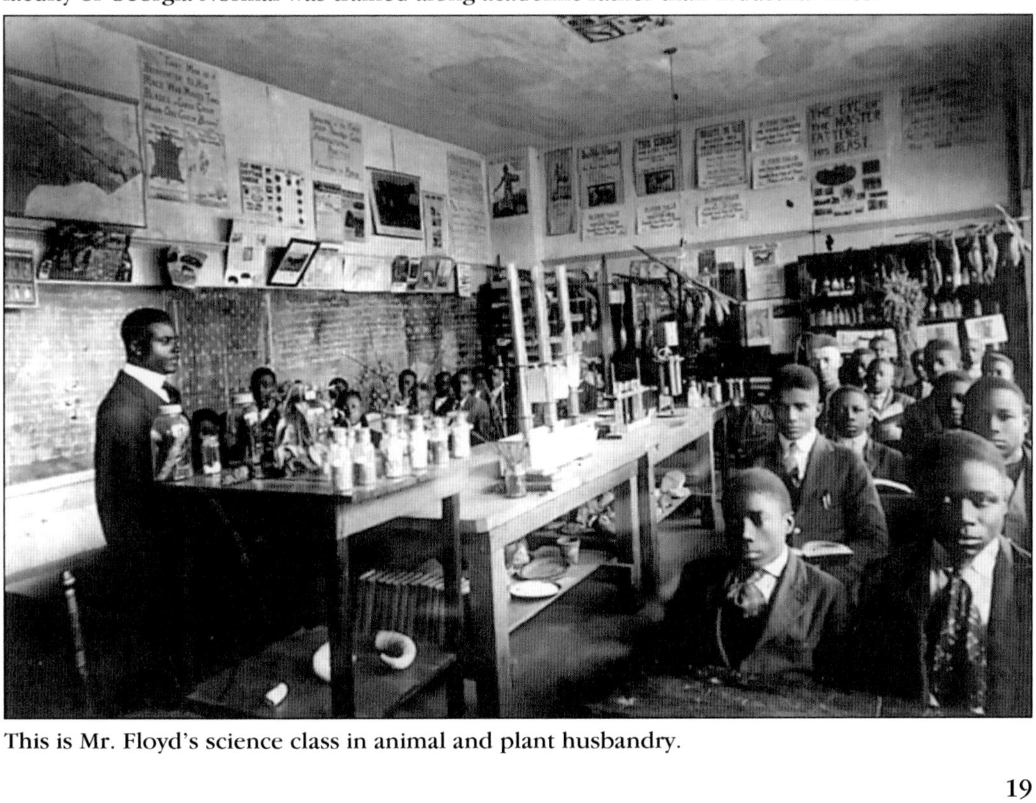

This is Mr. Floyd's science class in animal and plant husbandry.

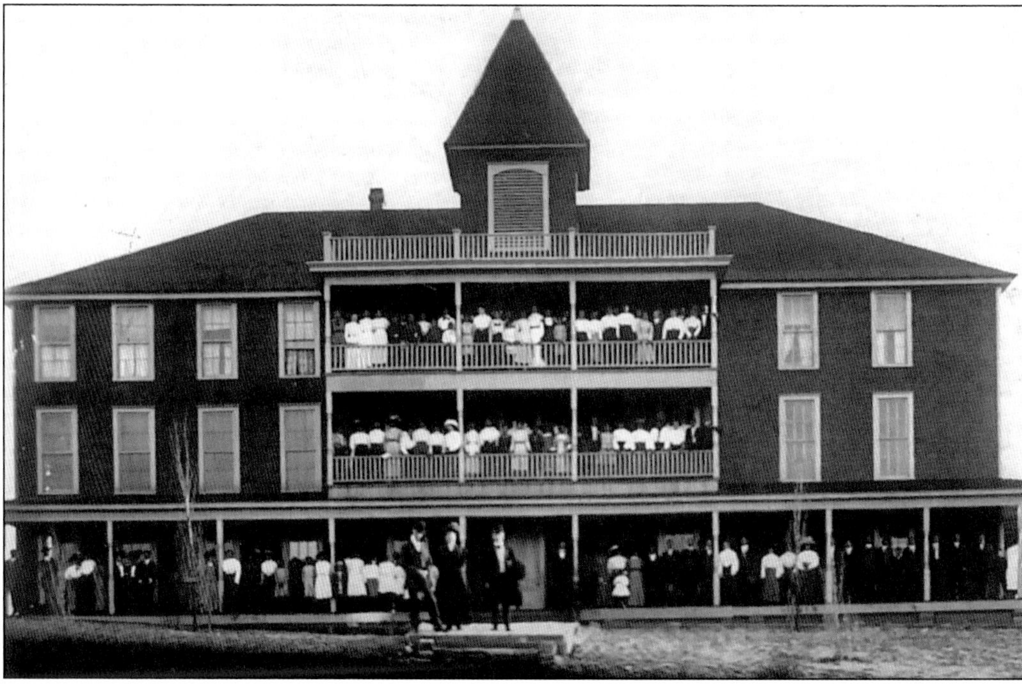

The first permanent building, begun in 1904 and named Peace Hall in honor of Miss Anna Hazard, was a three-story frame structure located on the Sand Hill. With the completion of this facility, the boarding department of the institute opened during the fall term, 1904.

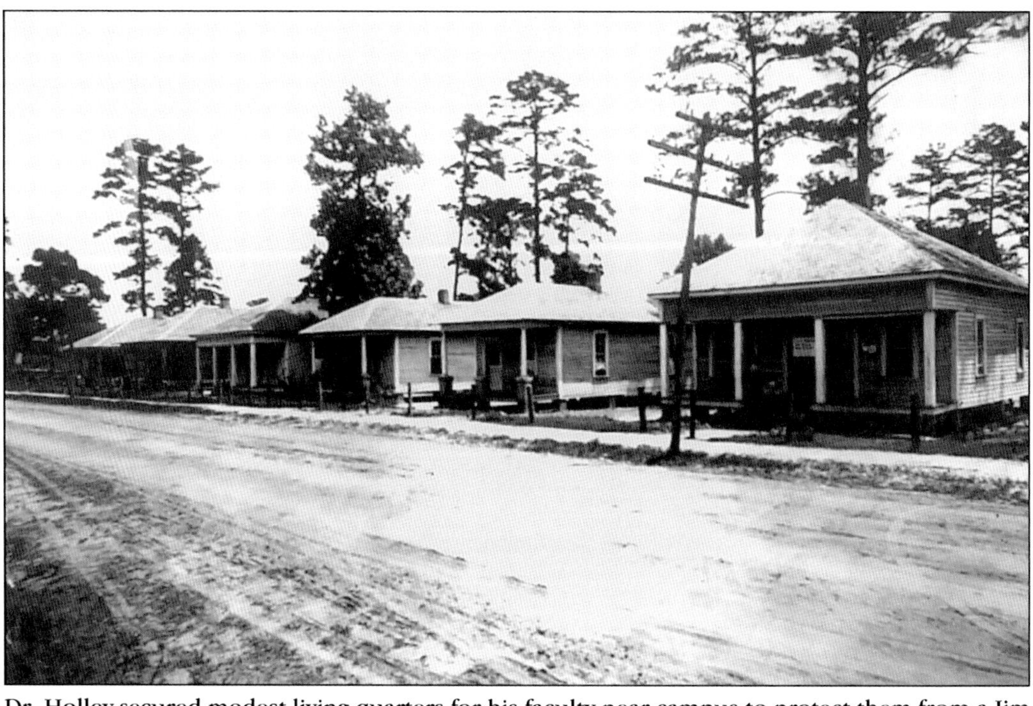

Dr. Holley secured modest living quarters for his faculty near campus to protect them from a Jim Crow society.

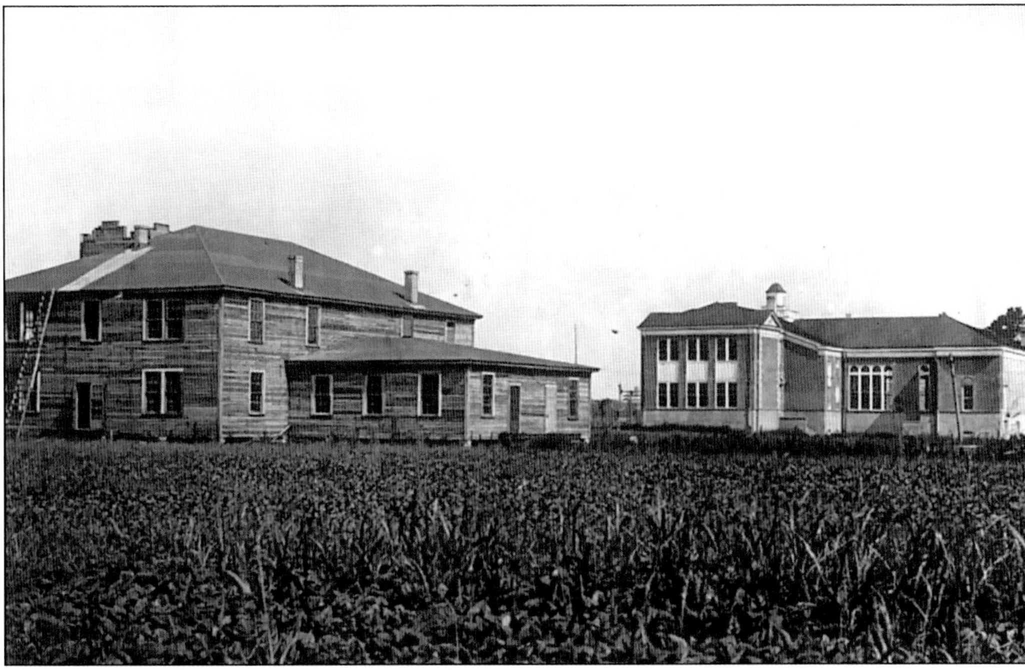

Completed in 1917, Caroline Hall was regarded as one of the best buildings in southwest Georgia. The brick building contained office space, recitation rooms, and a chapel capable of seating over 800 individuals. The new administration building took the name of the former president of Wellesley College, Miss Caroline Hazard of Peace Dale, Rhode Island.

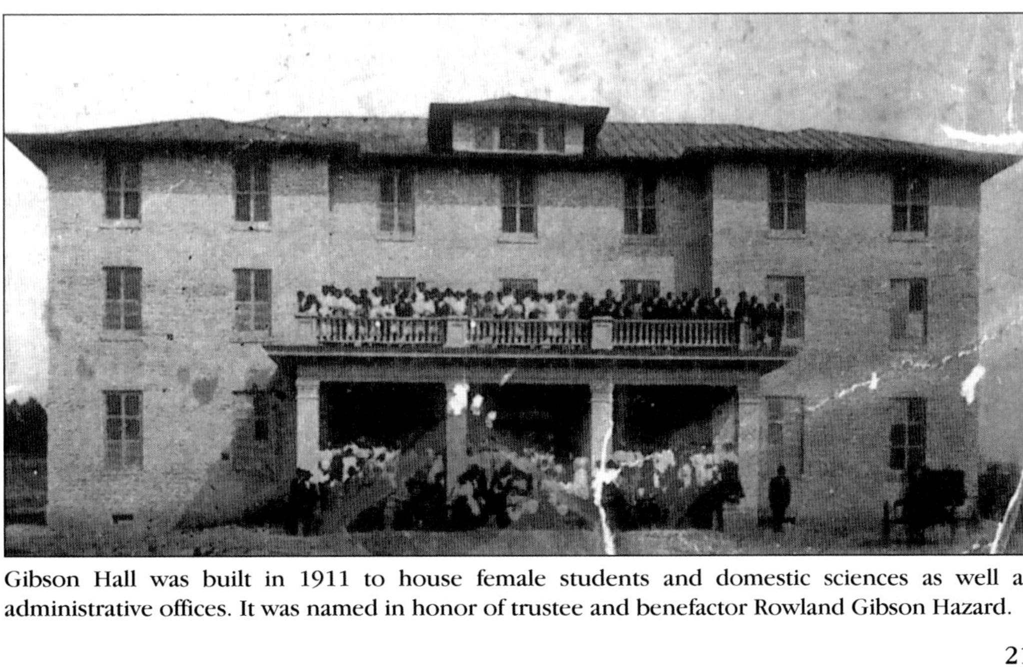

Gibson Hall was built in 1911 to house female students and domestic sciences as well as administrative offices. It was named in honor of trustee and benefactor Rowland Gibson Hazard.

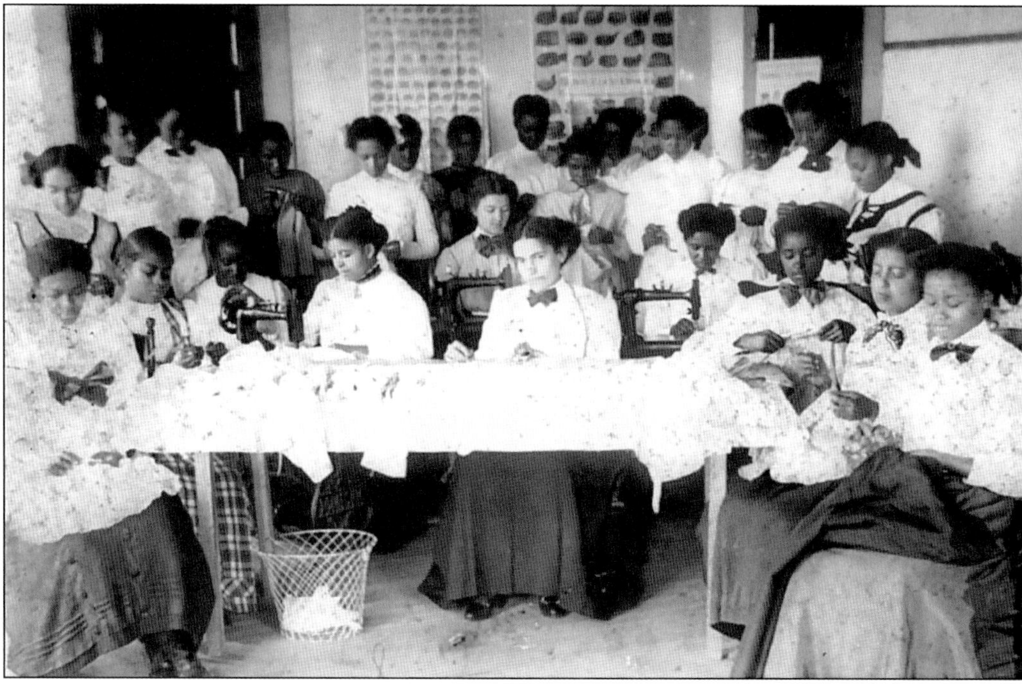

The two-year normal curriculum in home economics trained teachers for public schools with course offerings in sewing, canning, cooking, housekeeping poultry-raising, dairying, and gardening. In gardening students produced beans, potatoes, and corn. This foodstuff help offset the cost of living expenses on campus.

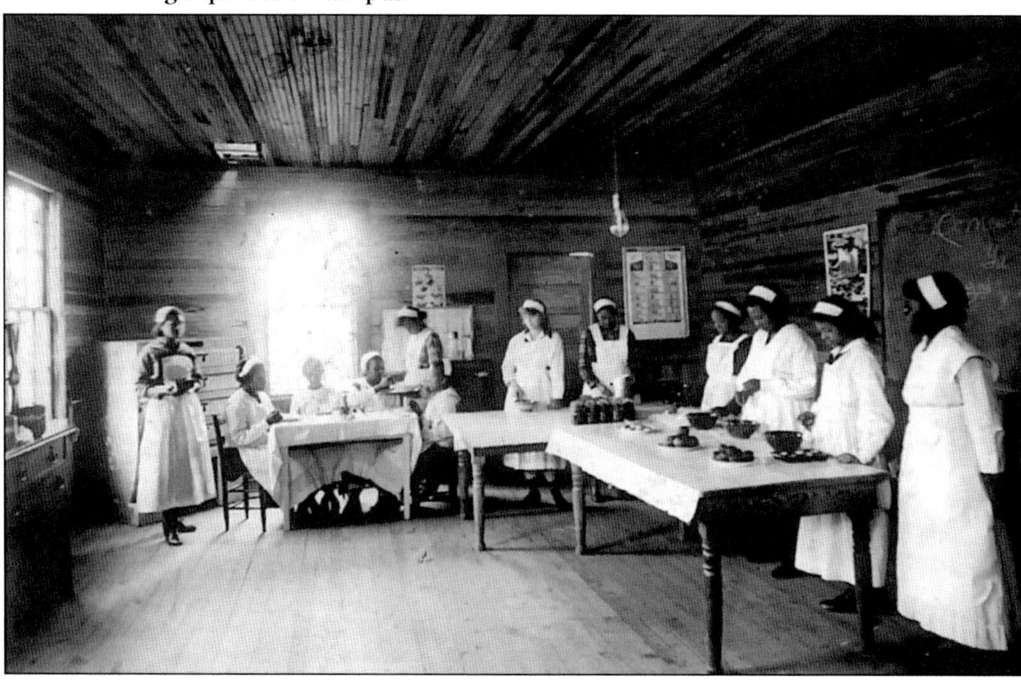

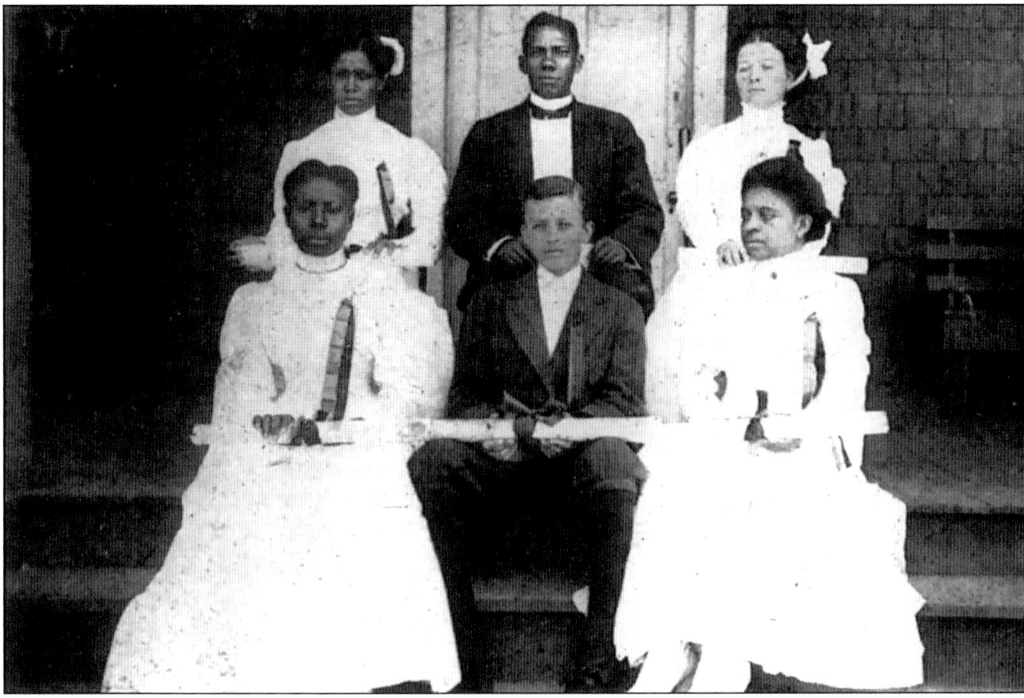

The second graduating class, *c.* 1910, of Albany Bible and Manual Training Institute, included among its graduates Anna Mathilda Hill and Elnora Lockett.

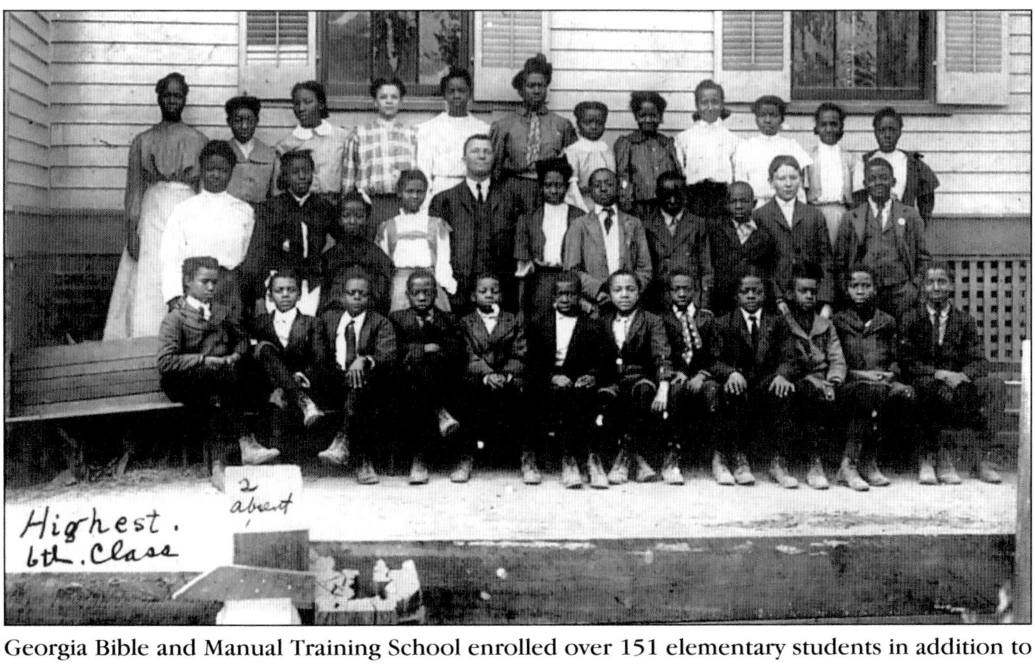

Georgia Bible and Manual Training School enrolled over 151 elementary students in addition to its secondary and normal students in 1915. Shown here is a sixth-grade class.

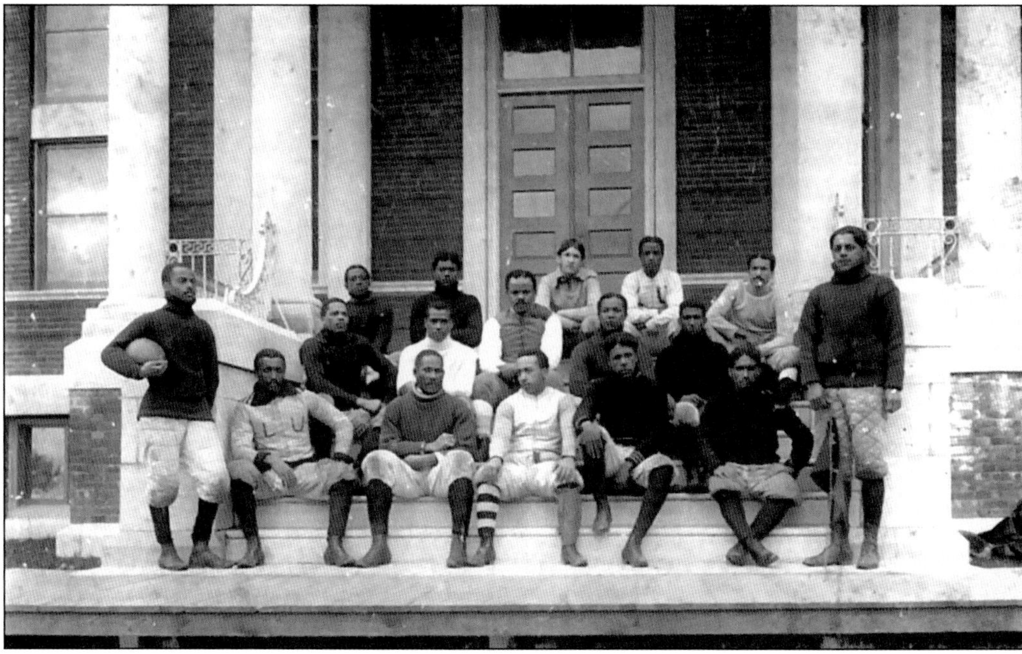

Georgia Normal athletics competed throughout various parts of Georgia, developing a good reputation in football, baseball, and basketball during the 1920s. In 1939, with support from Caroline Hazard, a 20-acre athletic field became a reality. Pictured above is the men's football team and women's basketball team below.

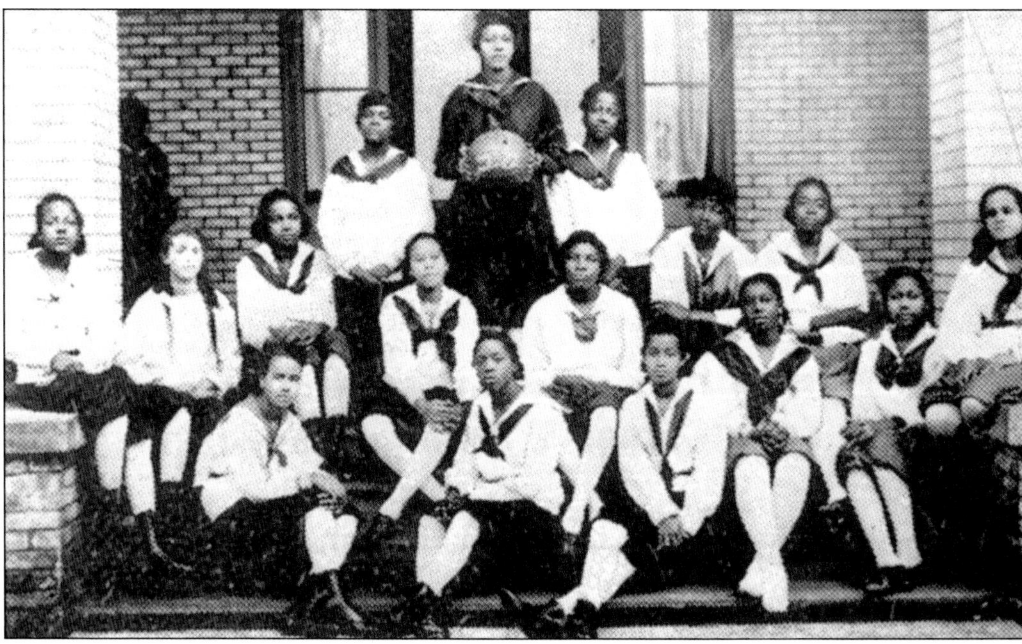

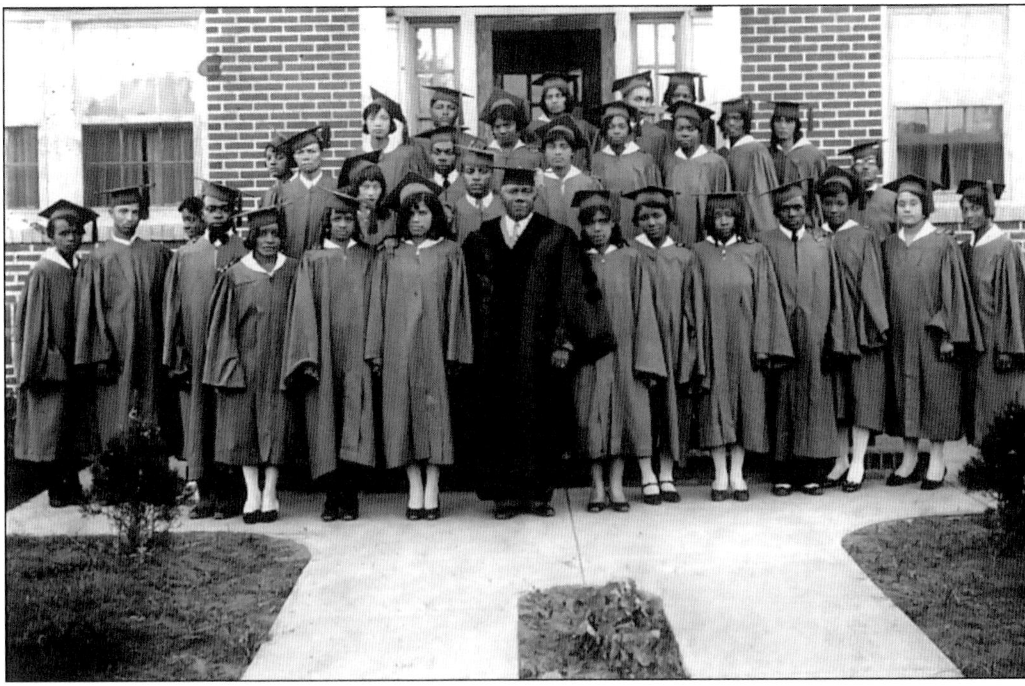

This is the Georgia Normal graduating class, *c.* 1935.

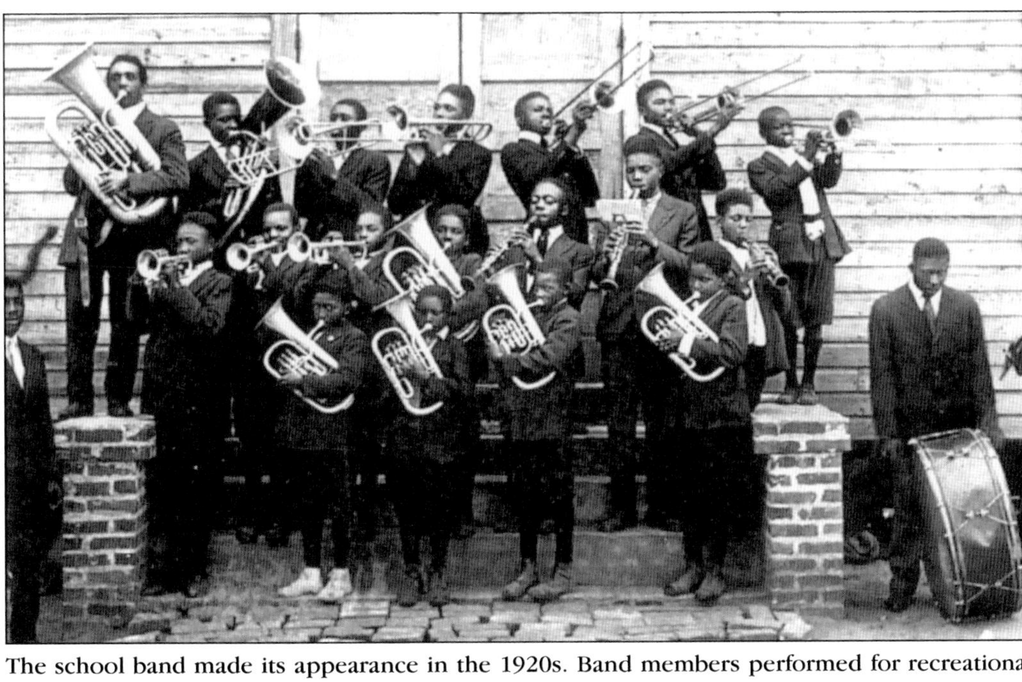

The school band made its appearance in the 1920s. Band members performed for recreational activities and gave concerts on special occasions.

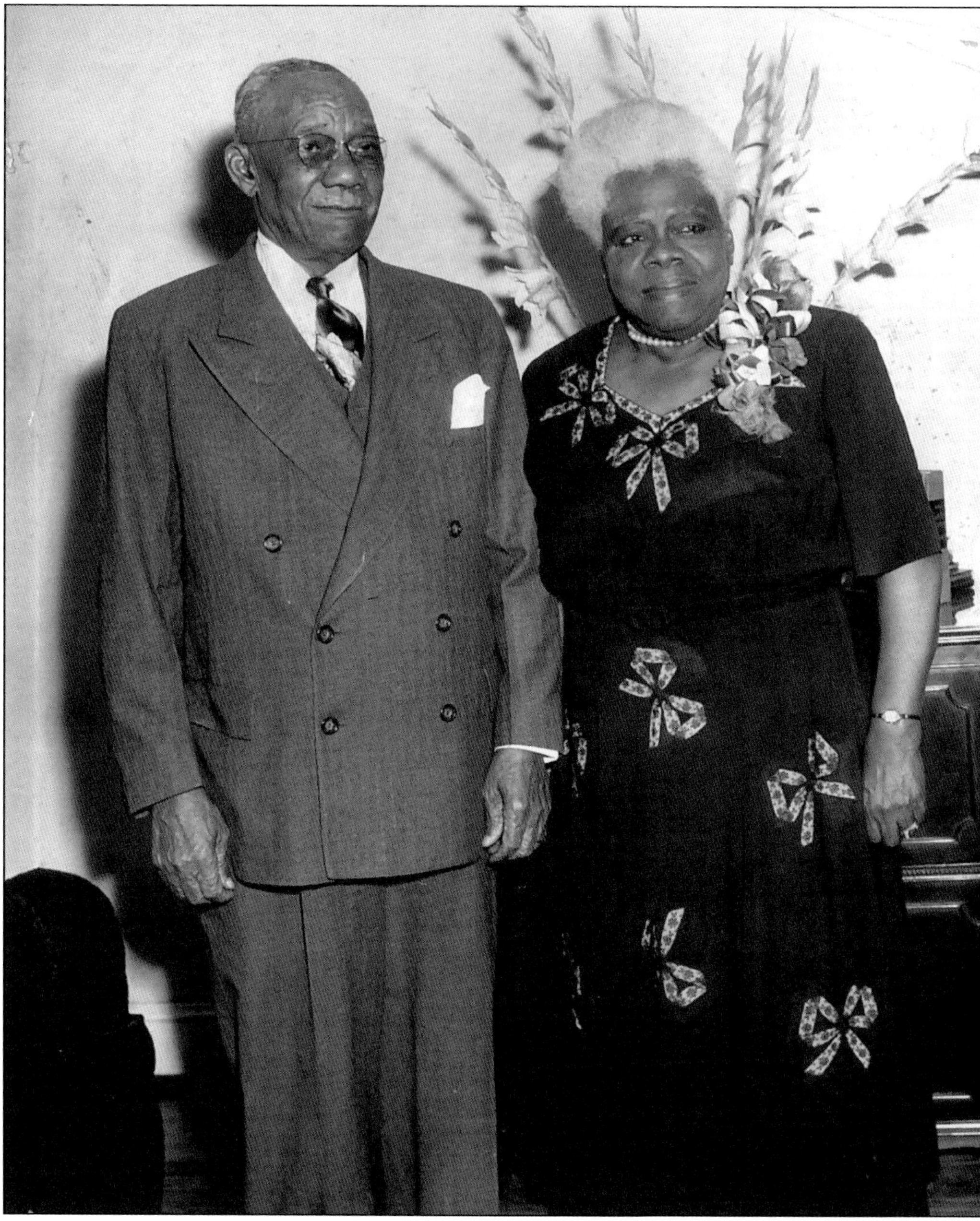

This is Dr. Joseph W. Holley, founder of Albany State University, and Dr. Mary McLeod Bethune, founder of Bethune Cookman College.

Two

Dr. Aaron Brown 1943–1953

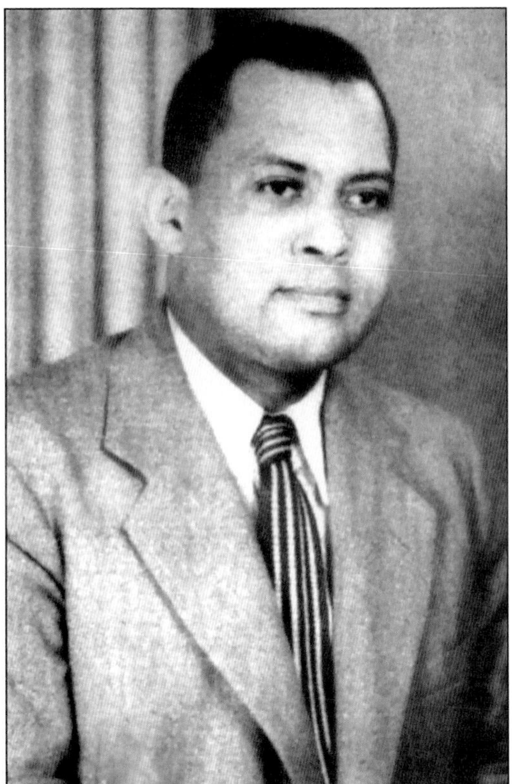

On July 1, 1943, Dr. Aaron Brown became the second president of Albany State College. A graduate of Talladega College, Dr. Brown assumed the awesome responsibility of providing educational experiences for interested persons in the midst of World War II. During his administration, the institution's name was changed to Albany State College. The college was upgraded to four-year status and became a degree-granting institution offering bachelor's degrees in elementary education and the arts and sciences. Many student activities, including the student council, Greek letter organizations, college annual, college newspaper, and athletic program expansions were begun during his term. In 1945, Brown's dream became a reality when the college was accredited by the Southern Association of Colleges and Secondary Schools. There were many improvements in the physical plant during his administration. Through dedication and vision, Dr. Brown initiated a new thrust in education at Albany State College.

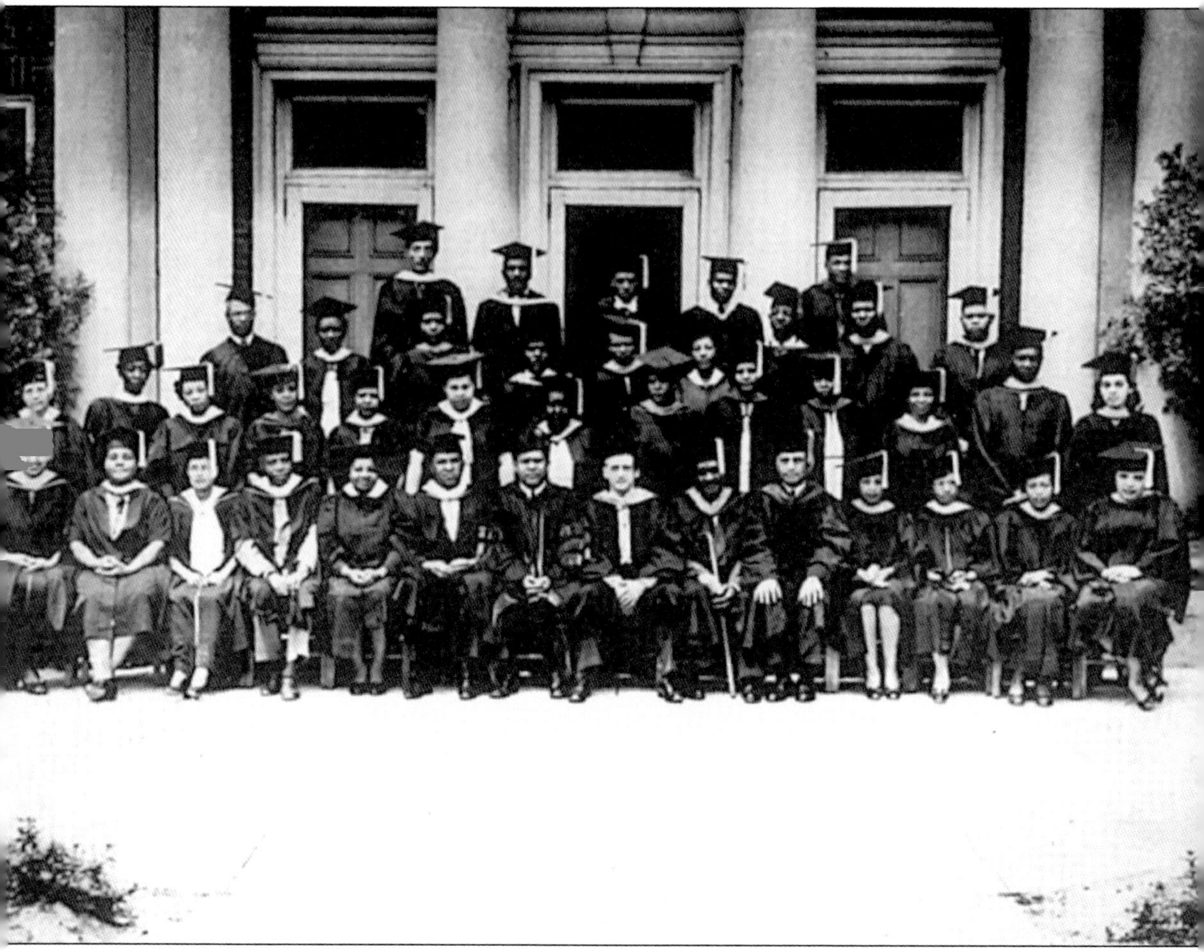

Here is the 1947–1948 faculty in academic regalia following commencement. Dr. Brown encouraged faculty development and assisted faculty members to do additional studies. President Brown believed in publishing in academic journals and local newspapers, and taking an active role in community service.

Dr. Richard J. Jeffreys served as Dean of Albany State during President Aaron Brown's administration. Jeffreys Hall, the former science building on campus, was named in his honor.

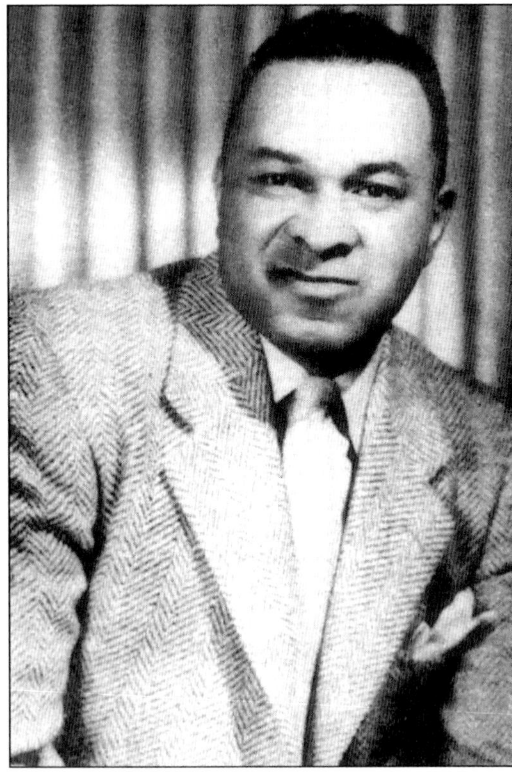

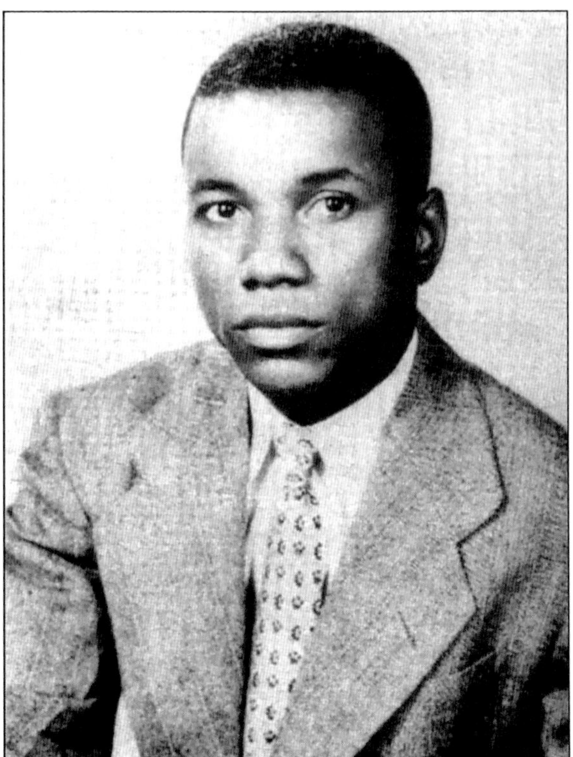

Dr. Charles J. Stanley served briefly as college registrar and professor of Social Sciences at Albany State during Dr. Brown's era.

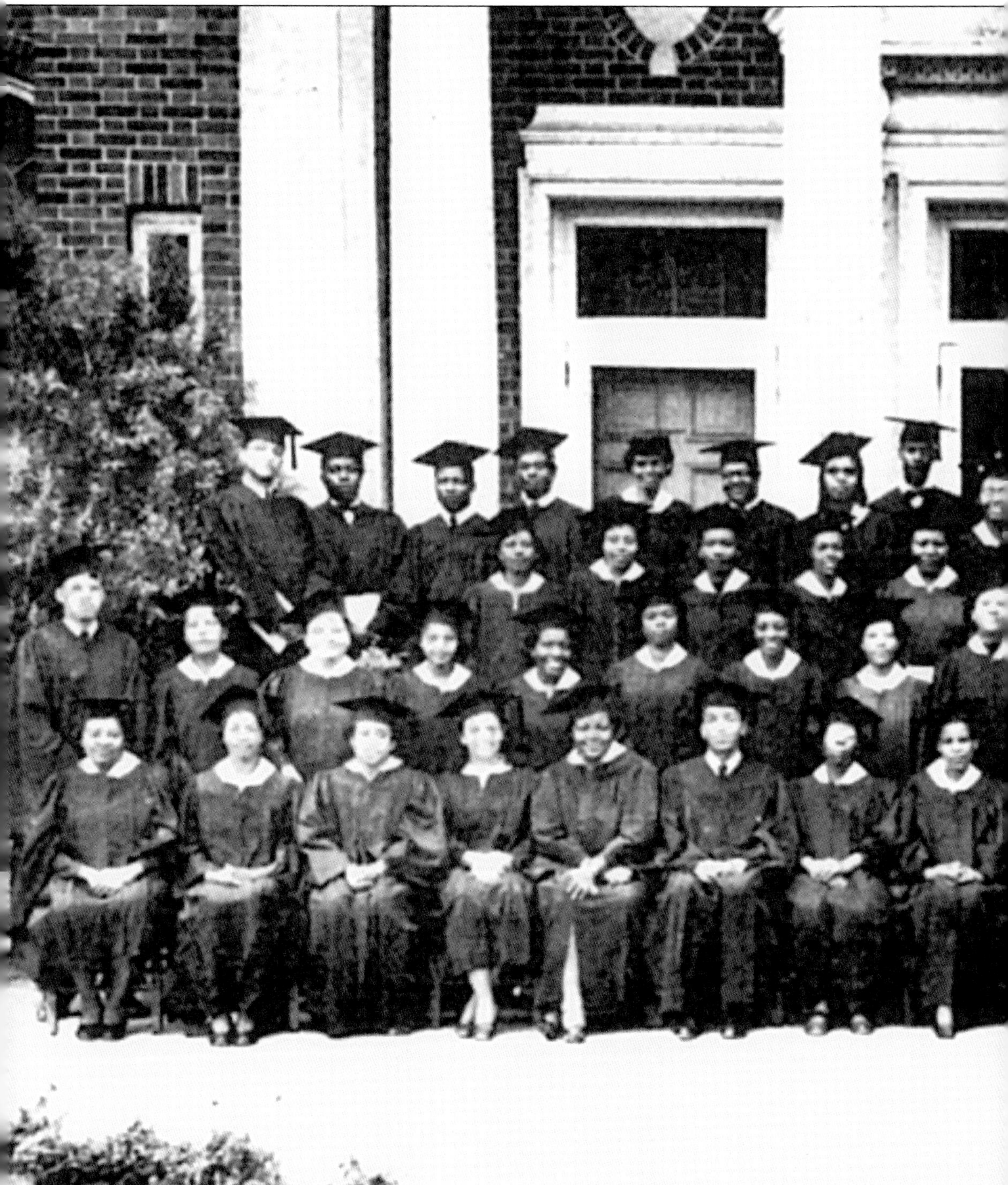

Following World War II, Albany State experienced an increased student population as an influx of war veterans enrolled. This was especially apparent by 1948 as the institution expanded and

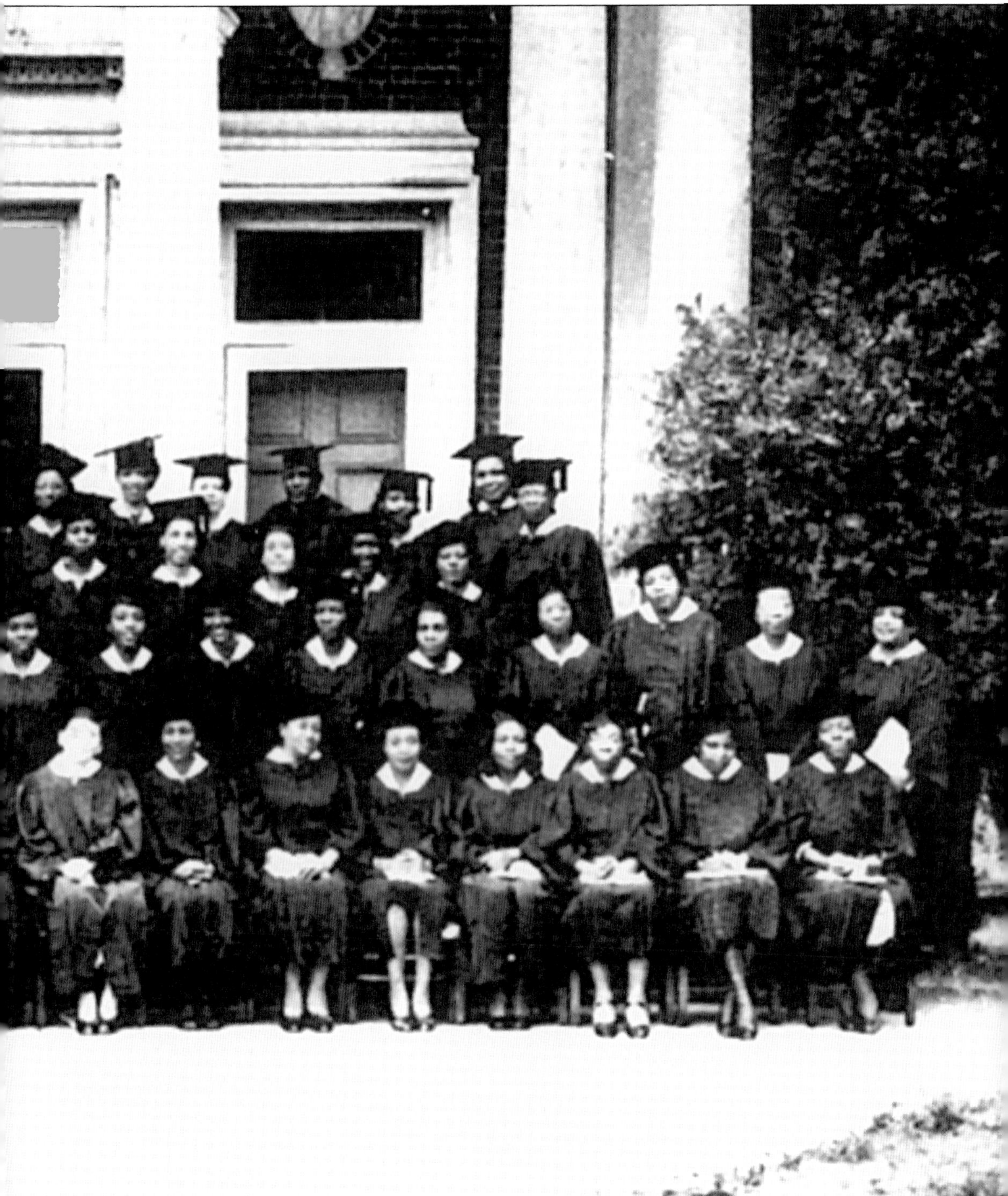

created new programs. Pictured above is the 1948 graduation class.

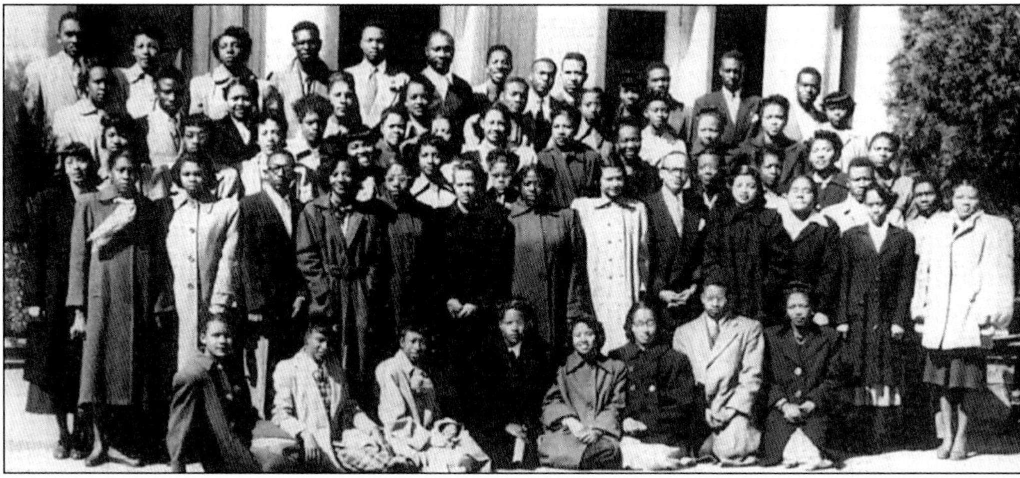

The National Association for the Advancement of Colored People was established on campus in 1943 by Savannah's branch of the NAACP Youth Council. President Brown encouraged students and faculty alike to join by launching a 1,000-membership drive in 1944.

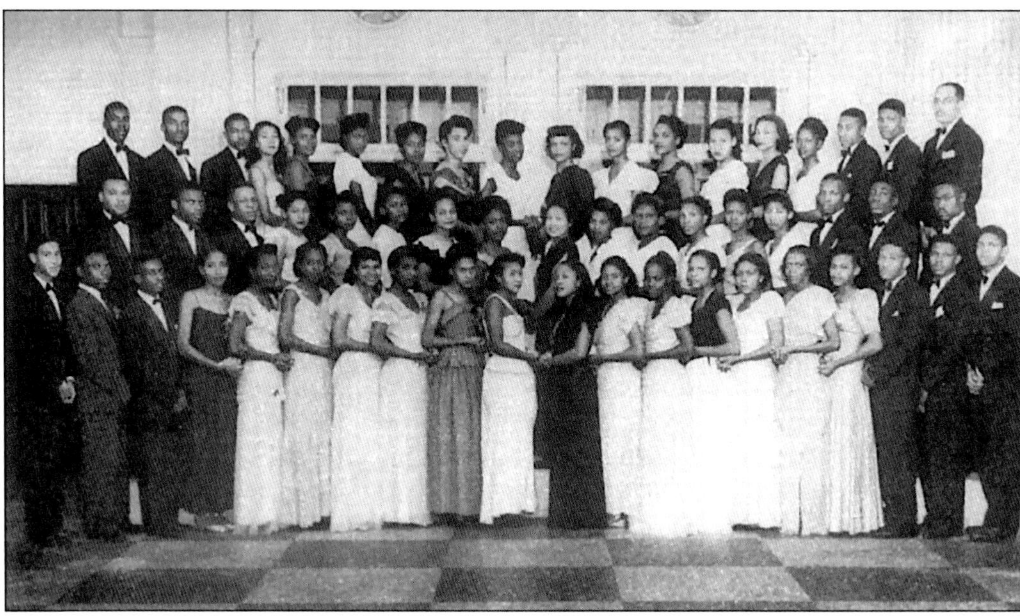

The concert choir, under the direction of Mr. James Elkins with Miss Brownie Mae Lattimore as accompanist, received strong letters of commendation for its tours throughout the South including Alabama, Ohio, Kentucky, and Tennessee. The choir appeared on the local radio station, WALB, each Sunday afternoon.

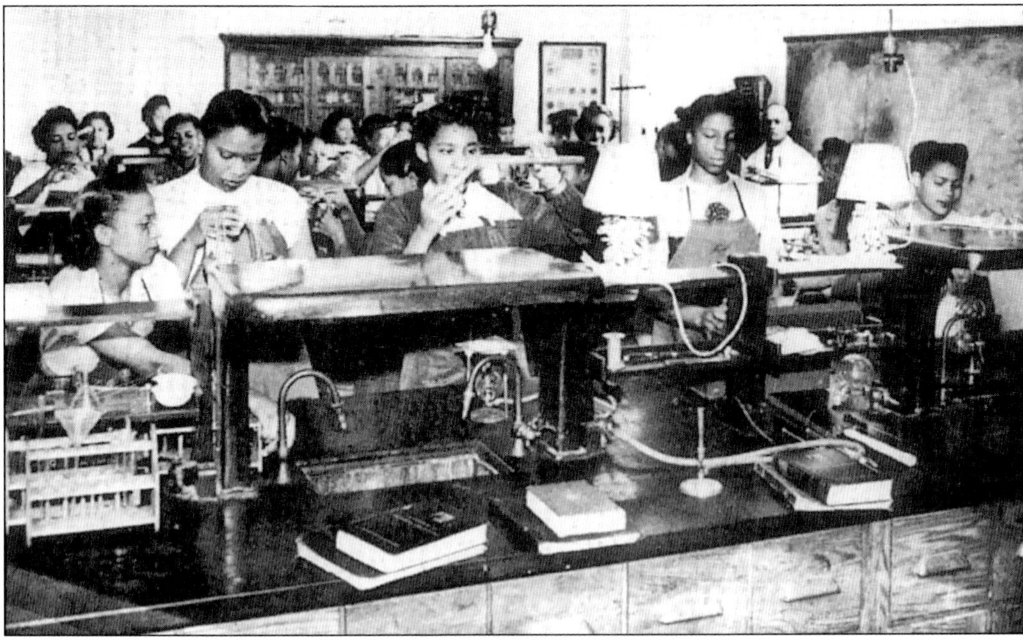

Albany State College created its College of Arts and Sciences and included a degree-granting program in chemistry to increase its male student population.

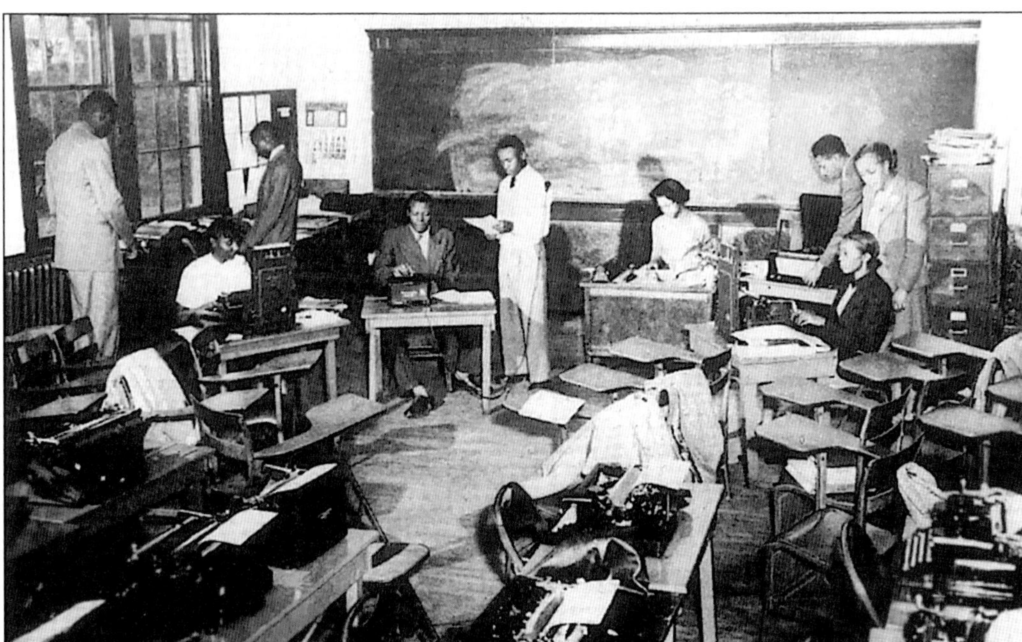

New courses were also implemented in Business Adminstration and Commercial Education to attract a more diverse student body as seen in this business machine class photograph in 1948.

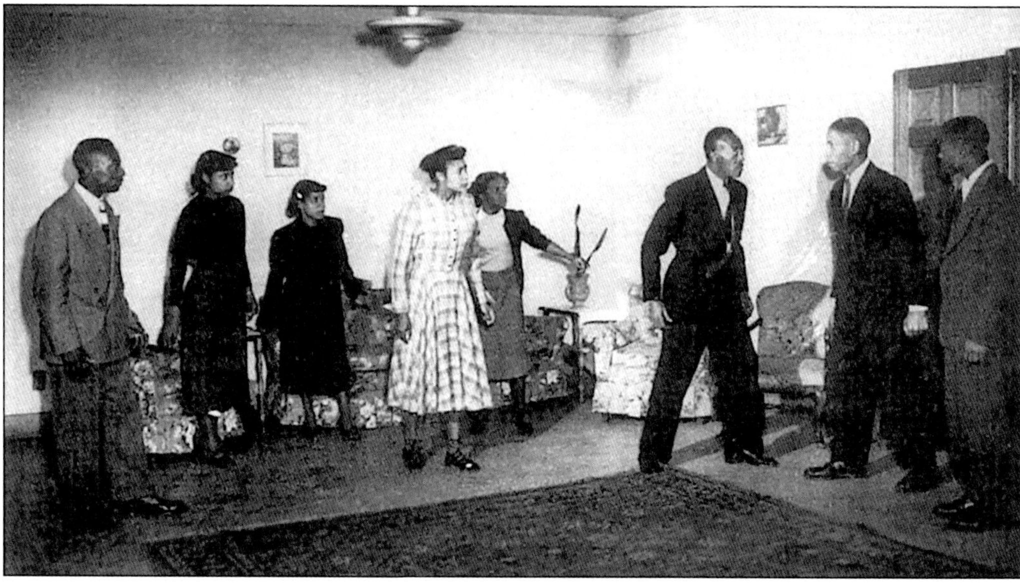

Pictured above is a scene from the Dramatic Club's performance of "Smilin' Through." Pictured below is a scene from "The Love Expert."

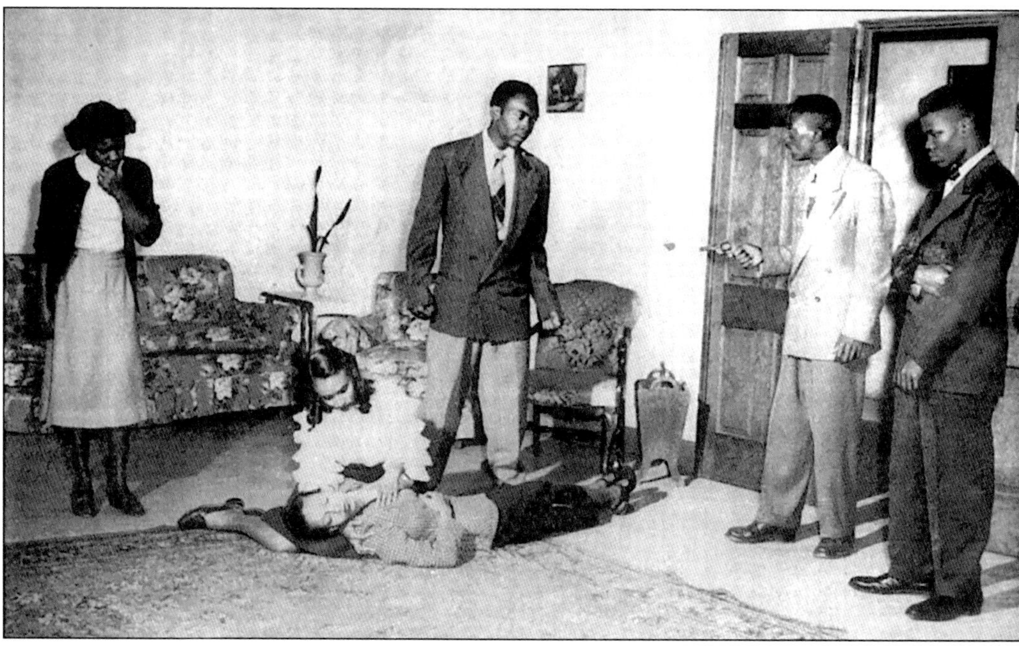

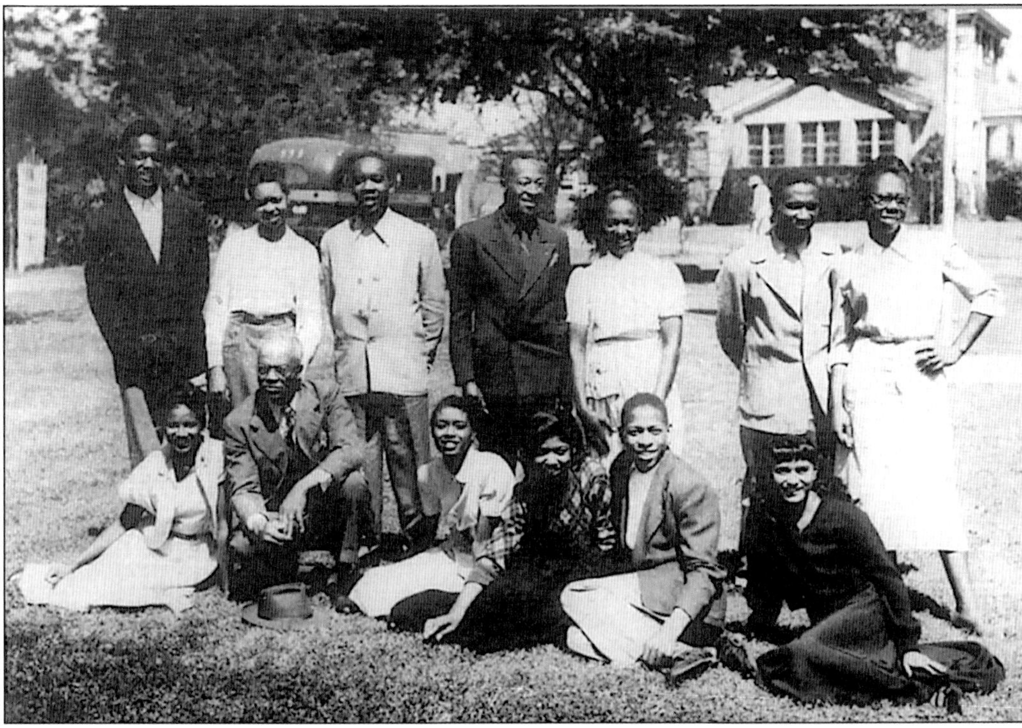

Mr. A.P. Turner organized the Dramatic Club in the fall of 1943. The club offered students an opportunity to develop the art of self-expression and offered training in stage management and design.

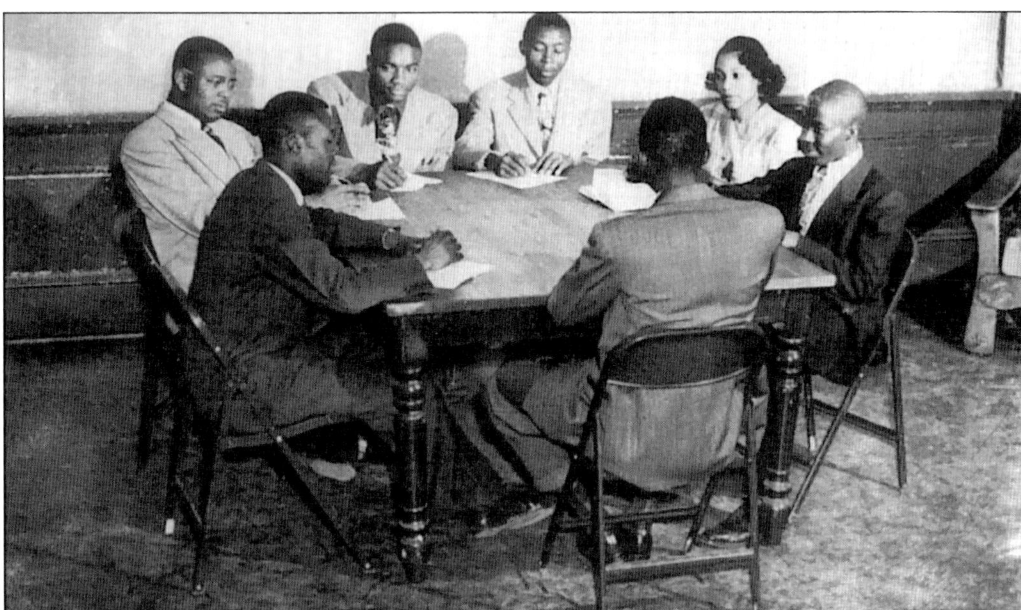

Mr. Sylvester Ashford, president of the student government, and Mr. Loran Hubbard, vice-president of the student government, are shown in a conference.

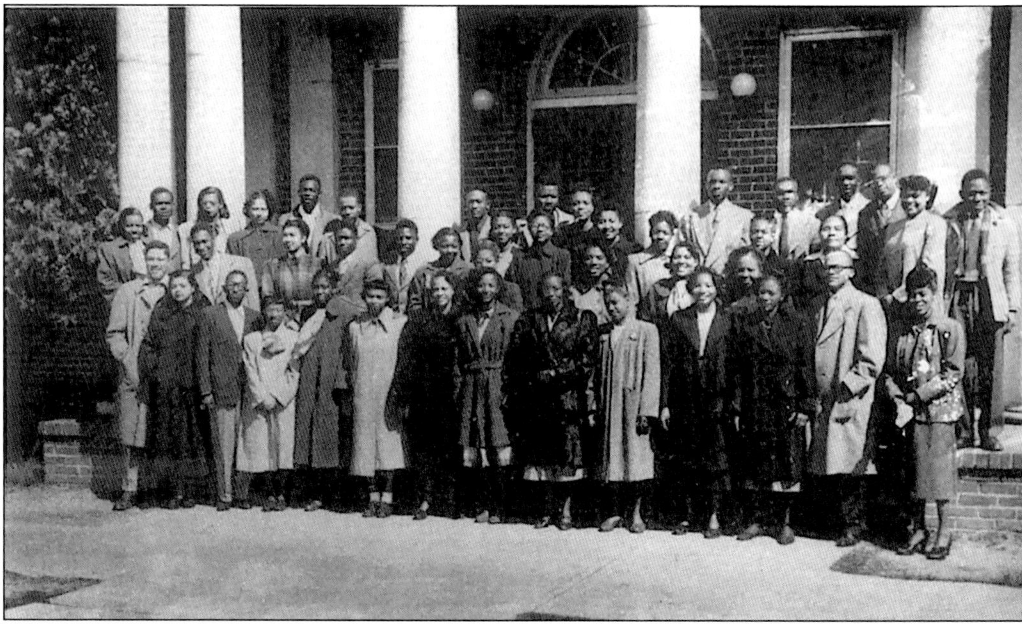

Organized by Prof. James E. Andrews in the mid-1940s, the Blue Key Honor Society was comprised of the highest honor students of Albany State. The society aimed to stimulate scholastic achievement in the fields of science, mathematics, and letters with open membership to students above the freshmen rank who maintained a scholastic average of "B" or above. Persons who have been in the society for five quarters consistently are considered "Fellows."

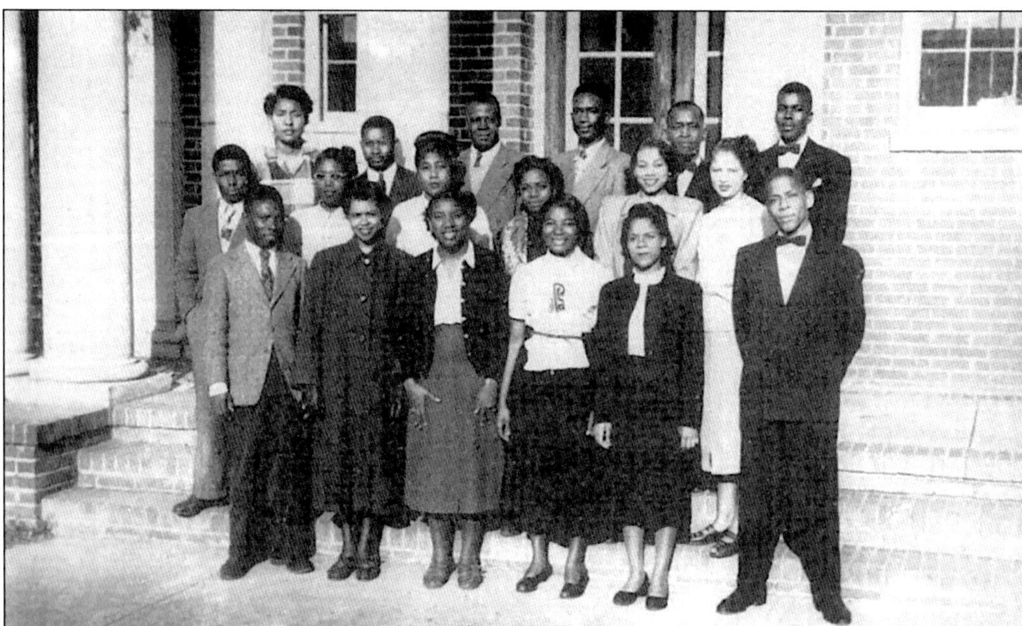

The Social Science Club was organized in October 1943 by Mrs. Troas L. Latimer, head of the social science department. The purpose of the club was to help pupils analyze, isolate, investigate, and interpret social science problems.

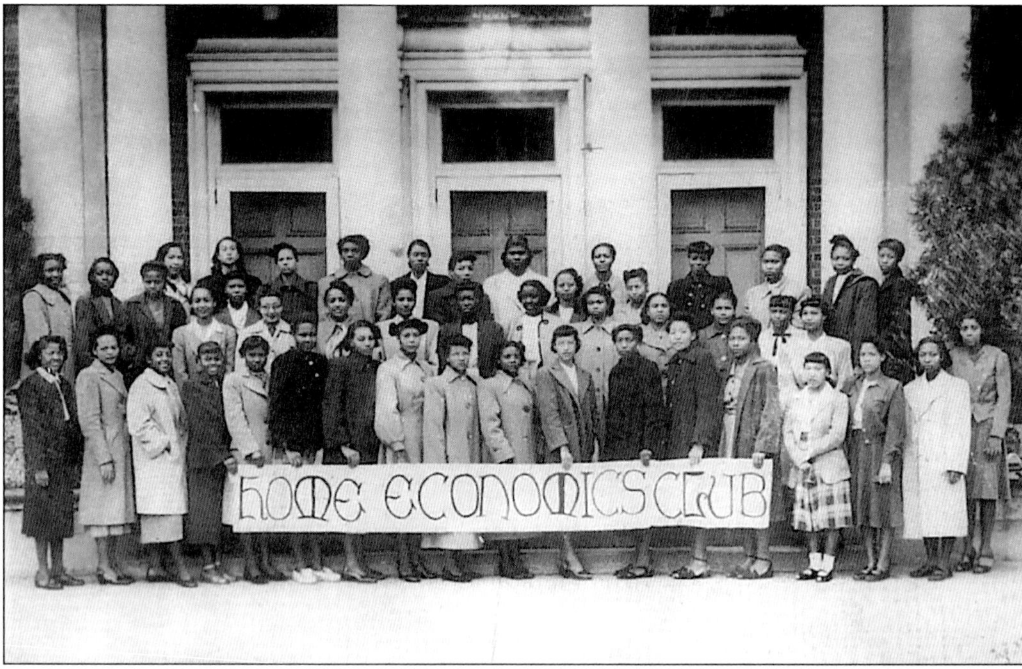

The aims of the home economics club were to acquaint its members with the economic problems of the world, the nations, and the home, and with the part each student can play in helping to solve these problems; and to acquaint its members with the methods and procedures employed in various phases of child development. "Better homes" might be considered the objectives of every home economics club. With better homes, we produced better lives and better standards of living.

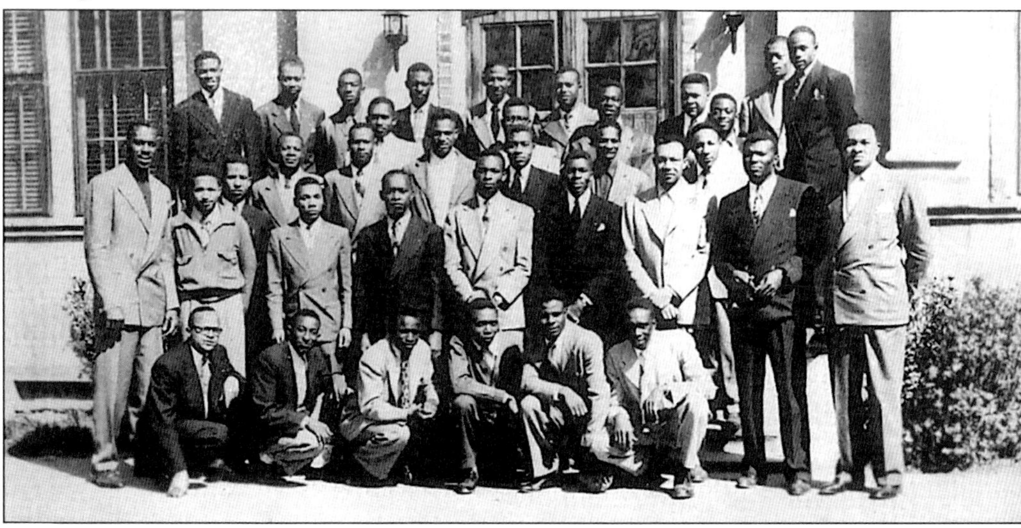

With the increased amount of students benefitting from the G.I. Bill following World War II, Beta Chapter of Georgia, Gamma Iota Alpha, represented honorably discharged veterans. The organization aimed toward the furtherance of brotherhood and fraternity, the solution of veterans' problems, and dissemination of information concerning veterans. In 1946 the Albany State freshman class consisted of 79 veterans who were organized by Prof. James E. Andrews, including one in the Women's Army Corps (WAC).

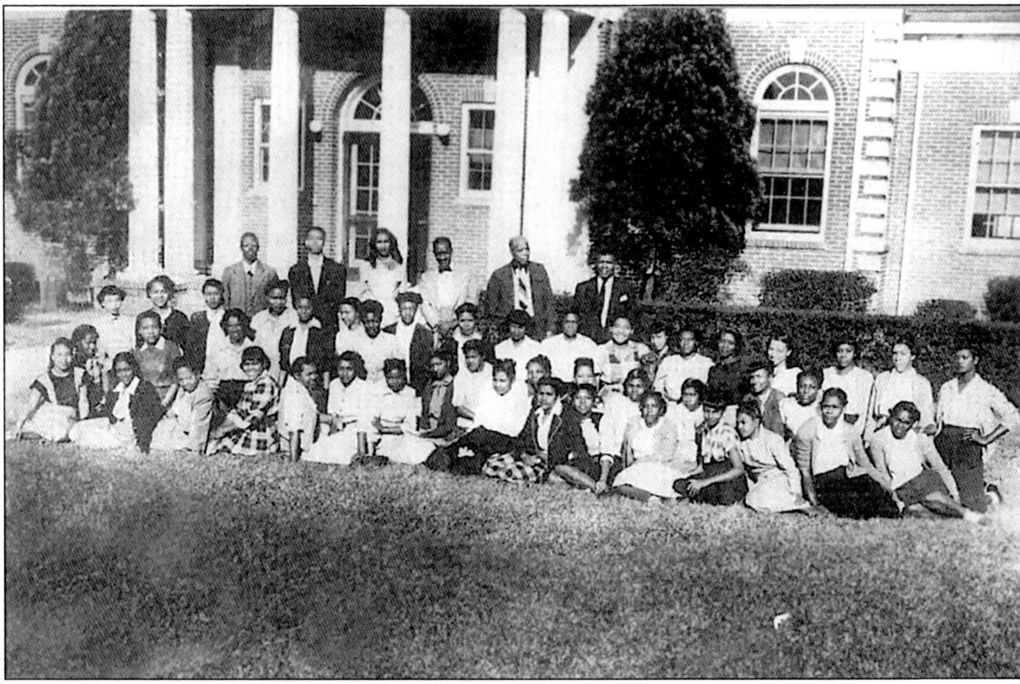

The Albany State College Sunday school had its beginnings almost with the college itself. Students were required to attend Sunday morning services that usually began with Sunday school followed by Sunday morning church services and ending with afternoon vespers.

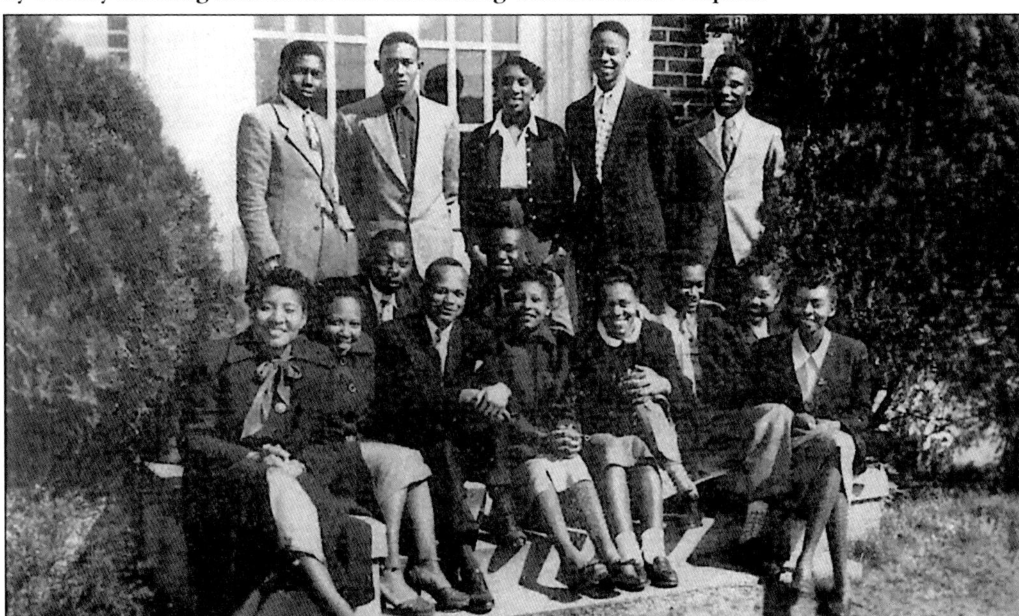

Students from different states came to Georgia to attend Albany State College. Year after year this number increased. In the session of 1946–1947 the out-of-state students of Albany State organized themselves unto a Cosmopolitan Club in order to associate and exchange ideas from the different sections of the country, and to express appreciation to Albany State College for its kindness to them. The membership of this club doubled over a period of two years.

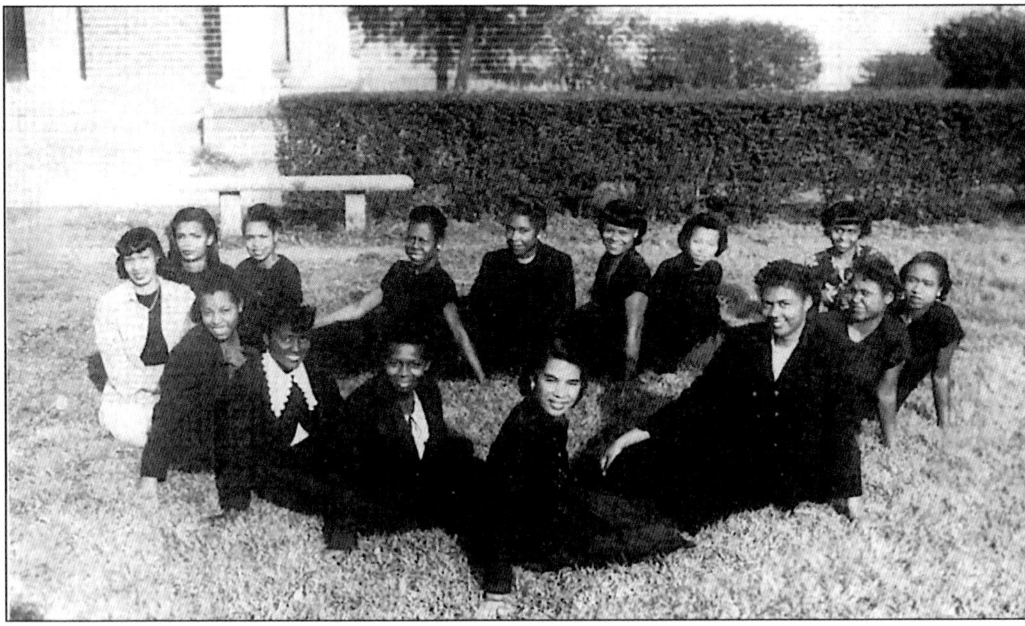

Pictured above, the Albany State College Young Women's Christian Association was organized on January 8, 1947 at Gibson Hall under the supervision of Mrs. O. Hamilton and Mrs. O.R. Wysinger. Below are the officers of the YMCA. Pictured from left to right are John Wilson, Perry Barrington, Alvin Terrell, and Carter D. Marshall.

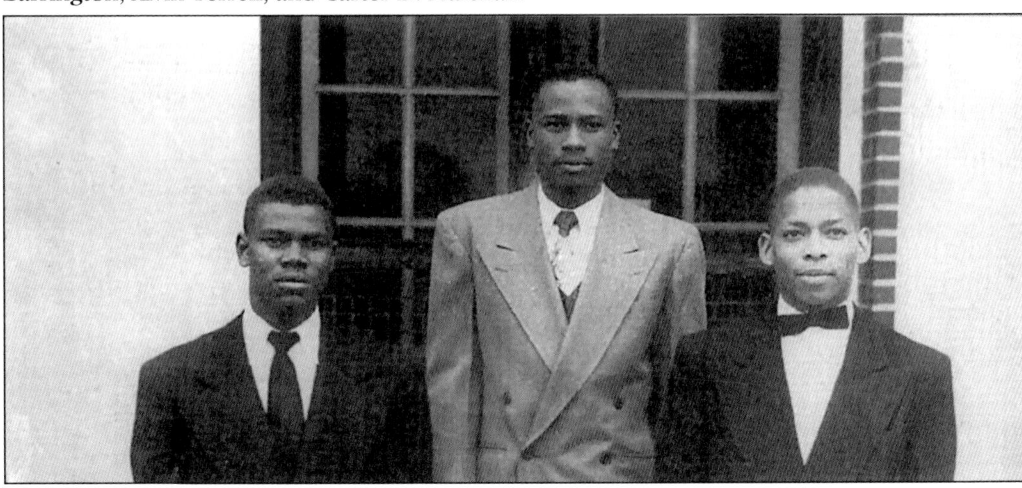

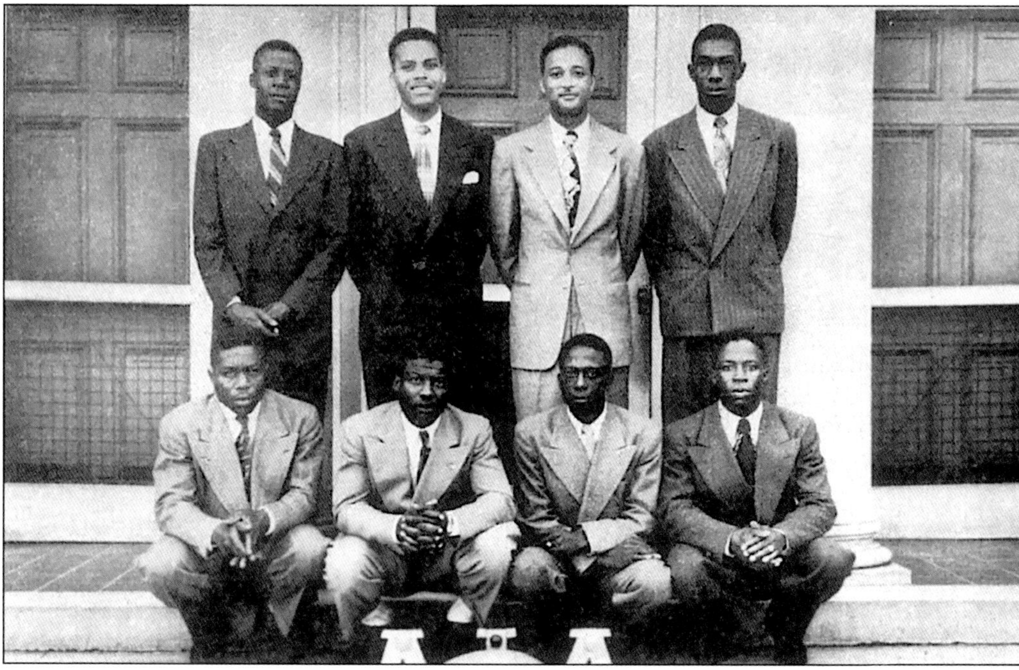

These are charter members of the Delta Delta Chapter of the Alpha Phi Alpha Fraternity.

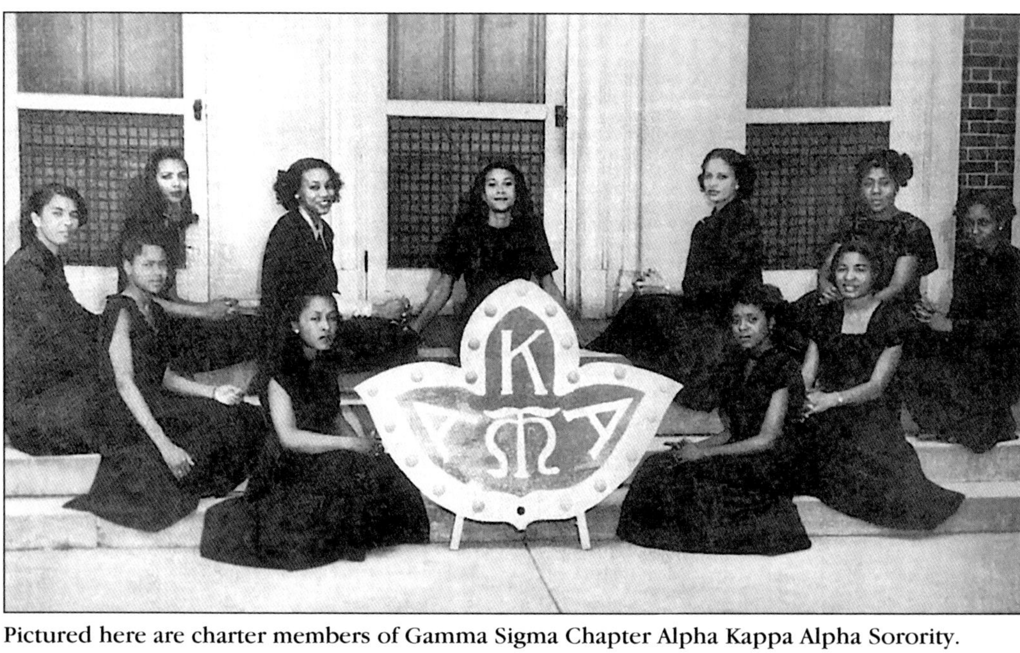

Pictured here are charter members of Gamma Sigma Chapter Alpha Kappa Alpha Sorority.

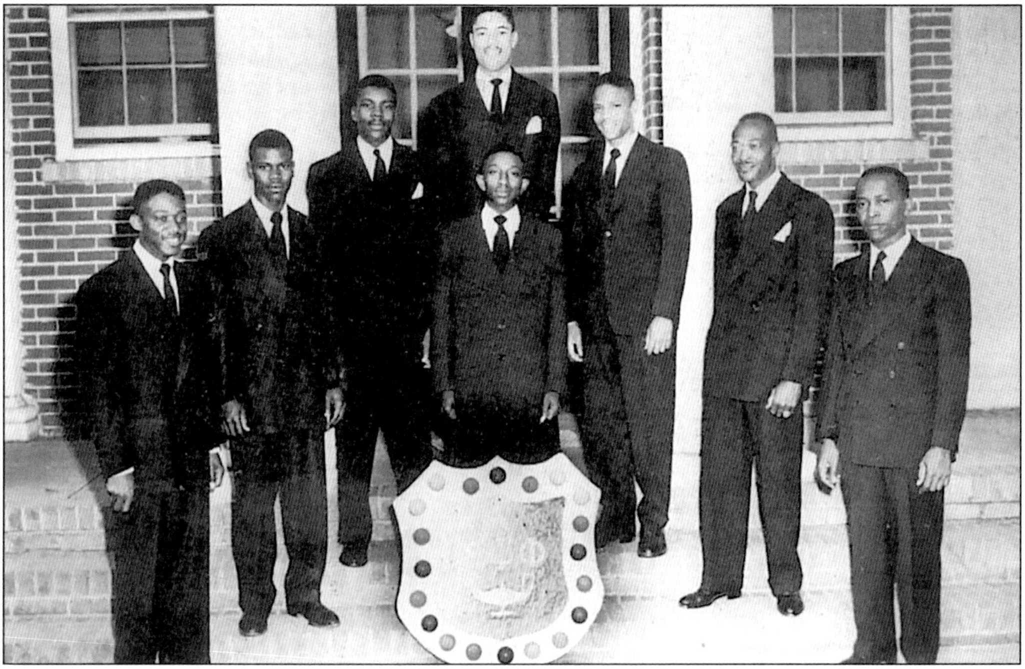

Charter Members of the Chi Epsilon Chapter of Omega Psi Phi fraternity are shown here.

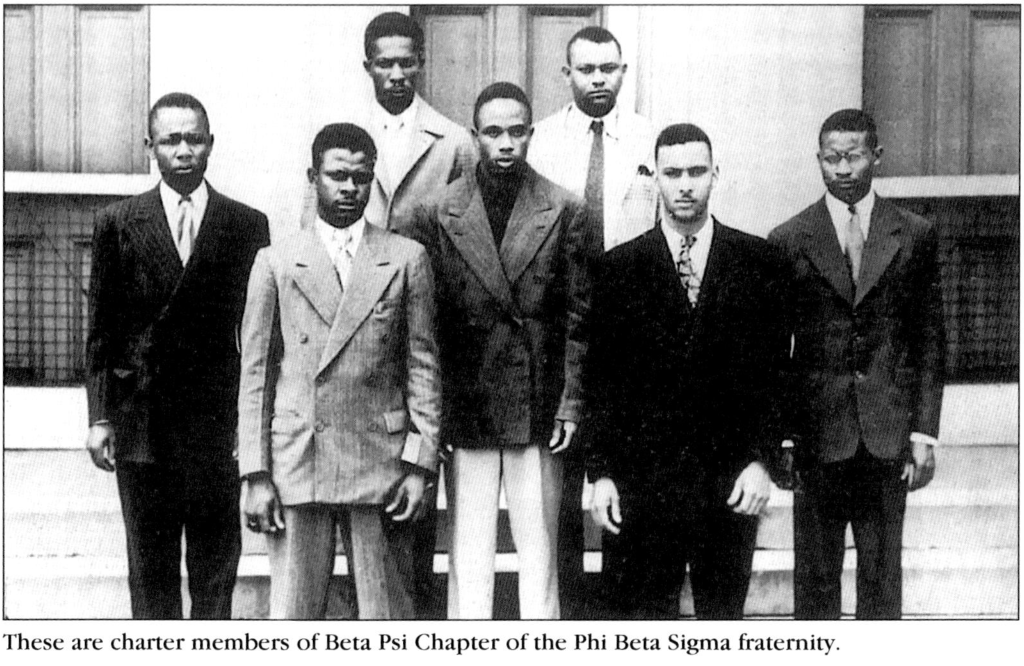

These are charter members of Beta Psi Chapter of the Phi Beta Sigma fraternity.

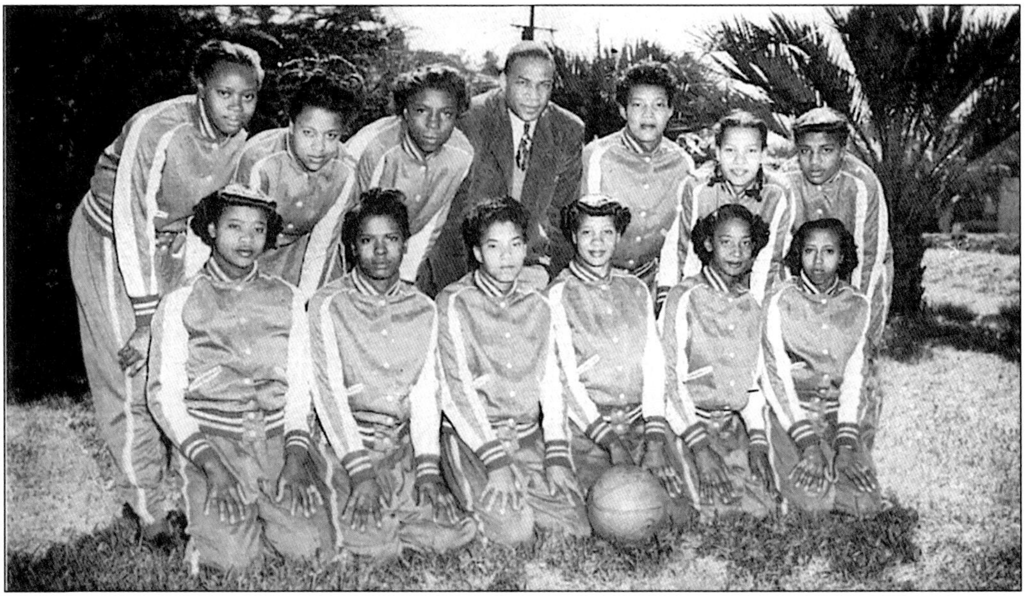

Pictured here is the 1948–1949 women's basketball team.

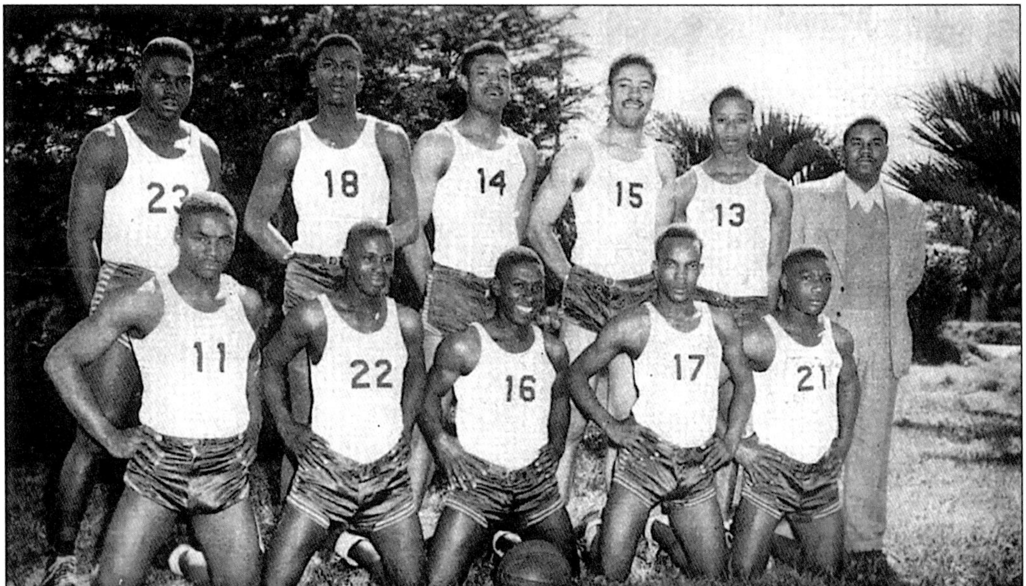

The 1948–1949 men's basketball team is shown here.

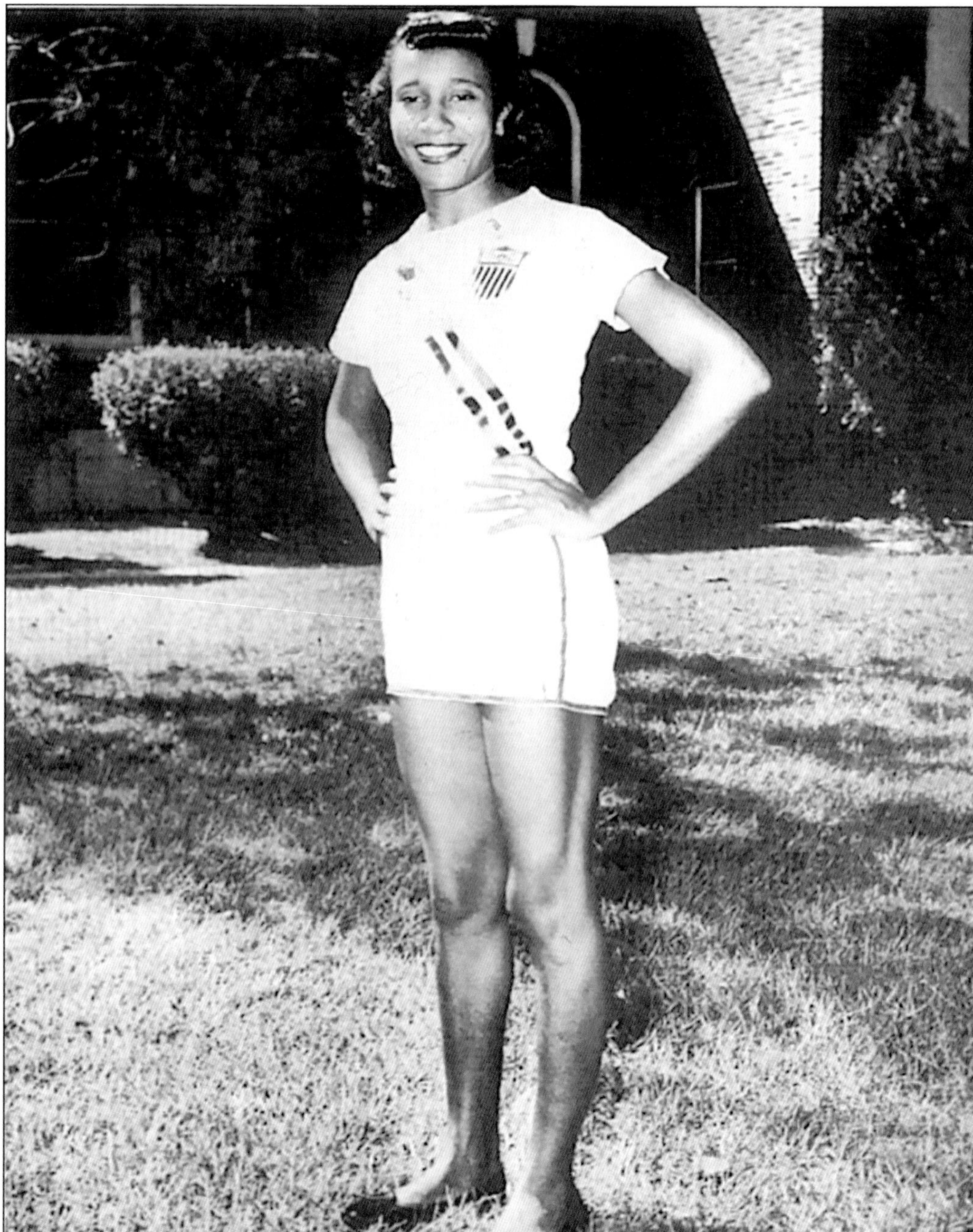

Alice Coachman, the only member of the United States's 1948 women's Olympic track and field squad to capture a gold medal for the United States and the first ever African-American female gold medalist, was born in Albany. In addition to being a track and field star, Alice was an outstanding basketball competitor. She transferred to Albany State College in 1947 where she continued her track work along with her home economics studies. In the 1948 A.A.U. conclave she established a new American women's record in the high jump when she cleared the bar at 5 feet, 4 and 13/16 inches. Alice soared to the unprecedented height of five feet, six and a half inches to win the 1948 Olympic women's high jump.

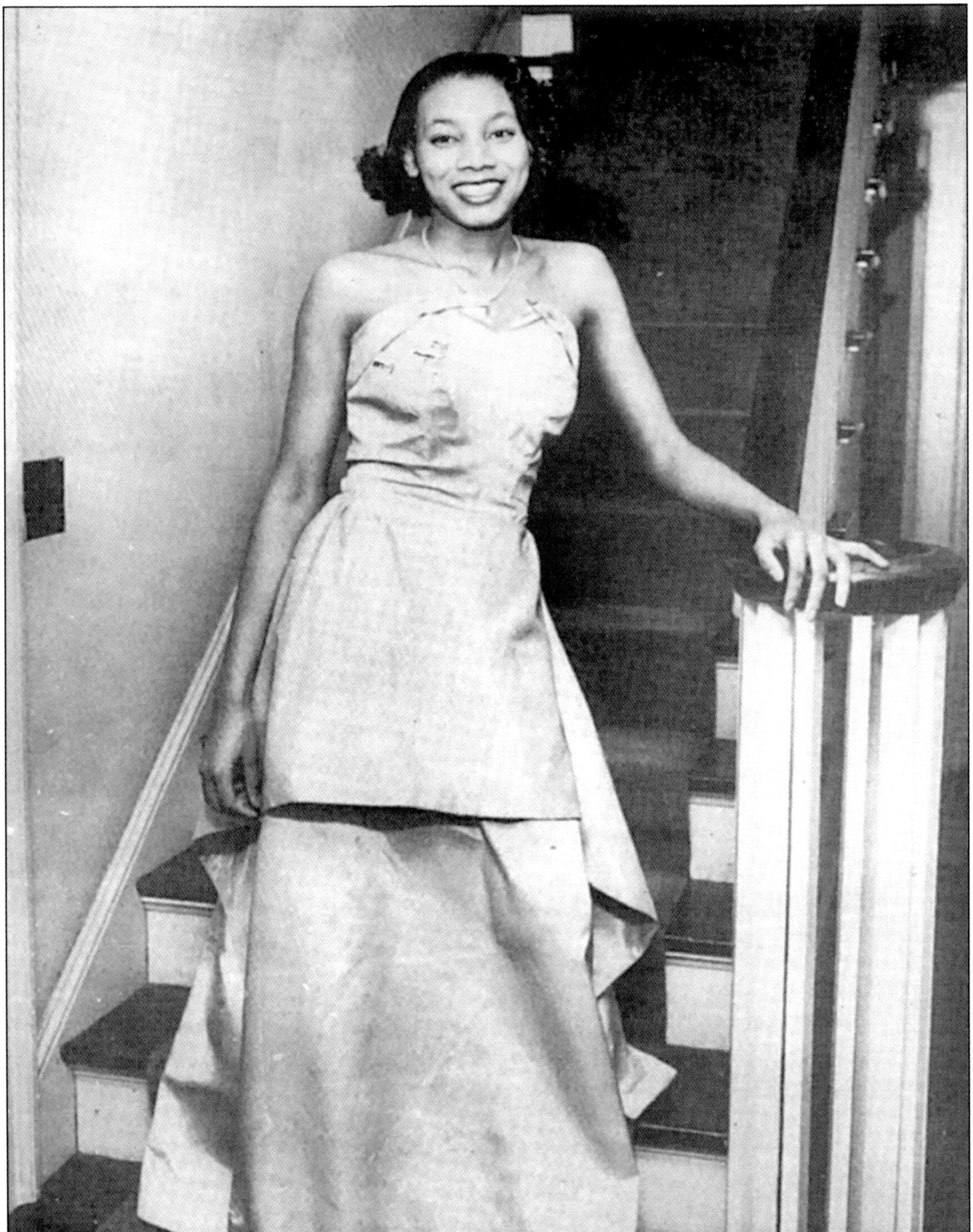

This is Beatrice Poole, Miss Albany State College 1948–1949.

Three

Dr. William H. Dennis Jr. 1953–1965

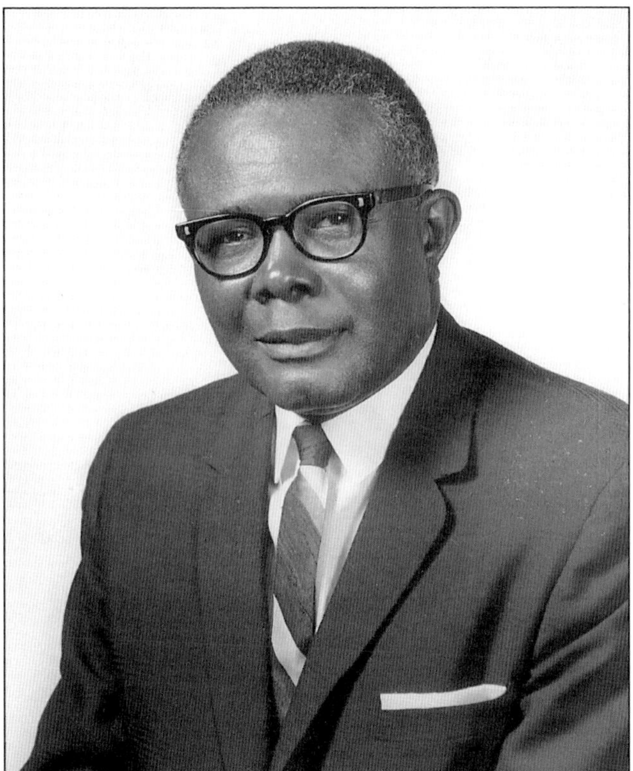

A graduate of Morehouse College and Columbia University, Dr. William H. Dennis Jr. was a member of the faculty at Albany State College. In 1953, he was appointed as the third president of the college. During his administration, the college underwent enormous expansion in student population, curriculum and institutional programs, and physical plant facilities. Growth in the physical facilities included an addition to the Hazard Laboratory School, a new library, a fine arts building, a science building, a gymnasium, a faculty housing complex, and three dormitories. To honor his dedication and contributions to education, Dean R.H. Simmons initiated the W.H. Dennis Jr. Lecture Series in 1972. This series has become an annual affair. During his tenure, Albany State College was the first African-American college to gain full membership in the Southern Association of Colleges and Secondary Schools.

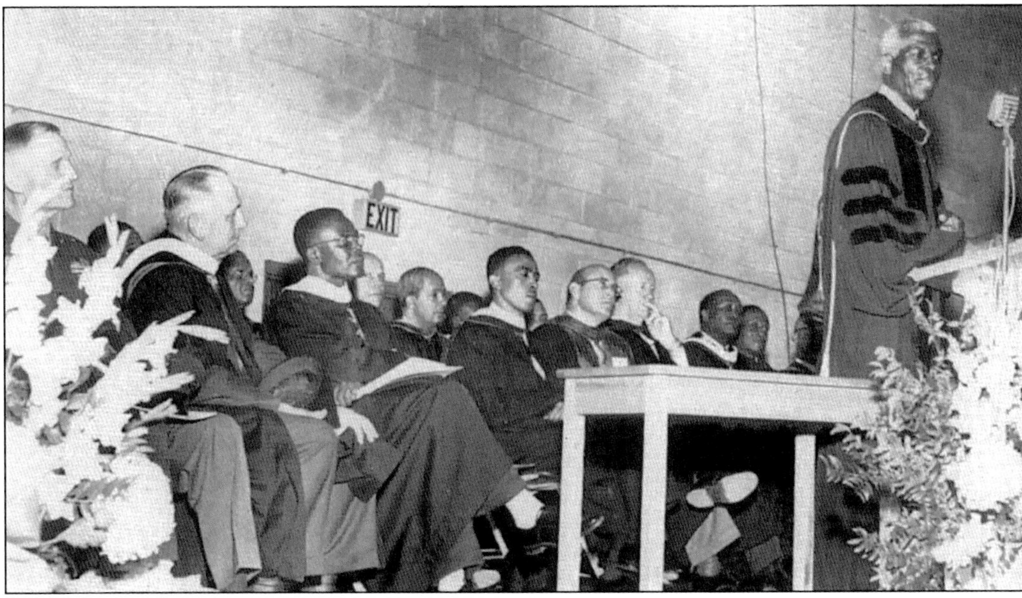

Dr. Benjamin E. Mayes, president of Morehouse College, delivered the inaugural address during the investiture of Dr. William H. Dennis, third president of Albany State, on November 3, 1955. The Honorable Robert O. Arnold, chairman of the University System of Georgia, represented the Georgia Board of Regents.

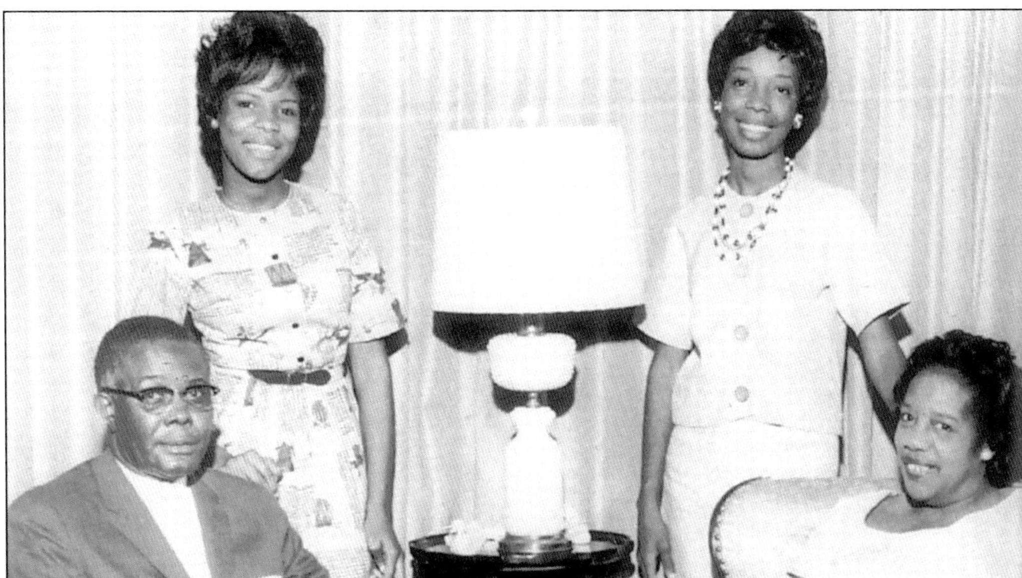

President and Mrs. William H. Dennis Jr. are pictured with daughters Gertrude and Rosalyn.

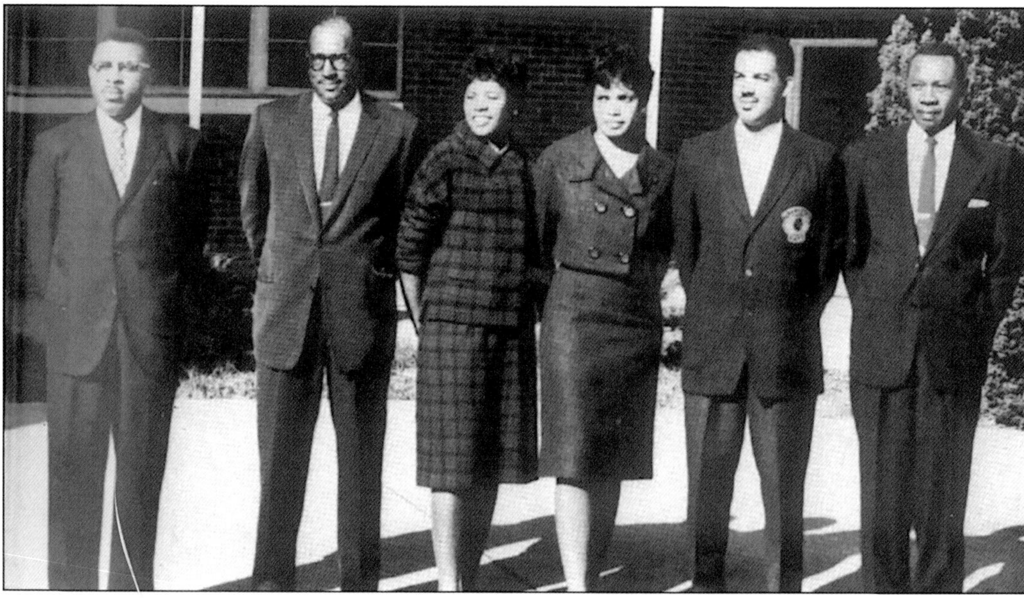

From left to right are faculty members and administrators of the Department of Health and Physical Education Robert Rainey, Dr. Charles Stancil, Obergenia Roberts, Betty Mclellan, O.W. O'Neal, and Forrest Kirkpatrick.

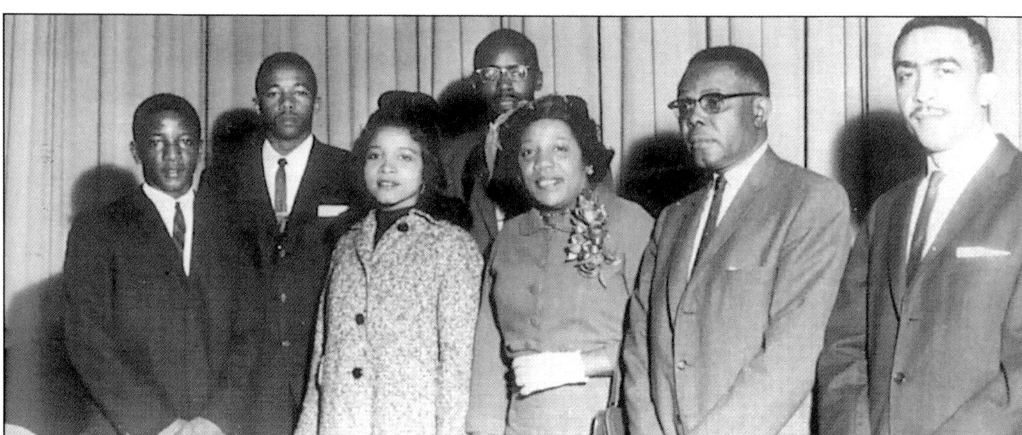

From left to right are student leaders Leviticus Roberts, Earnest Hester, and Ethel Heardman, with the Rev. R.B. Hooper, Mrs. W.H. Dennis, President W.H. Dennis, and Dean R.H. Simmons

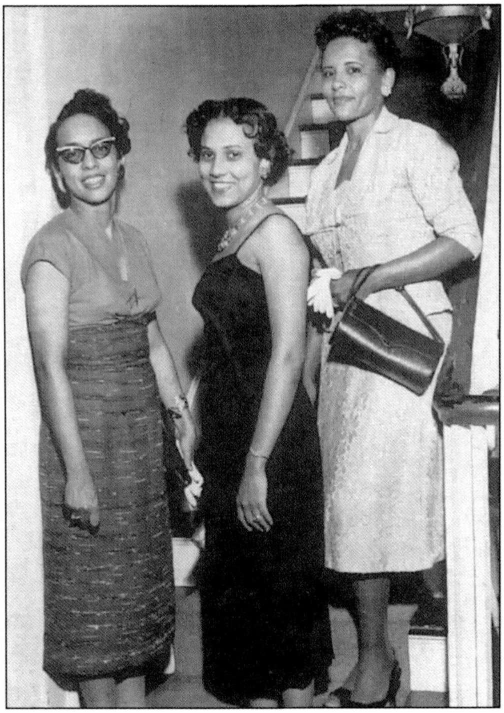

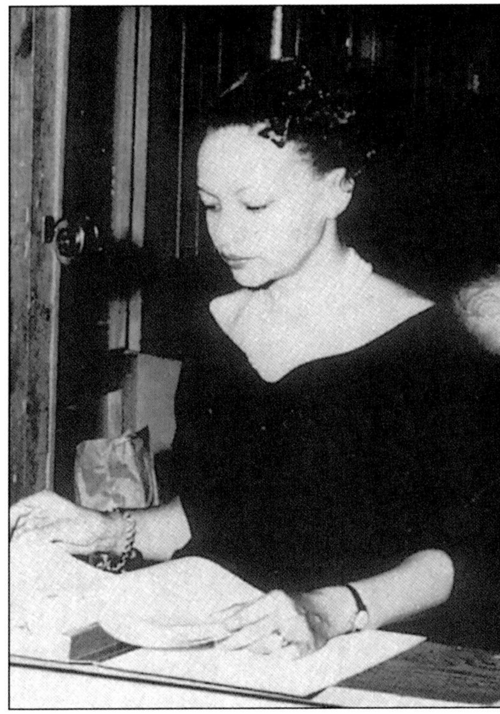

(*above, left*) Pictured are Helen Mays (registrar) with Anne S. Cheatham and Mary E. McCoy. (*above, right*) Aileen Harris was the business manager of auxiliary services.

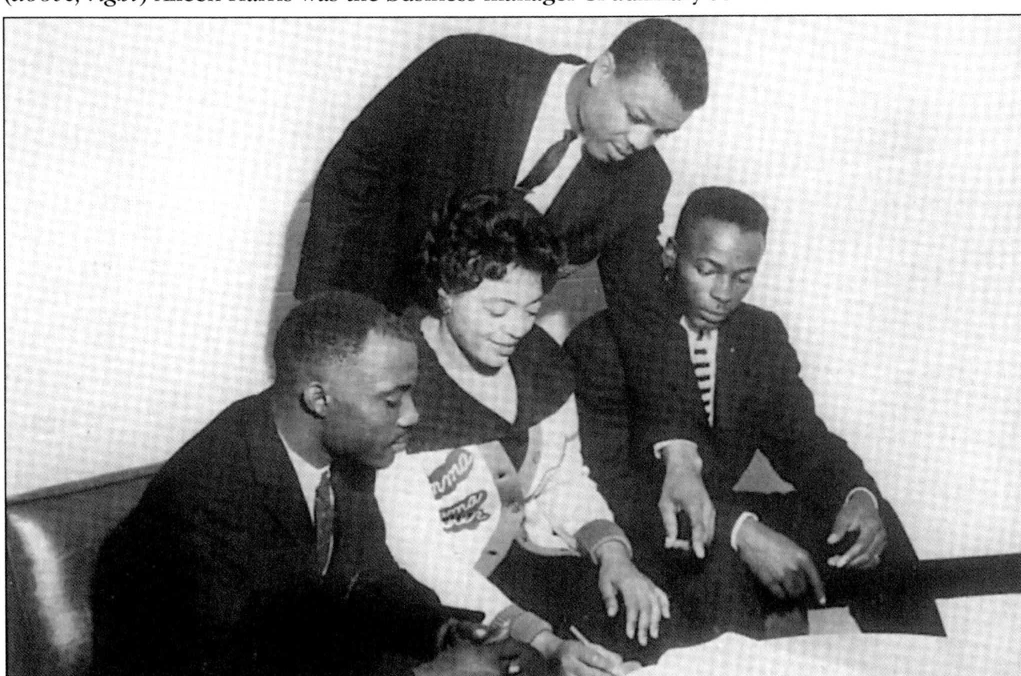

The officers of the 1960–1961senior class are (left to right seated) Ernest Strawter, vice-president; Mary Ford, secretary; and Eugene Conner, business manager. Standing is Robert Ervin, president.

The Student's Voice is the official organ of the Albany State student body.

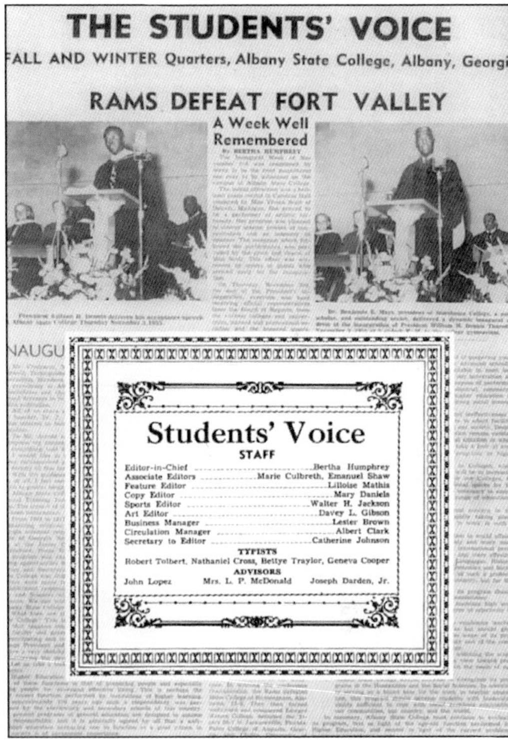

THE STUDENTS' VOICE

FALL AND WINTER Quarters, Albany State College, Albany, Georgia

RAMS DEFEAT FORT VALLEY

A Week Well Remembered

Students' Voice

STAFF

Editor-in-Chief	Bertha Humphrey
Associate Editors	Marie Culbreth, Emanuel Shaw
Feature Editor	Lilloise Mathis
Copy Editor	Mary Daniels
Sports Editor	Walter H. Jackson
Art Editor	Davey L. Gibson
Business Manager	Lester Brown
Circulation Manager	Albert Clark
Secretary to Editor	Catherine Johnson

TYPISTS

Robert Tolbert, Nathaniel Cross, Bettye Traylor, Geneva Cooper

ADVISORS

John Lopez   Mrs. L. P. McDonald   Joseph Darden, Jr.

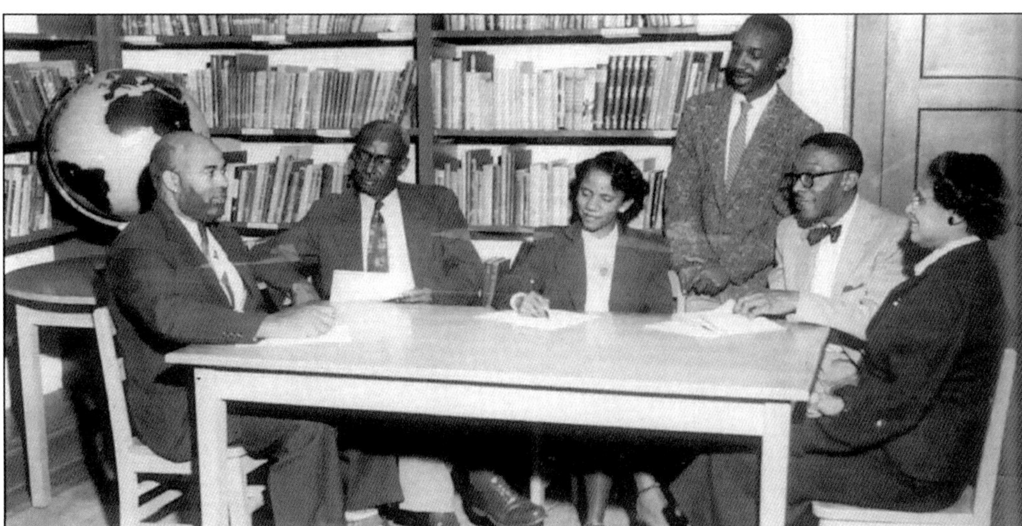

Albany State's Department of Education faculty, *c.* 1956, is from left (last names only) Garret, E.J. Granberry, Anne Gayles, ? Thompson, W.H. Dennis, and ? Turner.

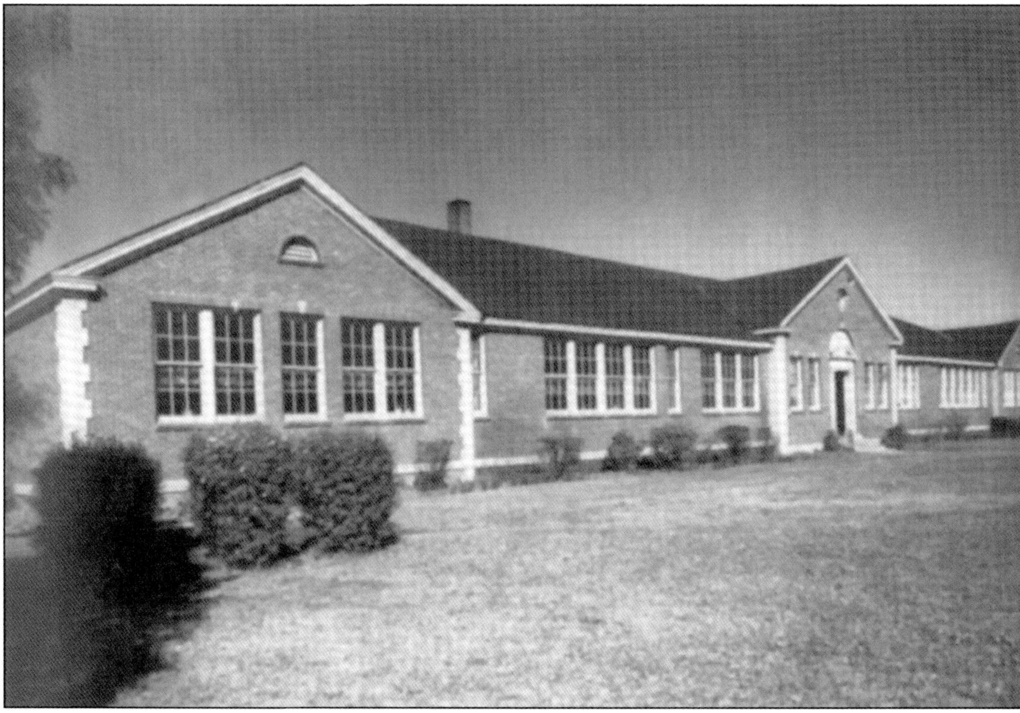

This is a picture of the Hazard Laboratory School, *c.* 1956.

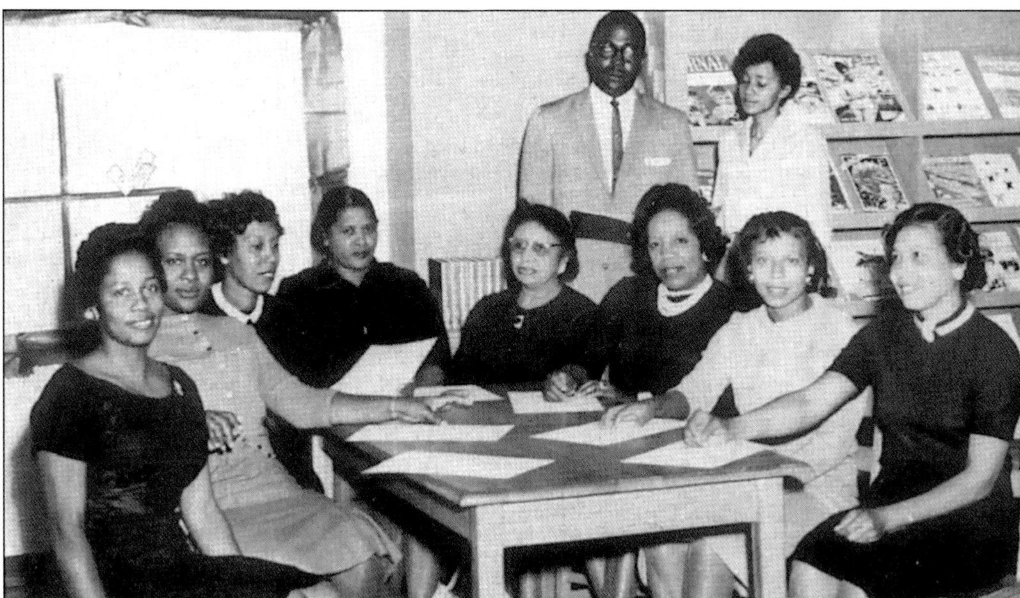

The nucleus of the laboratory school was comprised of the best and the brightest minds "in and out of the state of Georgia." The Hazard Laboratory School faculty in 1961, from left to right, were Miss M. Wilson, Miss B. Benson, Mrs. S.R. Gray, Mrs. M.L. Clark, Mrs. Susie Ellis, H.T. Hutchins (director), Mrs. W. Dennis, Miss M. Mallette, Mrs. L.P. Miller, and Mrs. Pearl Sanders.

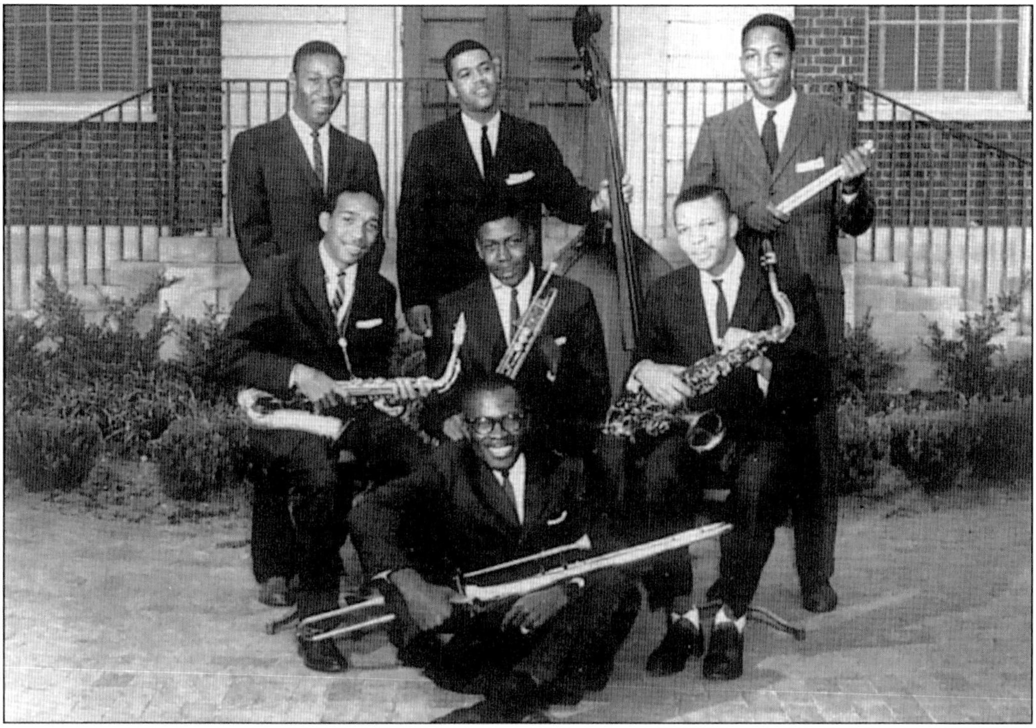

One of the most dynamic groups throughout Albany State history has been the Collegians Jazz Band. From left to right are Willie Banks, Samuel Stokes, Atwood Gervin, Matthew Carrington, Moses Turner, Albert Smith, and Jerome Terry, *c.* 1956.

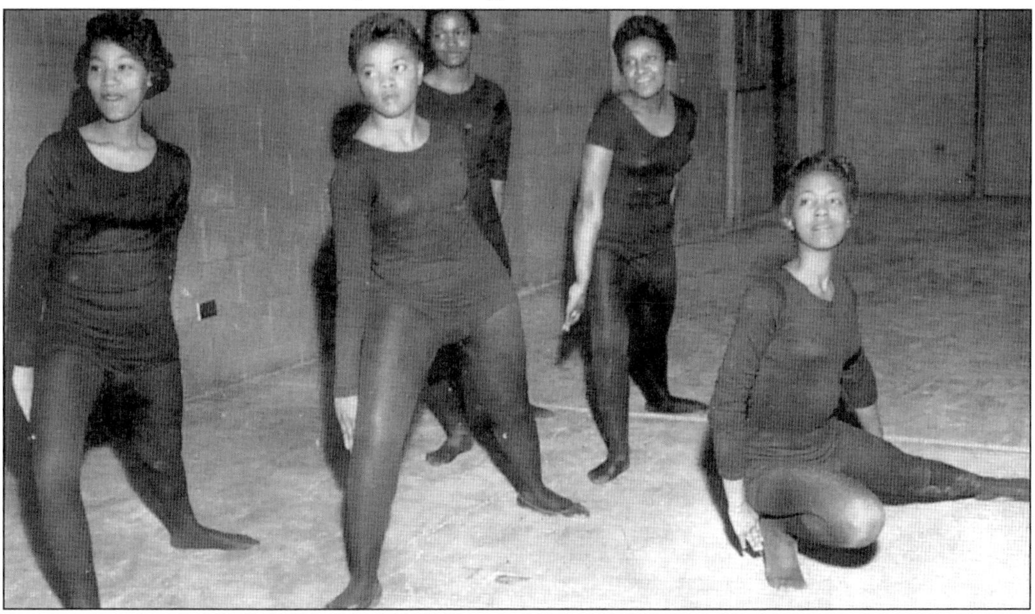

The Dance Group, under the direction of Miss C.L.Y. Height, interpreted various dances year round. Creative dances were presented during half time at many of Albany State's basketball games. From left to right are Lenora Hollaway, Lula G. Troup, K. Francis Houston, Marva Slaton, and Sybil Richardson, *c.* 1956.

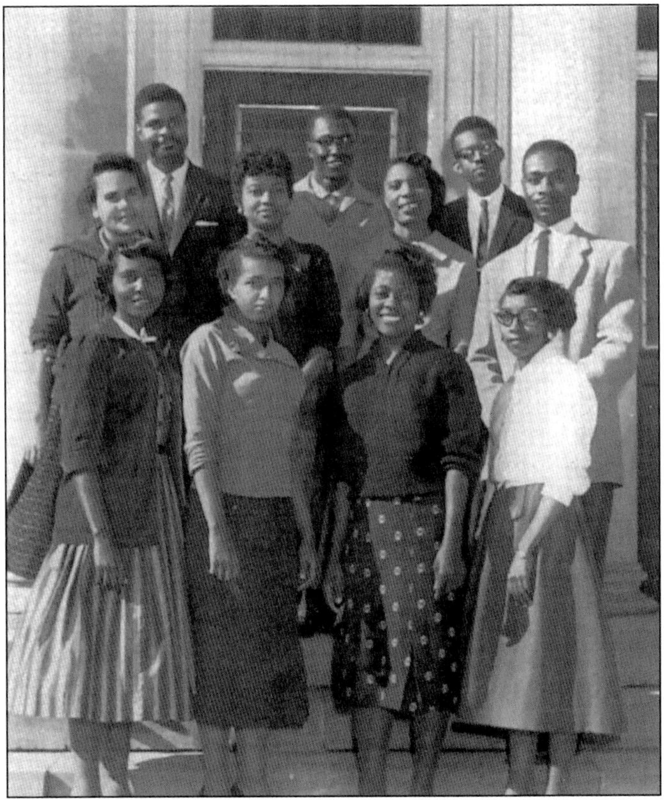

For the first time in the school's history, 11 students were nominated and accepted by Who's Who Among Students in American Colleges and Universities. Those accepted were (first row, from left to right) Francis Wilson, Barbara Sanchious, Josephine Federick, and Rosie Allen; (second row) Lucia Smith, Gladys Battle, Louie Marshall, and George Crawford; (third row) William H. Bryant, Raymond McIntyre, and Robert Tolbert, *c.* 1956.

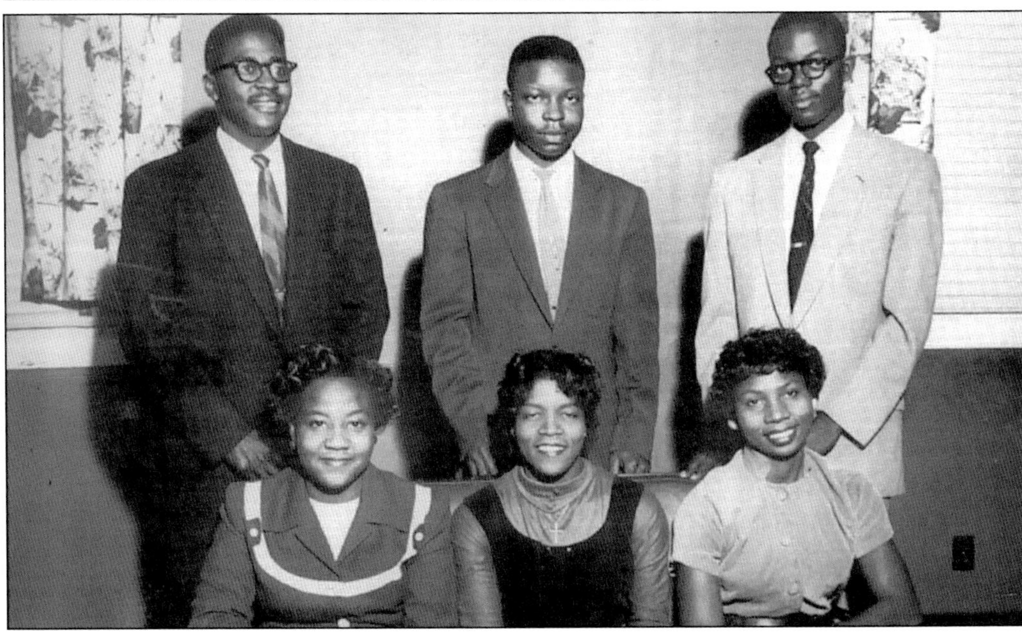

Charter members of the Alpha Iota Chapter of Alpha Kappa Mu National Honor Society are pictured here. Membership into this organization represents the highest academic achievement of an undergraduate career. To be eligible, a student must have a cumulative grade point average of 3.3 and a junior classification. This photograph is *c.* 1956.

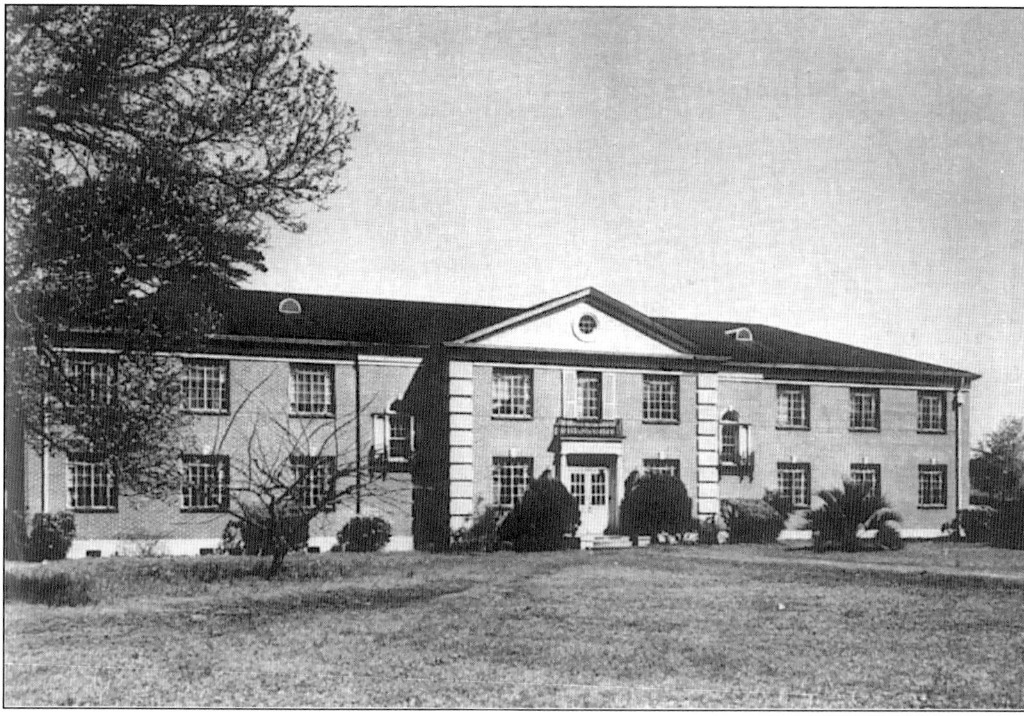

This is Davis Hall, a dormitory for upper-class men, *c.* 1956.

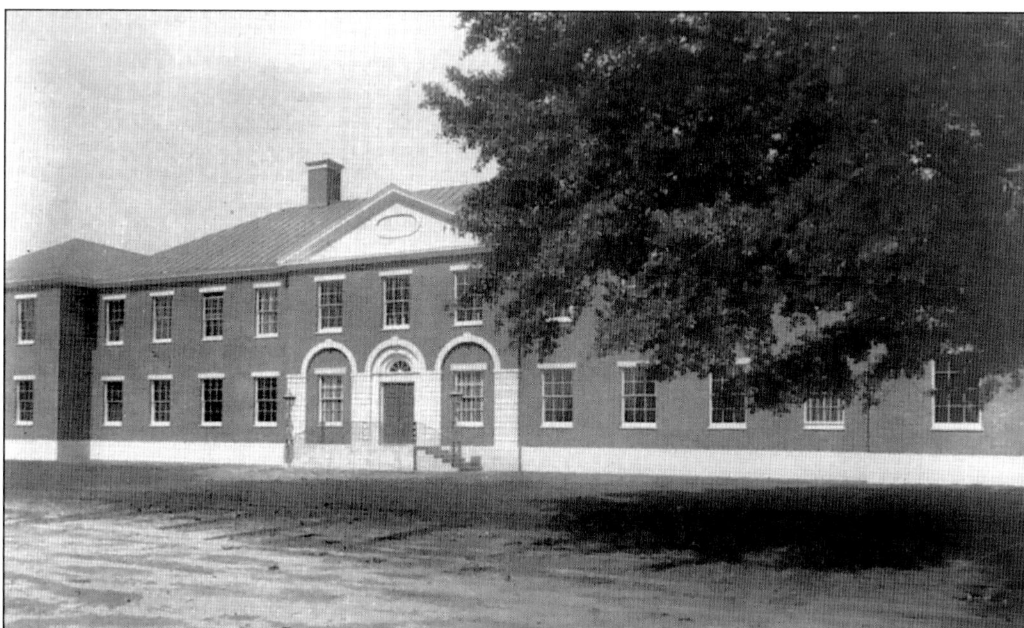

Jeffreys Hall, a science building, is shown here *c.* 1956. It was named for former dean Richard L. Jeffreys.

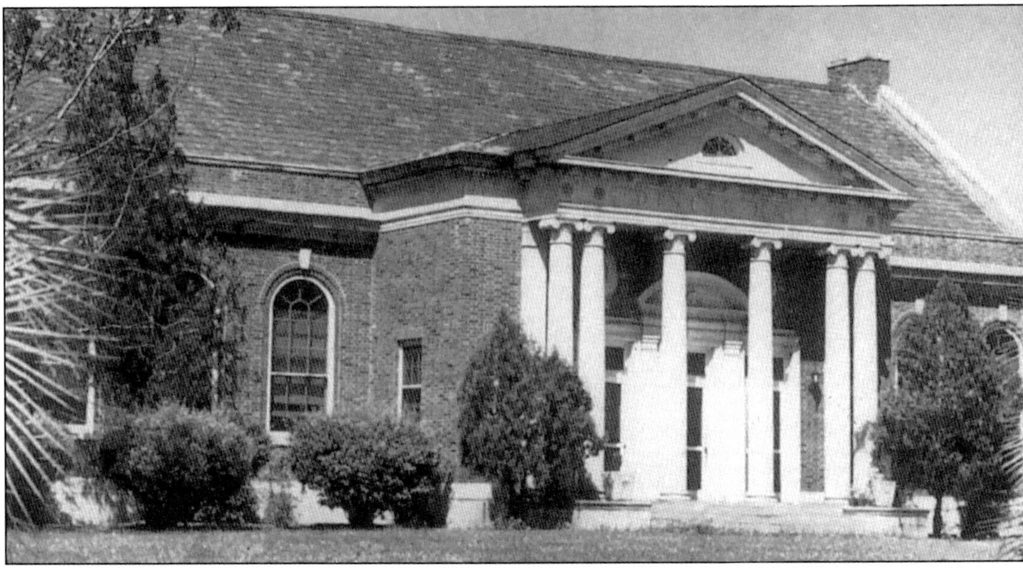

The University dining hall, built in 1931 and pictured *c.* 1956, was named for the former department of business head, Mrs. L. Orene Hall.

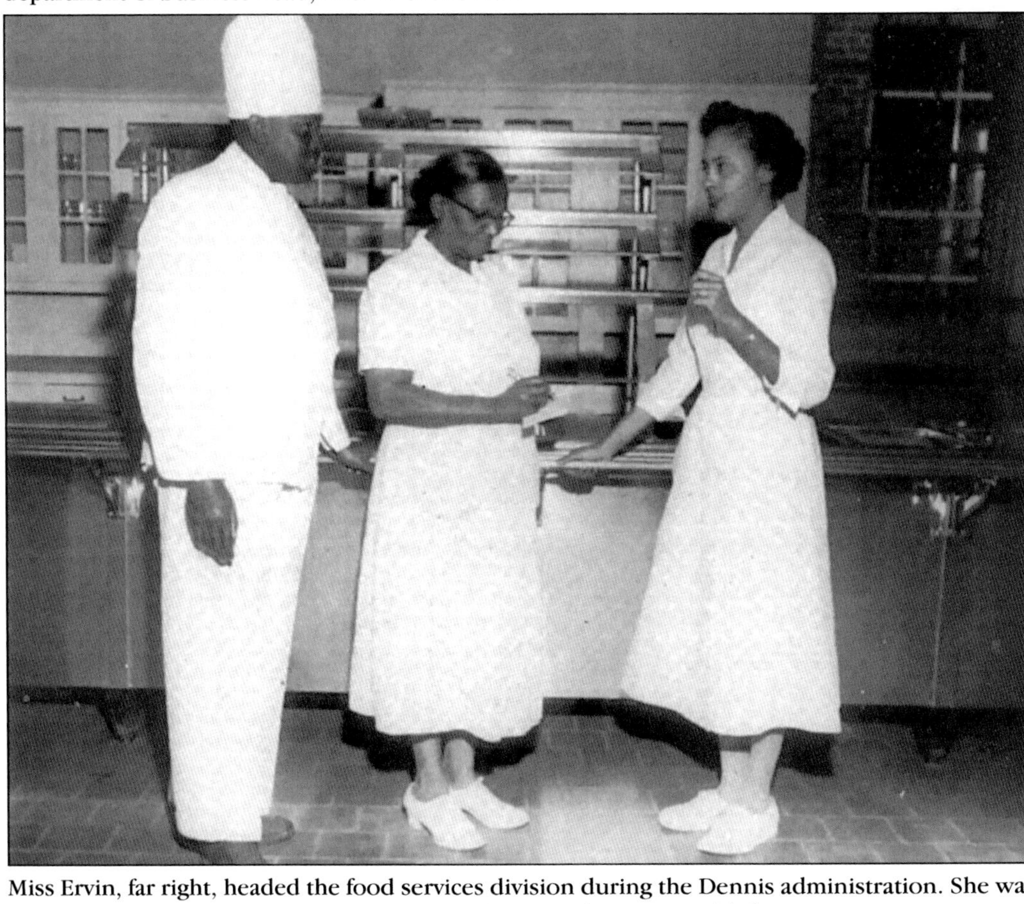

Miss Ervin, far right, headed the food services division during the Dennis administration. She was ably assisted by Miss Northington, center, and Mr. Jordan, pictured left.

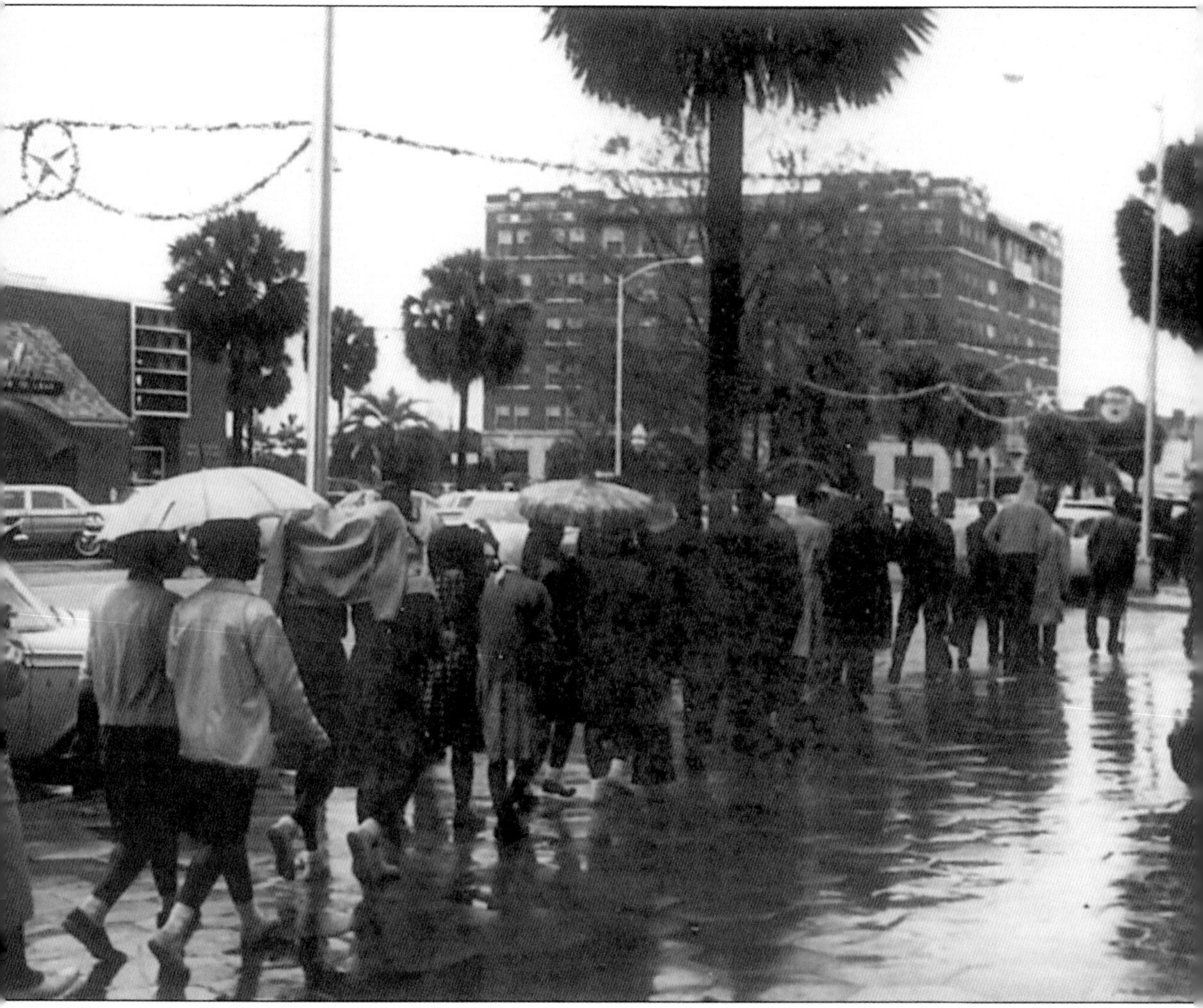

October 1961 was a watershed in Albany State's history. Three young activists—Charles Sherrod, Cordell Reagan, and Charles Jones of SNCC—arrived in Albany and initiated the Albany Civil Rights Movement. Two students from Albany State were arrested: Bertha Gober of Atlanta and Blanton Hall of Athens. These arrests galvanized the Albany community and brought national attention to the area. As a result Dr. Martin Luther King Jr., Ralph Abernathy of SCLC, and Tom Hayden of SDS journeyed to the city.

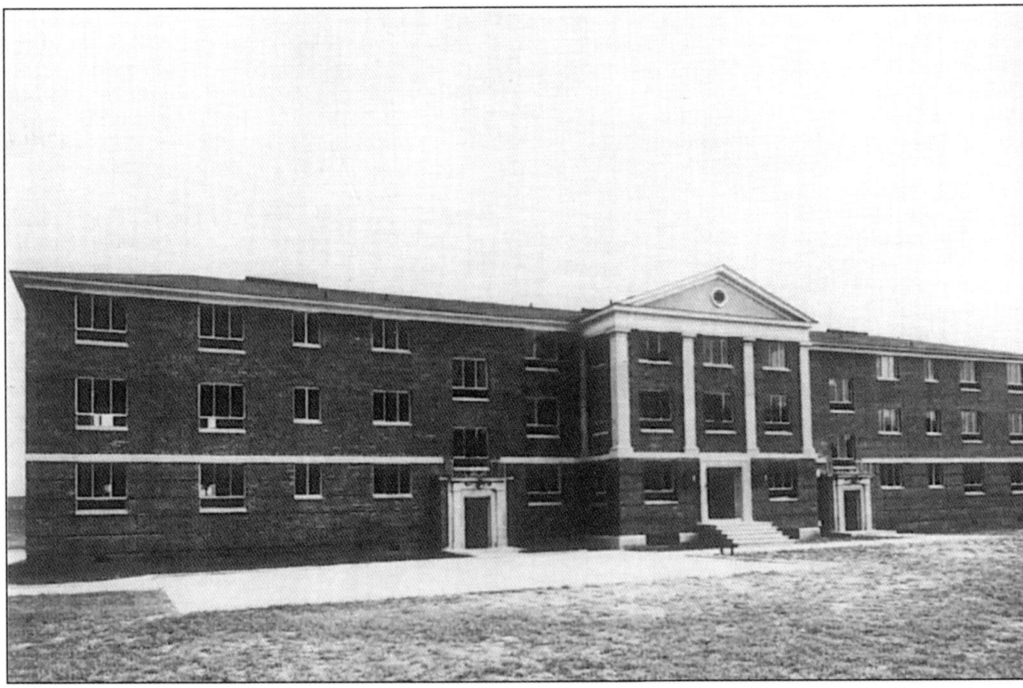

McIntosh Hall was a dormitory for upper-class women. It is shown here *c.* 1956, and was named for early trustee Henry M. McIntosh.

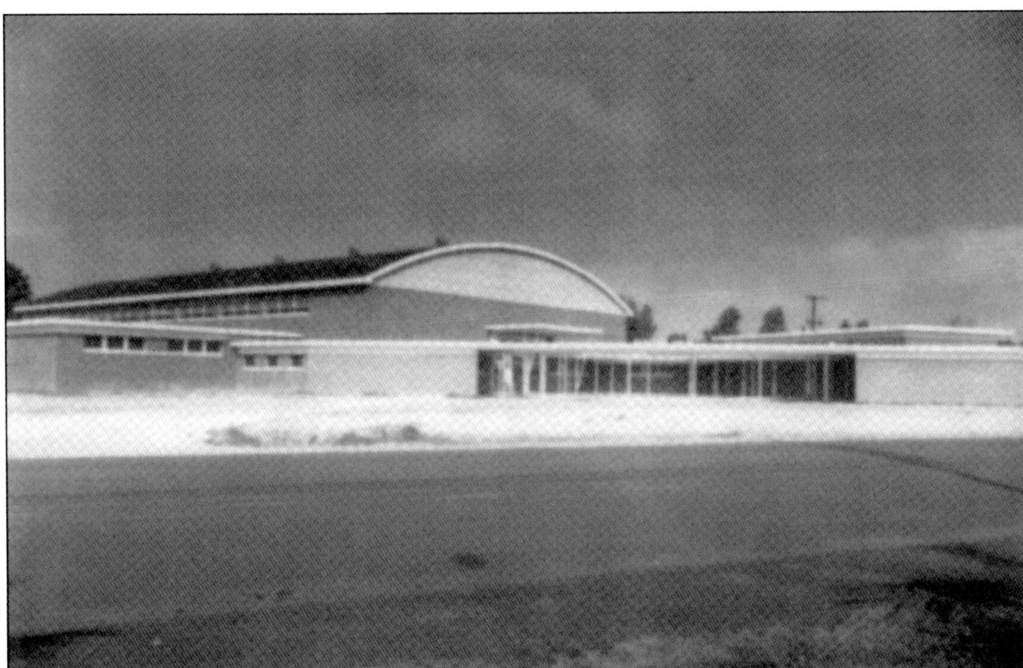

Sanford Hall was the new gymnasium, shown here in 1956.

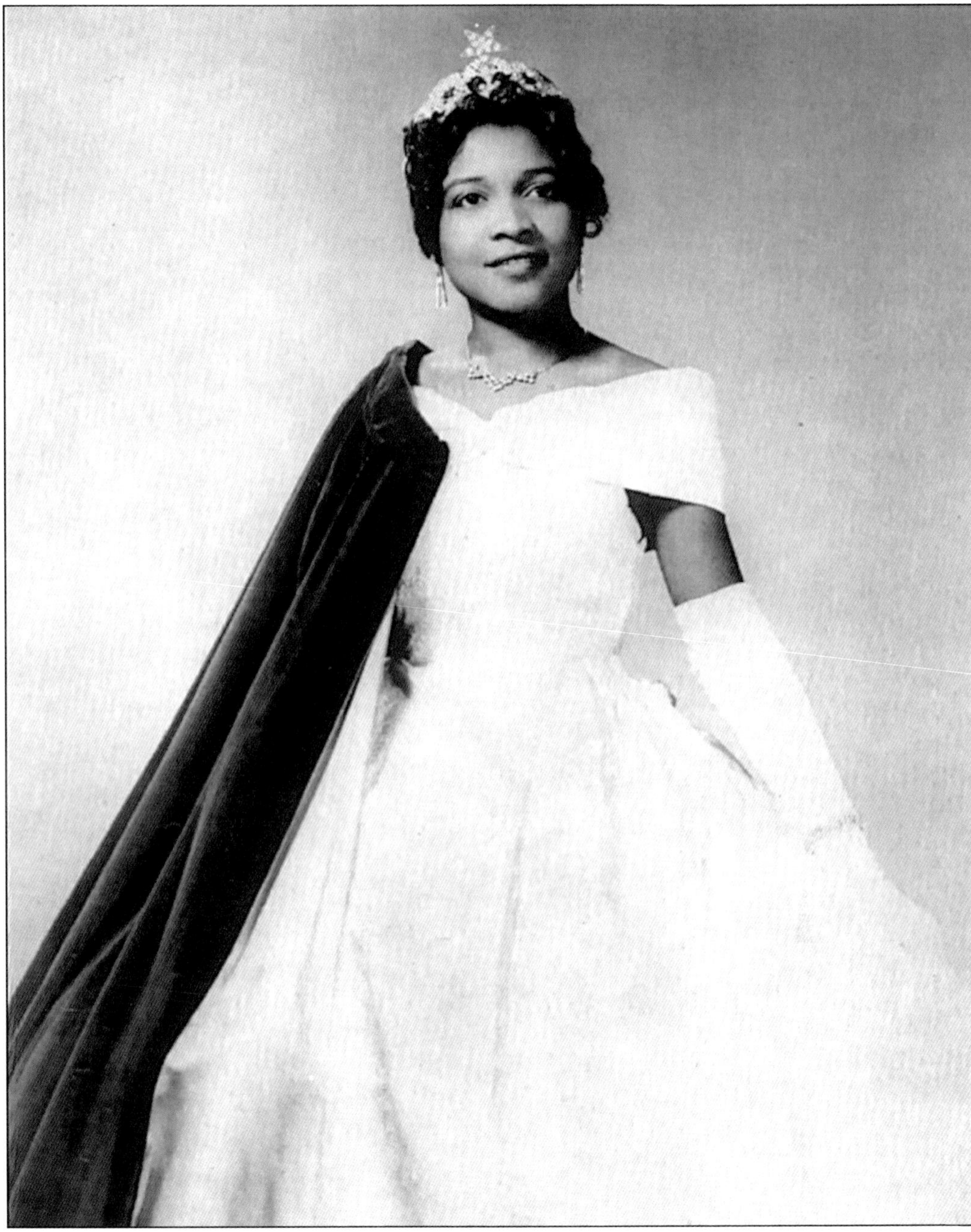

This is Ethel Hardeman, Miss Albany State 1960–1961.

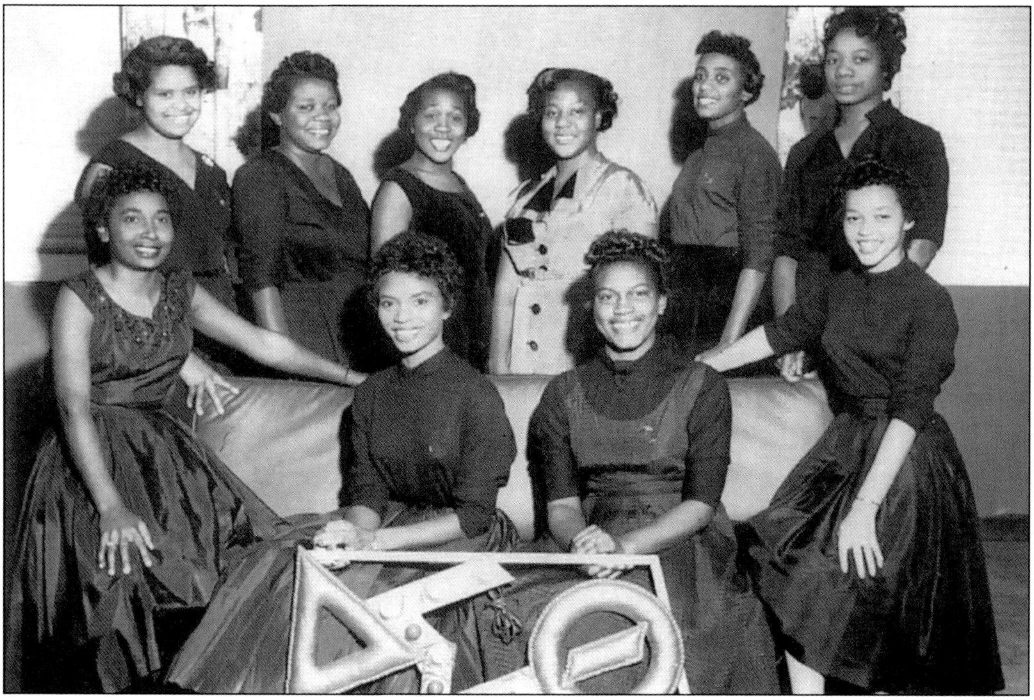

Pictured here are members of Delta Sigma Theta sorority, *c*. 1956. They are (from left to right) Annette Harris, Maeretta Mitchell, Bettye Neal, Cecil Andrews, Alma Byrd, Jean Beall, Erlene Cruel, Mary Daniel, Pansy Wilson, and Eloise Nelson.

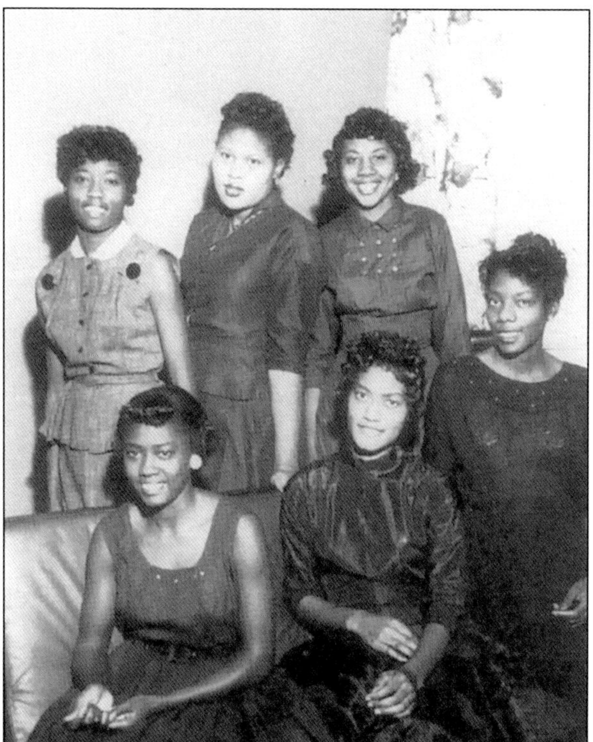

The following members of the Zeta Phi Beta sorority, Pi Beta Chapter, in 1956 were: (from left to right) Carrie Davis, Doris McKenzie, Elizabeth Robinson, Queen Davis, Mary Kate Smith, Irene Wright, and Nina Walker.

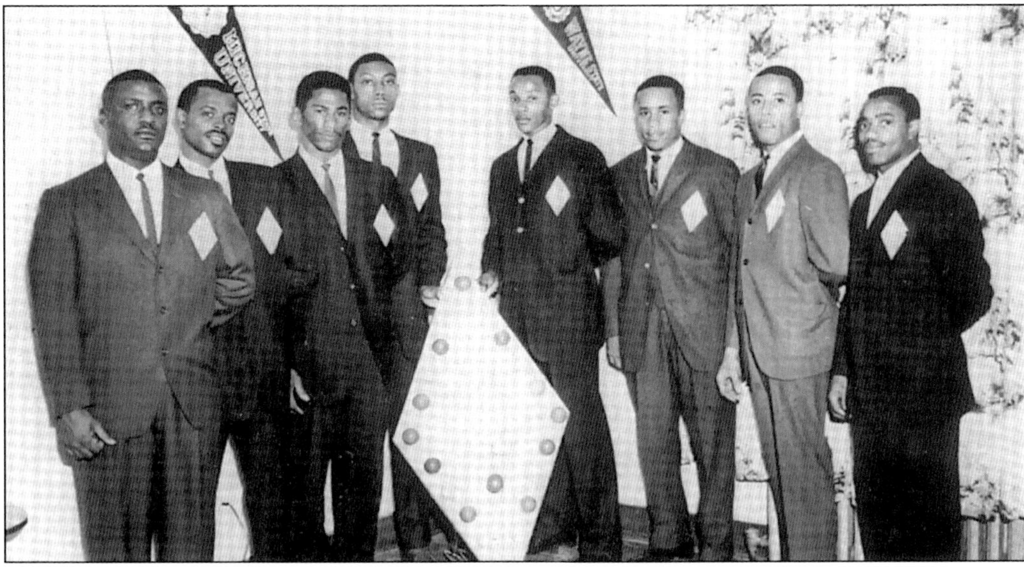

The members of Kappa Alpha Psi fraternity, Delta Xi Chapter, are (from left to right) Charles Frazier, Tim Duhart, Milton Bostic, Marion Dious, Charlie Fambro, Early Williams, Jacob Bentley, and Frank Scott. This photograph is from *c*. 1961.

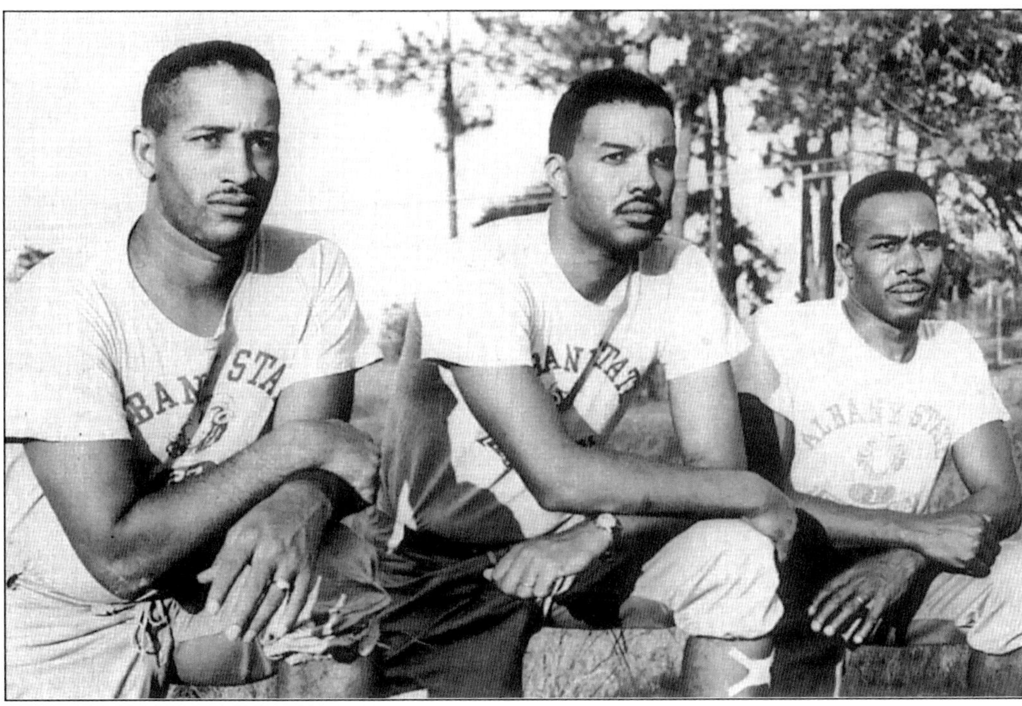

The brain trust of the "Golden Rams" in 1960 is shown in a characteristic pose. Head coach and director of athletics O.W. O'Neal Jr. (center) is flanked by line coach C.K. Dunson (left) and backfield coach J.C. Mitchell.

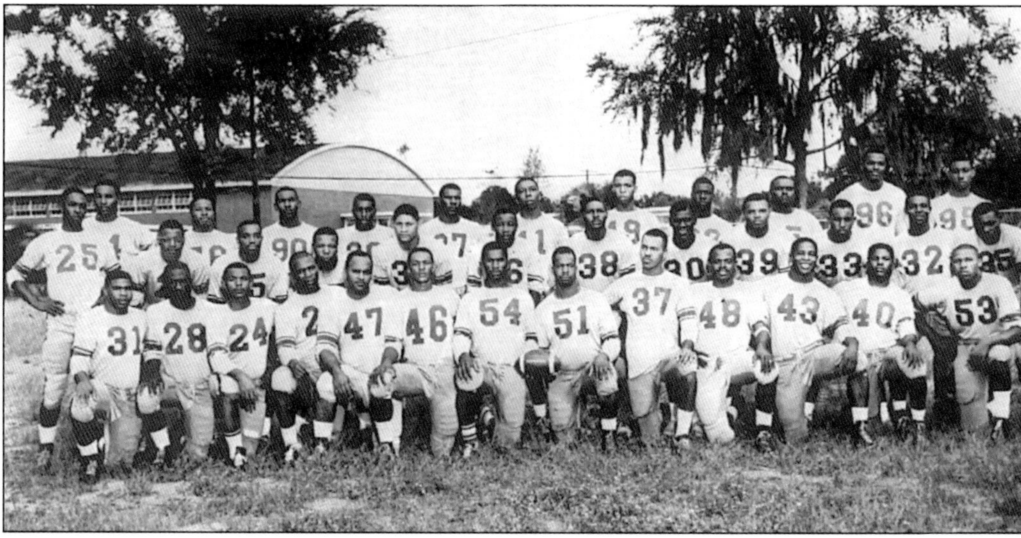

The 1960–1961 Albany State College Golden Rams are pictured here. In the first row (from left to right) are Ed Nelson (FB), Ransom Hill (HB), Willie Townsend (HB), Garfield Stephens (E), Clifton Bradley (T), Charlie Fambro (T), co-captain Milton Bostic (QB-E), co-captain Robert Bowens (C), Art Gamble (QB), Tem DuHart (G), Abner Mackey (T), Earl Summerline (G), and Dave Horne (E). In the second row (from left to right) are Jesse James (HB), Curtis Taylor (QB), Frank Scott (HB), Clayton Furlow (HB), Oscar Webster (FB), Henry Wison (HB), Eddie Coleman (G), Howard Magwood (G), Stanley Jones (G), Charles Price (G), Brister Hightower (G), and Jesse Ivory (HB). In the third row (from left to right) are Calvin Hention (T), Charles Peters (G), Armond Farrar (E), Jerry Hancock (HB), Bill Parkman (FB), Robert Wiley (T), Charles Goins (E), Leamon Wiley (C), Sherman Bailey (C), Steve Jackson (T), and Marion Dious (T).

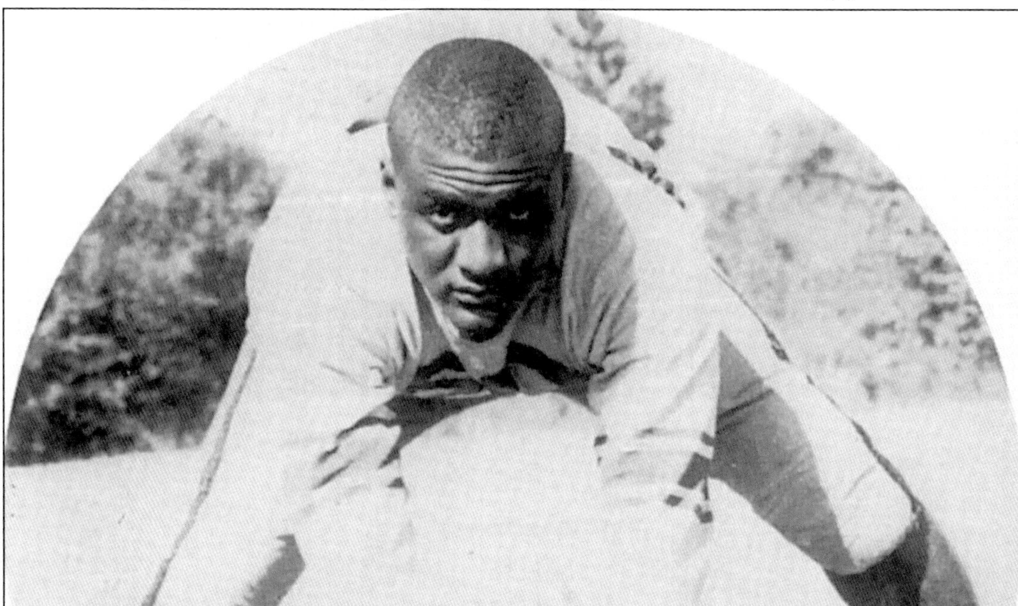

Charles Frazier, an All-Conference center, anchored the Golden Rams for their unblemished record of 1960. The 1960 football team was a second in African-American history following Tennessee with its unblemished record of 1939.

Four

Dr. Thomas Miller Jenkins 1965–1969

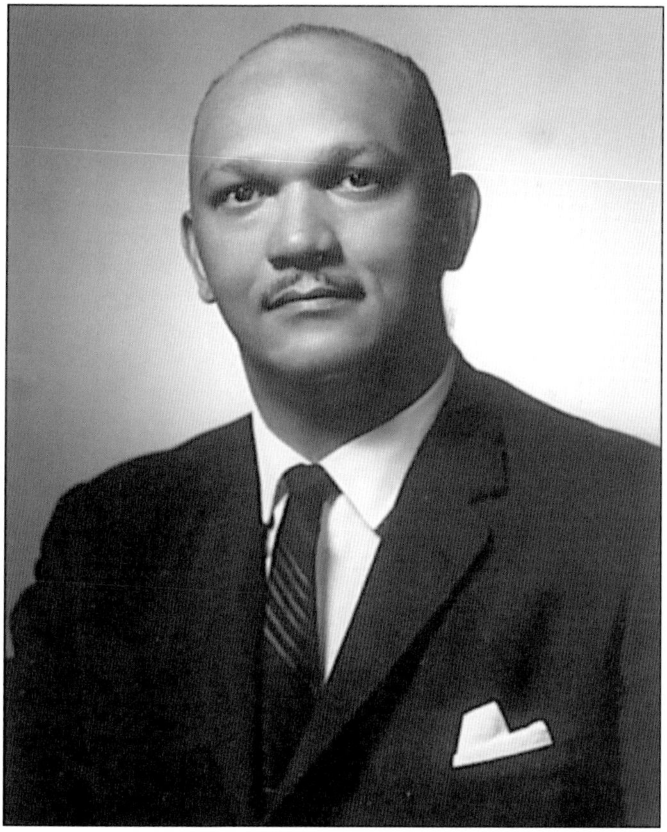

Dr. Thomas Miller Jenkins, a graduate of West Virginia State College and Boston University, was inaugurated as the fourth president of Albany State College on July 1, 1965. The college continued to grow in service and in scope during his administration. Faculty and staff were upgraded and a massive plan for expansion was initiated. A new health center, duplex faculty apartments, and the Dennis Student Union were erected during his tenure. The science, nursing, and business buildings were renovated to meet the demands of new and varied curricula. The college also made great strides in the area of community involvement.

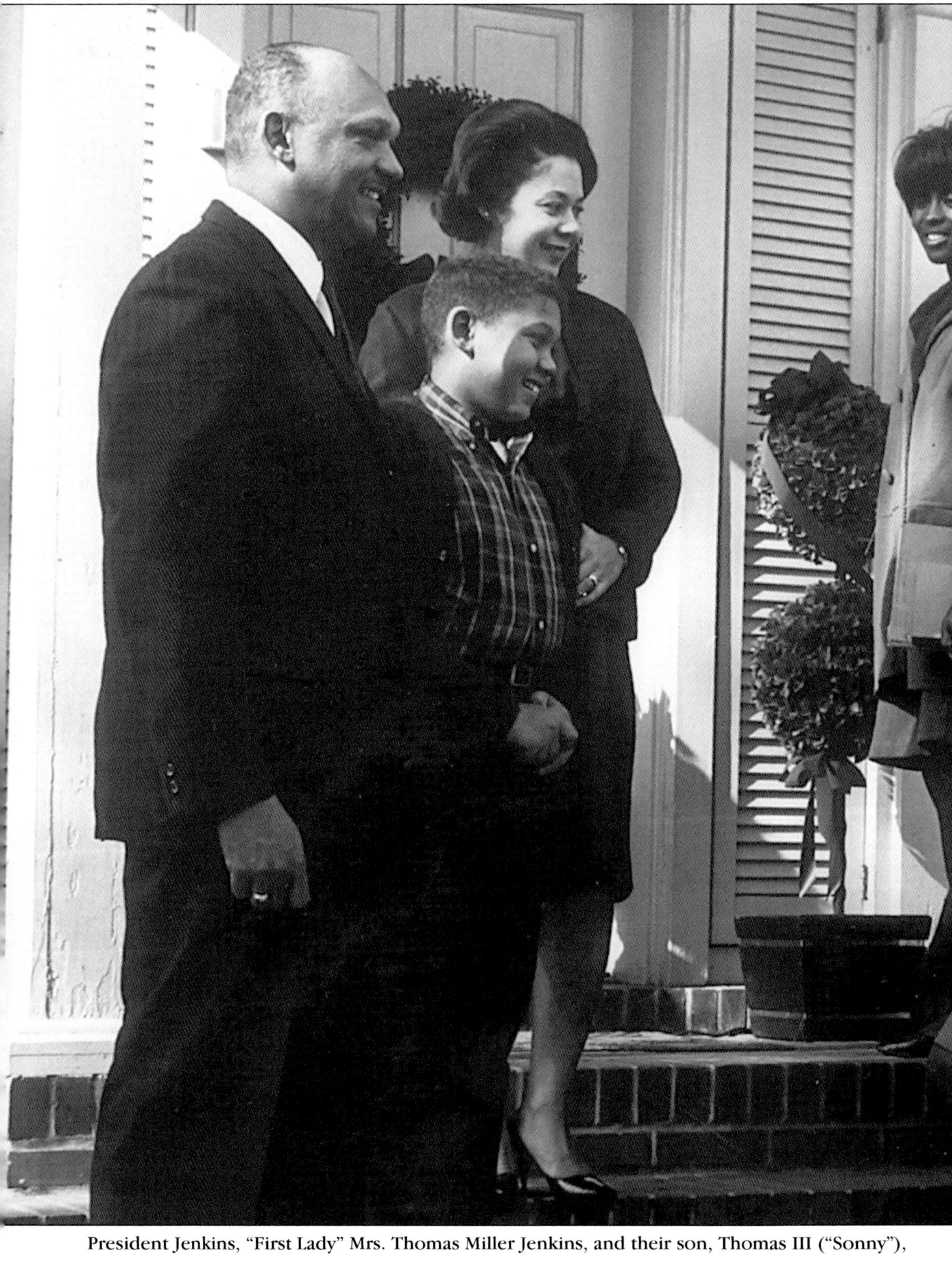

President Jenkins, "First Lady" Mrs. Thomas Miller Jenkins, and their son, Thomas III ("Sonny"),

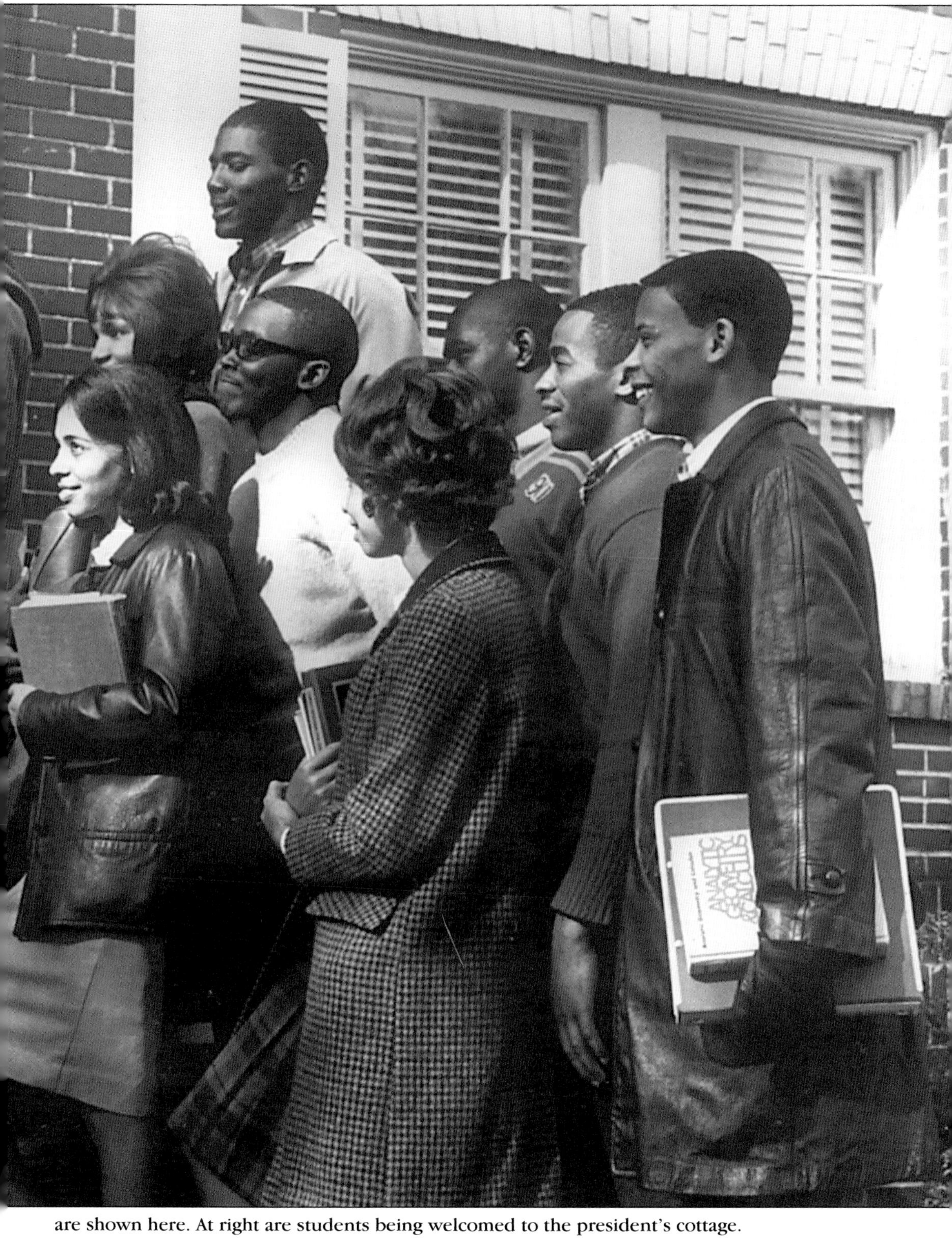

are shown here. At right are students being welcomed to the president's cottage.

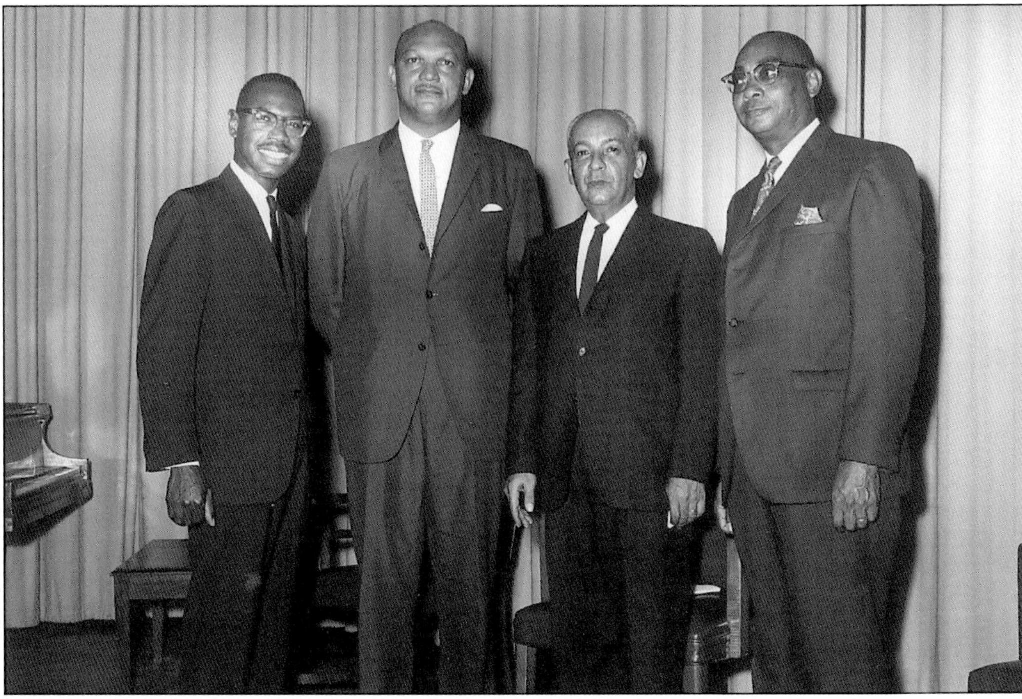

Ben C. Hampton, President Jenkins, unidentified, and Dr. William E. Lightfoote are pictured here.

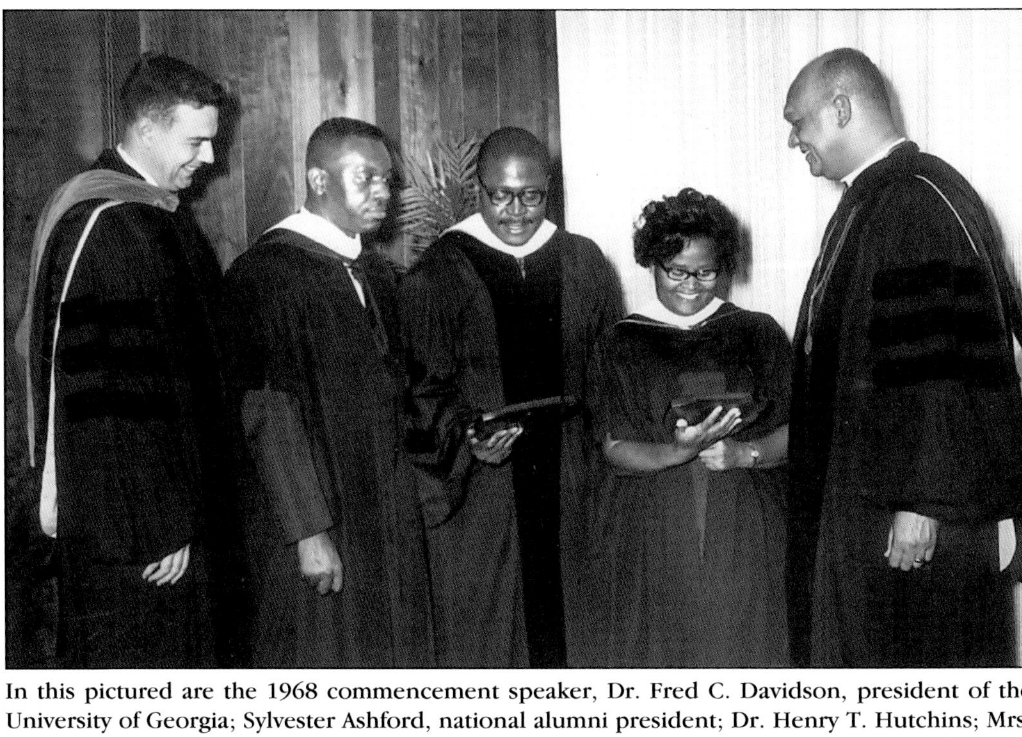

In this pictured are the 1968 commencement speaker, Dr. Fred C. Davidson, president of the University of Georgia; Sylvester Ashford, national alumni president; Dr. Henry T. Hutchins; Mrs. Gladys Ward McCullough, composer of Albany State's alma mater; the two distinguished Alumni Award recipients; and President Jenkins.

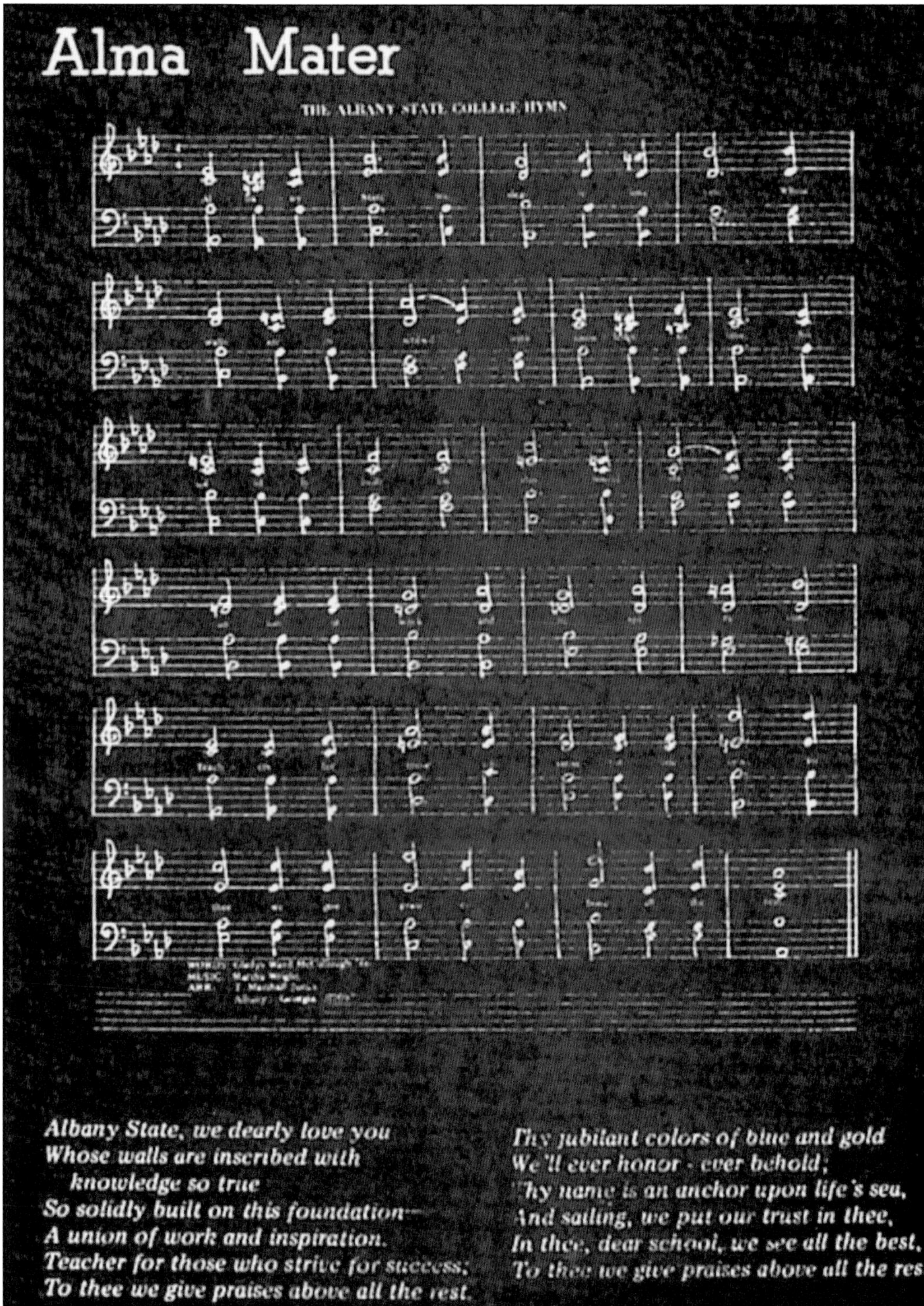

Albany State University's alma mater lyrics were written by Gladys Ward McCullough '46. The music was written by Martha Wright.

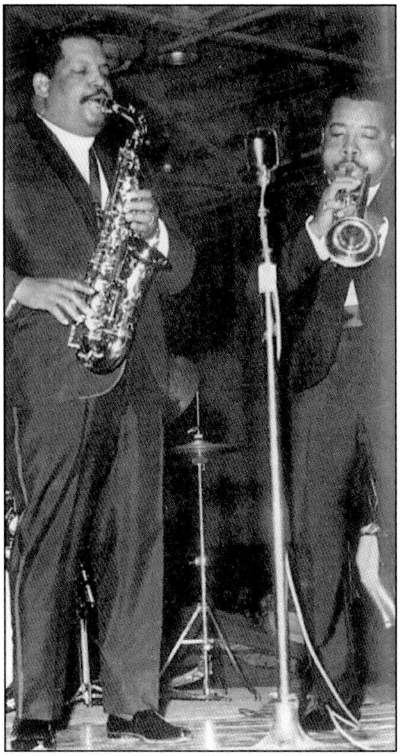

During Negro History Week Observance *c.* 1967, Cannonball and Nat Adderly, the famed brother jazz musicians, performed brilliantly in Sanford Hall.

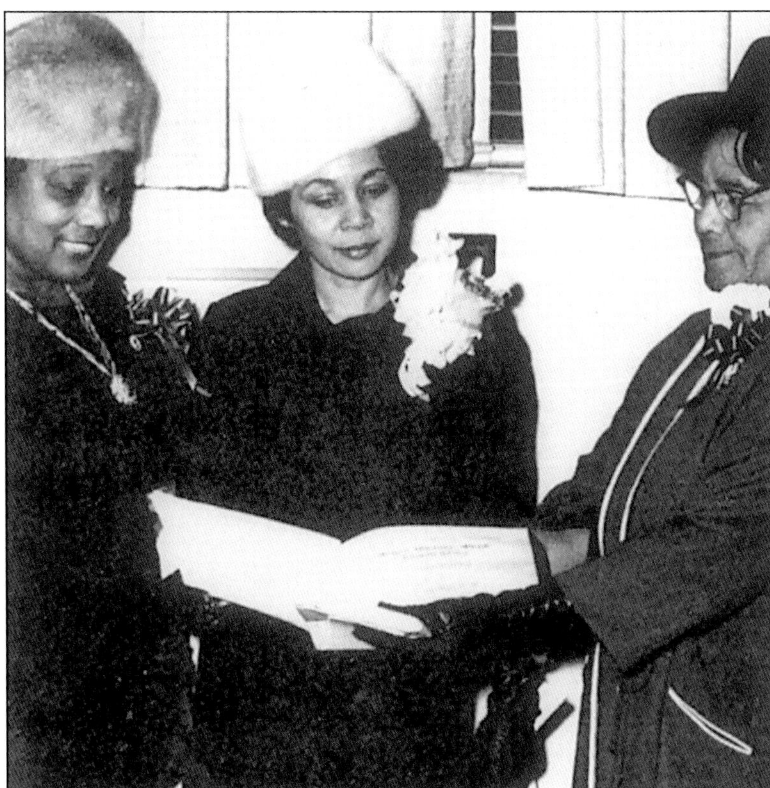

Mrs. Mamie B. Reese, Mrs. Evelyn K. Jenkins, and Mrs. Troas Latimer look over Sigma Rho Sigma program during Negro History Week. Mrs. Latimer founded Sigma Rho Sigma Honor Society and was an associate professor of history at Albany State. She taught from 1943 to 1966 in the division of social science.

Miss Albany State 1967–1968 and her attendants are seen here. From left to right are Velma Thomas (first attendant), Louise Brown, Miss Albany State, and Mary Parrish (second attendant).

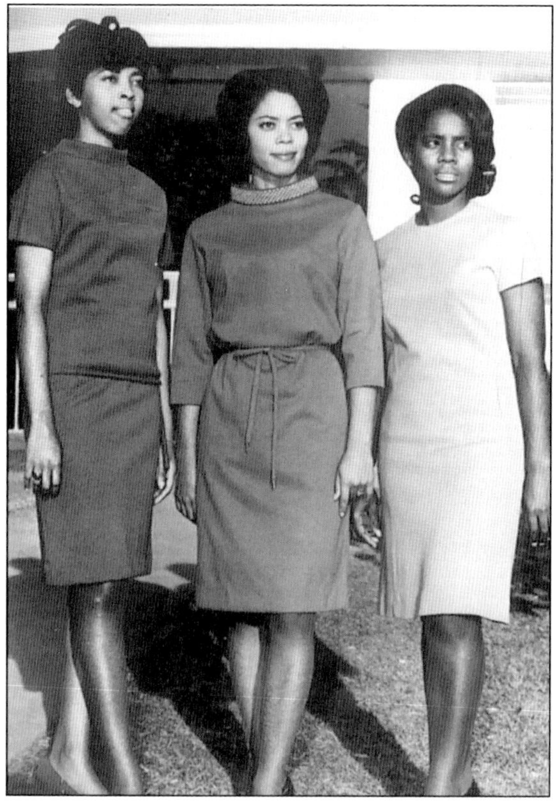

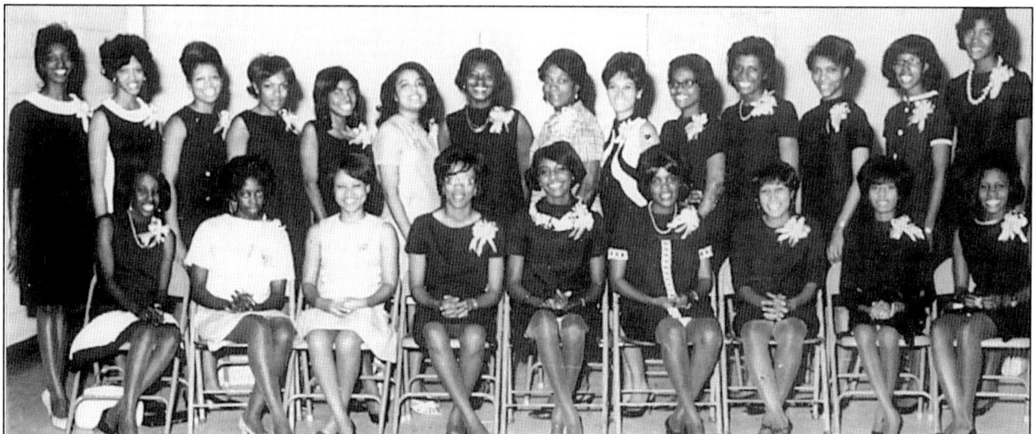

The Albany State Key Boarders is an organization of the campus's office managers and secretaries.

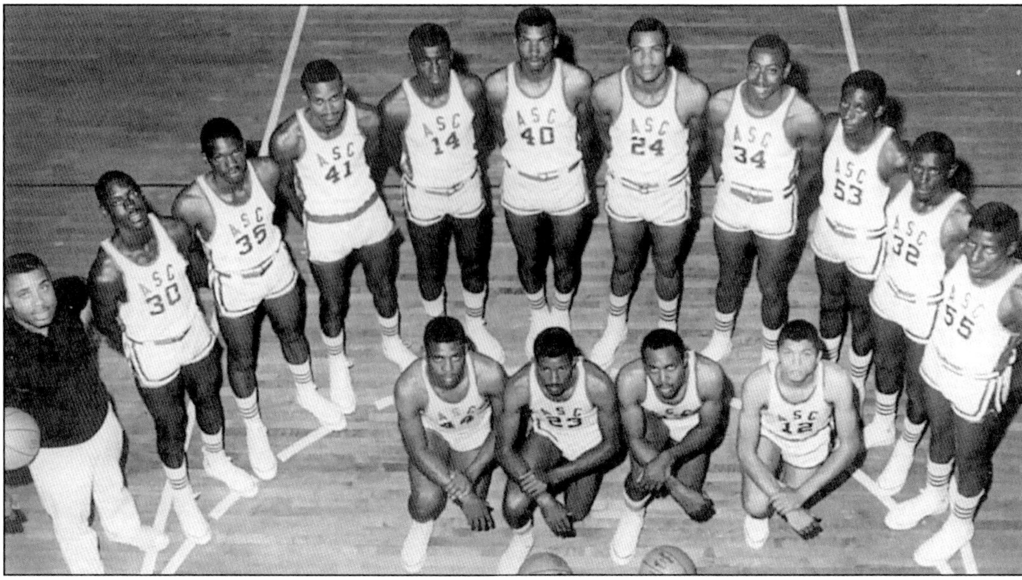

The 1967–1968 Rams squad won SEAC, NAIA, and District Championships. Kneeling from left to right are James Brown, Ted Anderson, Percy Richardson, and Howie Harlow. Standing from left to right are Coach Robert Rainey, Mack Daughtry, Joe Poitier, Paul Davis, Wilbert Jones, Mel Jones, Jimmy Reams, James Anderson, Gary Greene, John Davis, and Clarence Ellis.

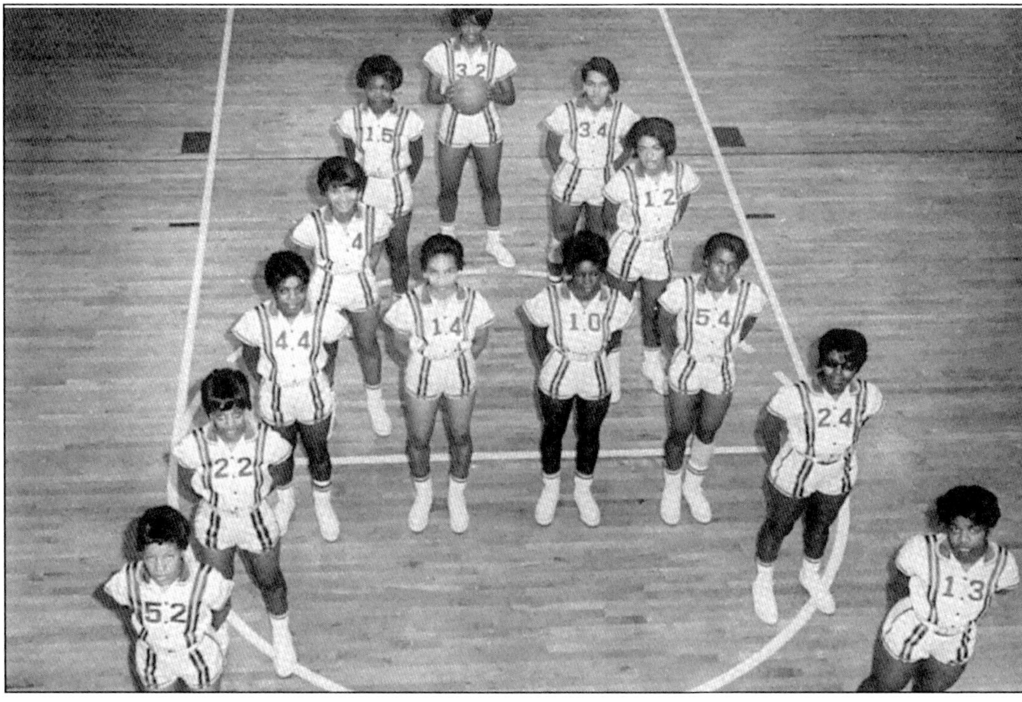

The 1967–1968 Ramettes were conference champions. Pictured in the center are Ruby Griggs and Earline Scott. Counterclockwise are Gwendolyn Haywood, Cora Winfrey, Ruth Williams, Glendora Scoot, Mae Lizzie Johnson, Demeris Jefferson, Jacquelyn Benjamin, Johnnie Hicks, Jonnie Baugh, Jacquelyn Walker, and Mary Wynn. The Lady Rams, or Ramettees," were coached by Miss Edith P. Daniels, also known as "Miss D."

Coach Edith P. Daniels, called "Miss D," was the mastermind behind ASC women's athletics for more than two decades, beginning in the 1960s.

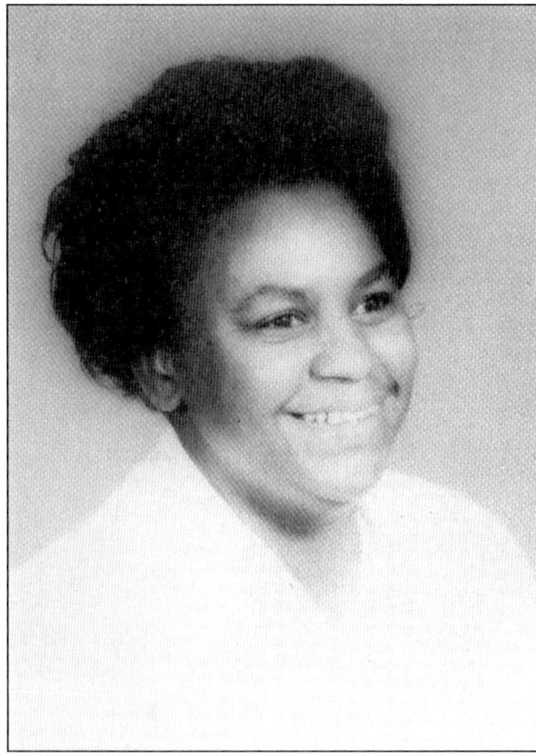

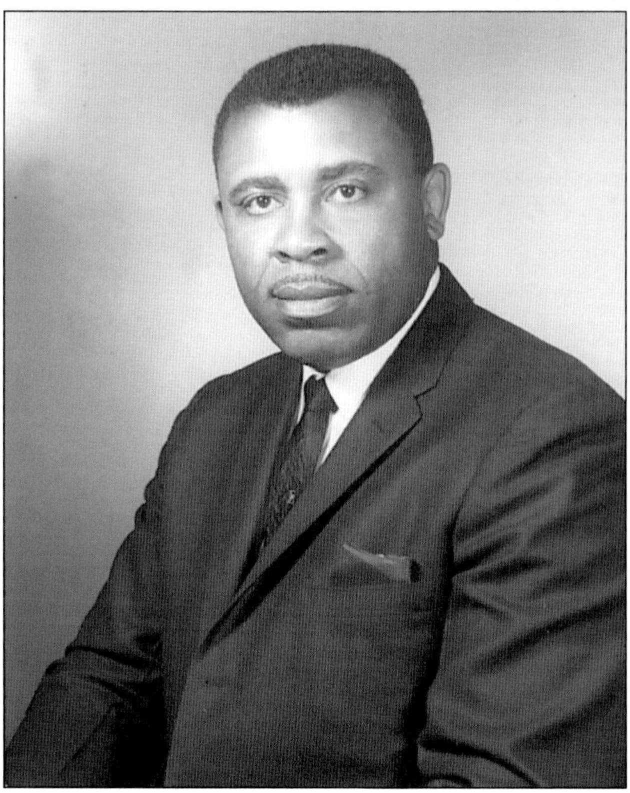

Robert Rainey began his coaching career at Albany State in 1960. Rainey, a native of McGhee, Arkansas, went to Albany to launch his college coaching career with experience as a high school coach and as a professional basketball player with the Kansas City Monarchs.

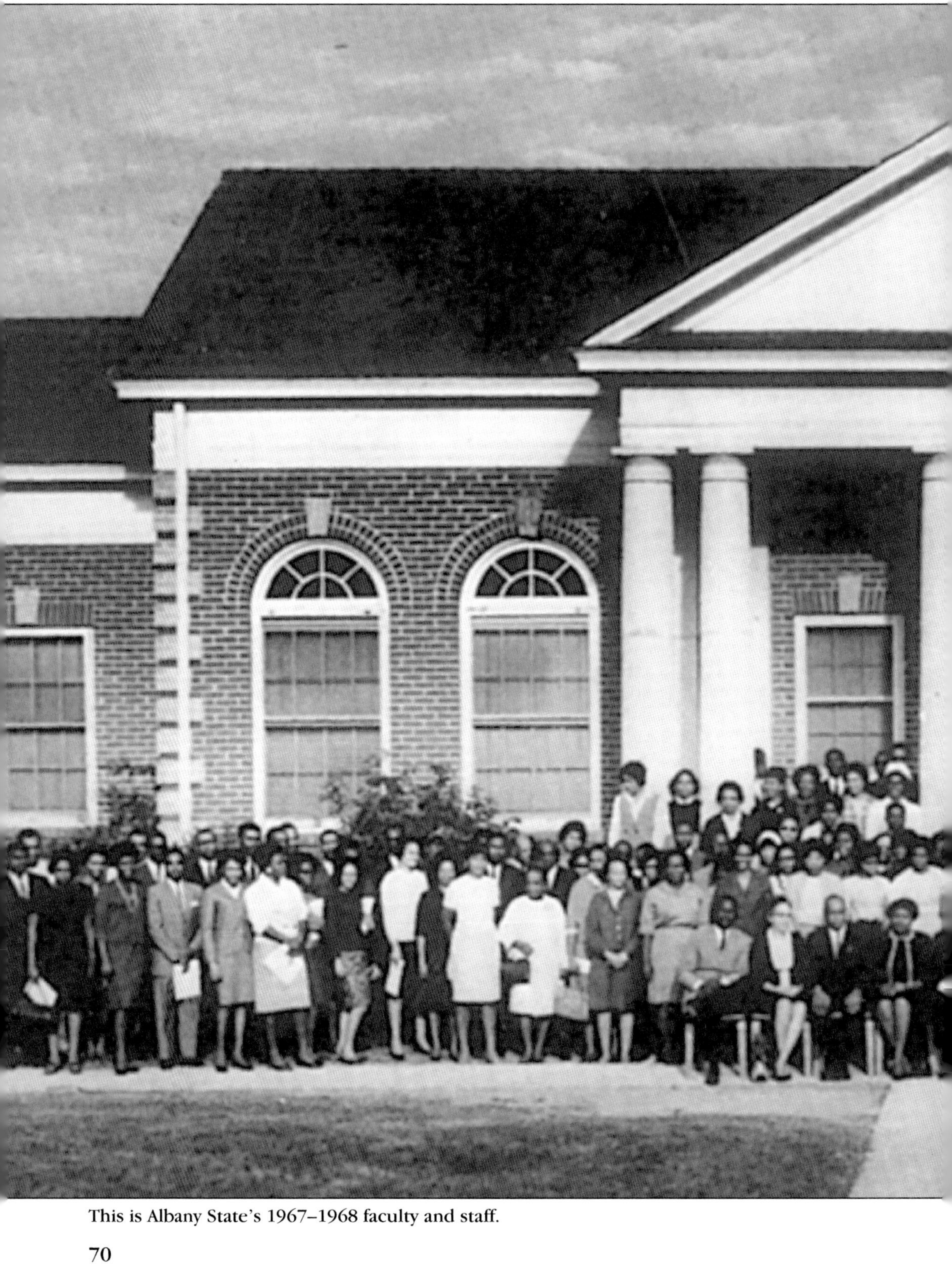

This is Albany State's 1967–1968 faculty and staff.

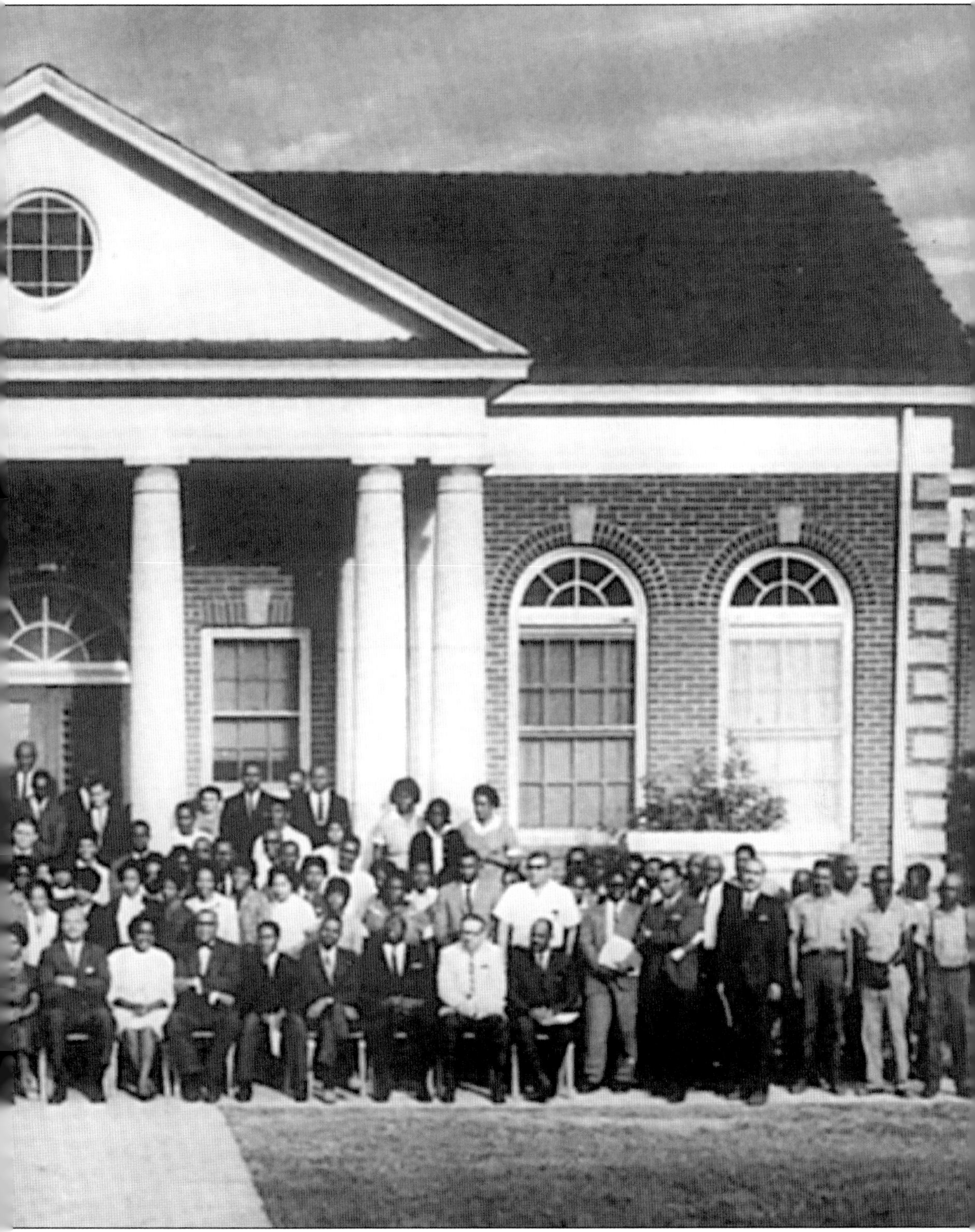

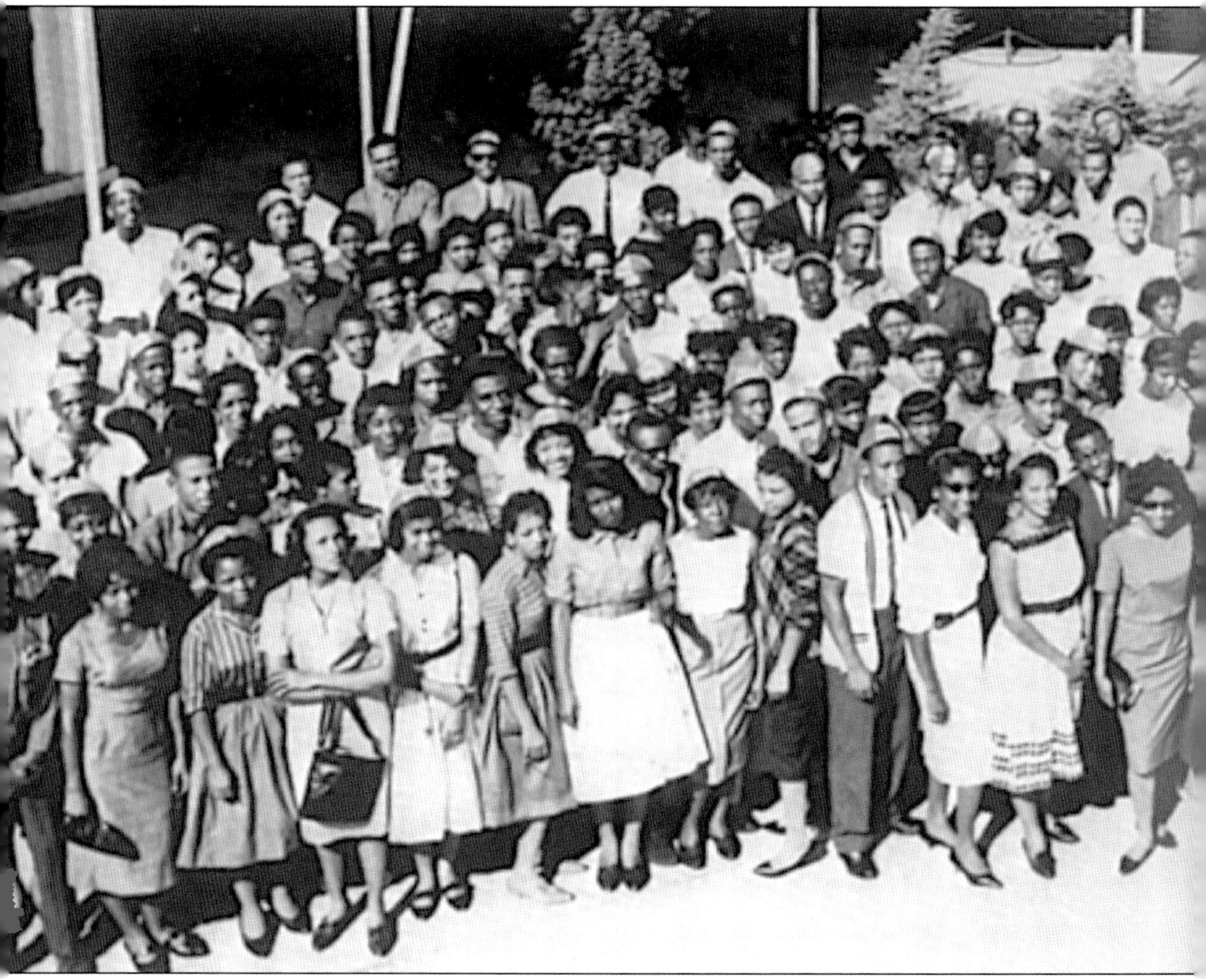

The freshmen class of 1961 had "A past to cherish, a future to fulfill."

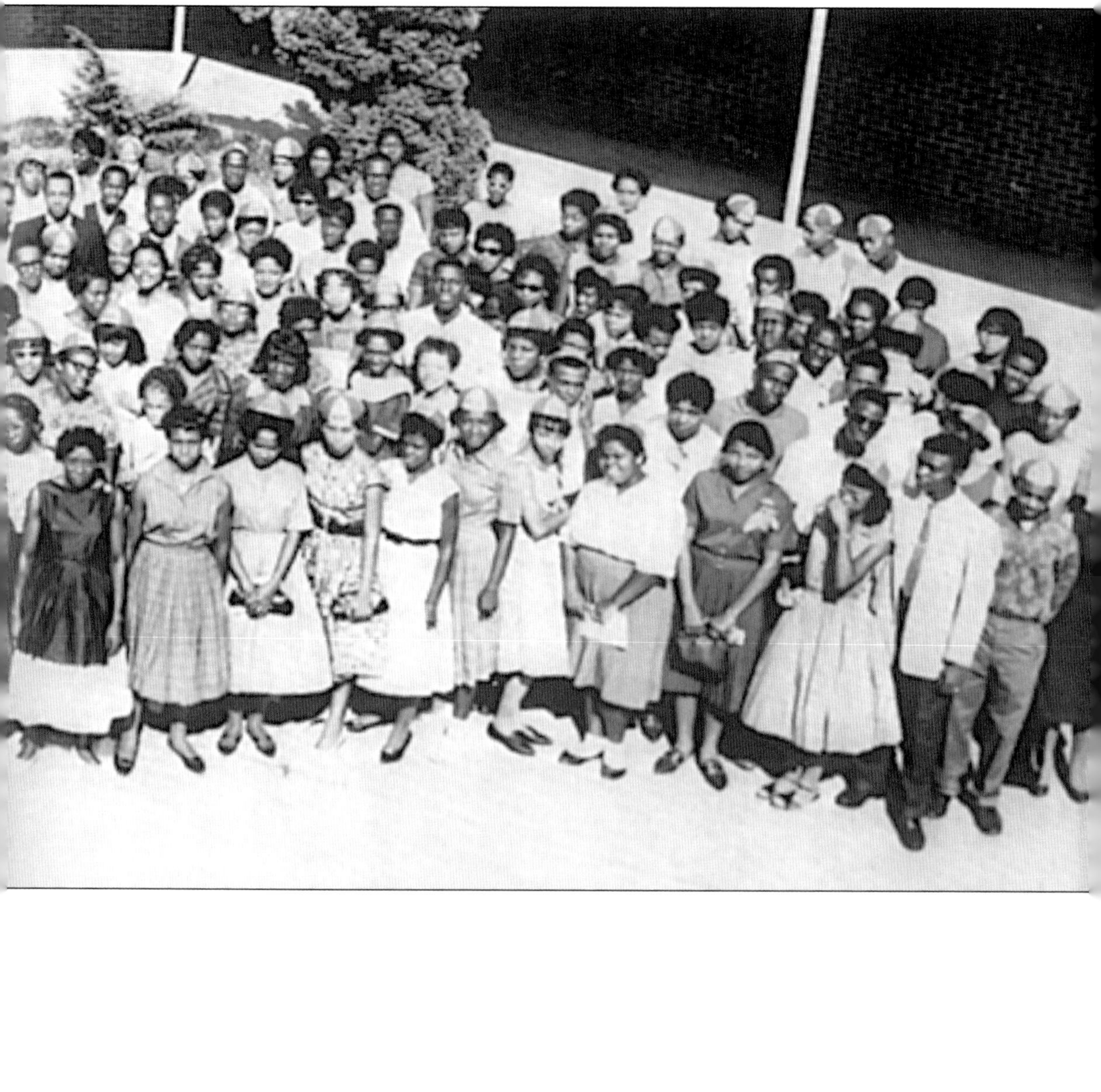

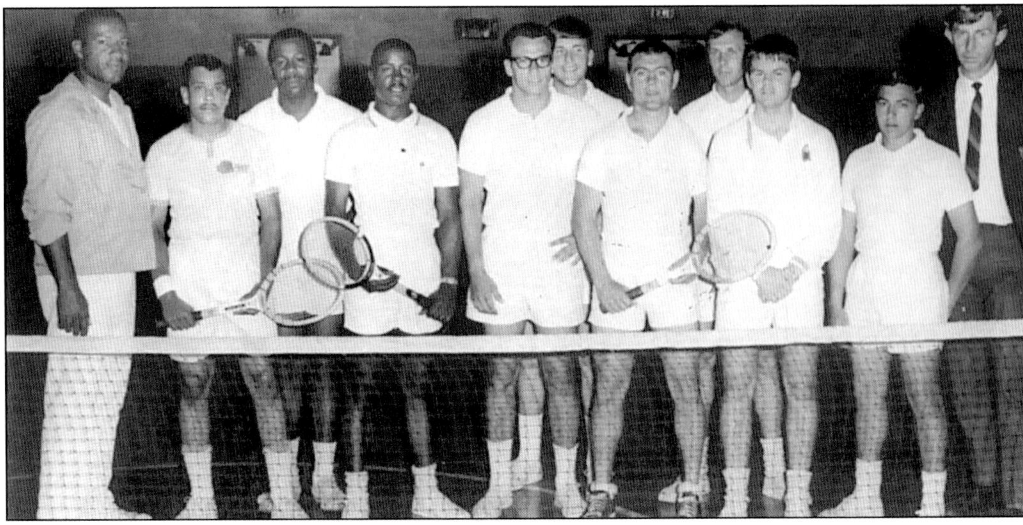

Albany State Tennis coach Dr. Bobby Lee is pictured with members of the tennis squad. Seen from left to right are Coach Lee, Mike Anthony, Jim Breland, and John Dean. The Transylvania College (Kentucky) tennis team, on the right, opposed the Ram netters during regular season competition.

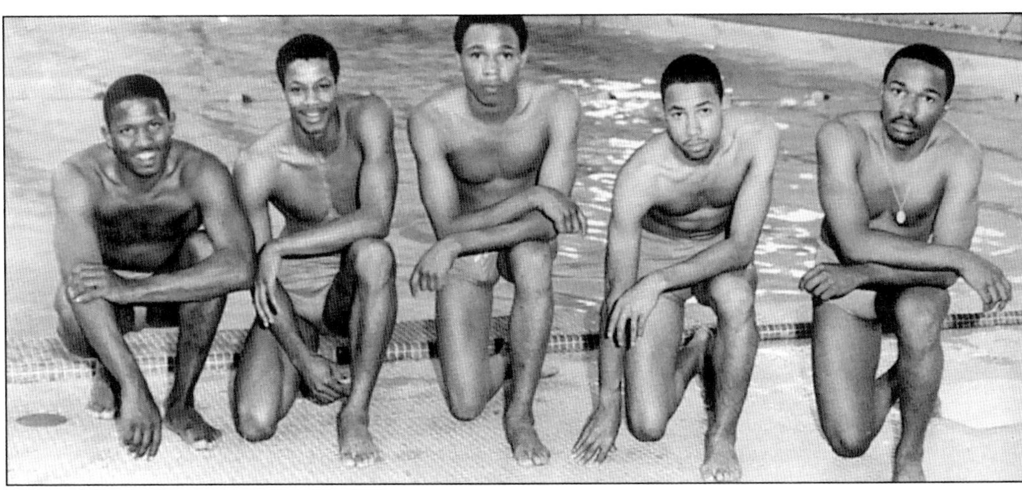

Members of the first intercollegiate swimming team at Albany State are, from left to right, Stacy Bell, Ernest Ward, William Pouncil, Charles Williams, and Grady Caldwell, who would later serve as director of student activities at Albany State.

Five

Dr. Charles Leonard Hayes 1969–1980

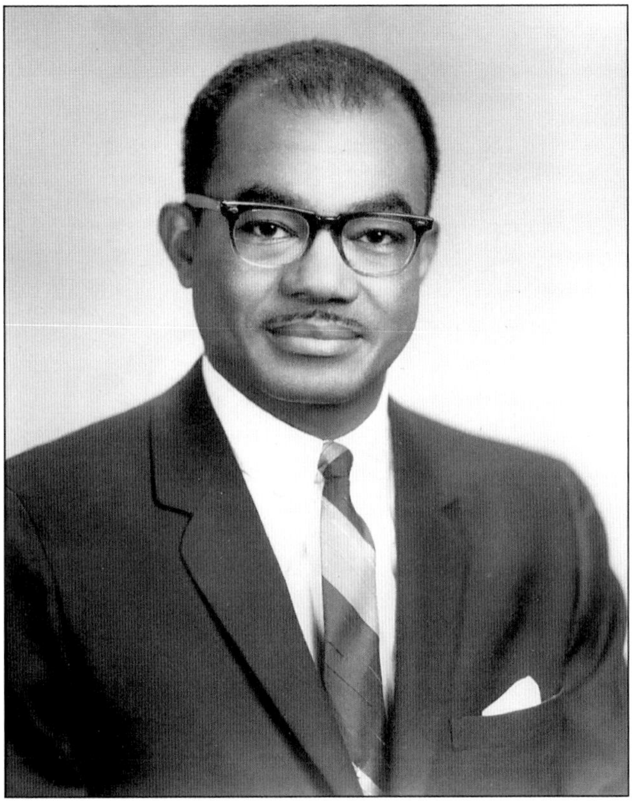

Dr. Charles Leonard Hayes, the fifth president of Albany State College, assumed this role October 1, 1969. A graduate of Leland College and a recipient of the M.Ed. from Loyola University in Chicago and an Ed.D. from Colorado State University in Greely, Dr. Hayes was responsible for much of the growth of the institution. During his administration, the college's enrollment grew, campus facilities were expanded, the National Council for the Accreditation of Teacher Education certified teacher education programs, and the Department of Nursing was reorganized as a division. The faculty was upgraded, and graduate study was provided through an agreement with the Georgia State University and Valdosta State College. Other examples of innovative programs included the college's dual degree program with Georgia Institute of Technology for those students who major in engineering and/or technology, and the Army officer program with Fort Valley State College, which qualified a student to apply for a commission as a second lieutenant in the United States Army Corps. Through Dr. Hayes's efforts, the institution was able to supplement its state support with numerous governmental and non-governmental grants.

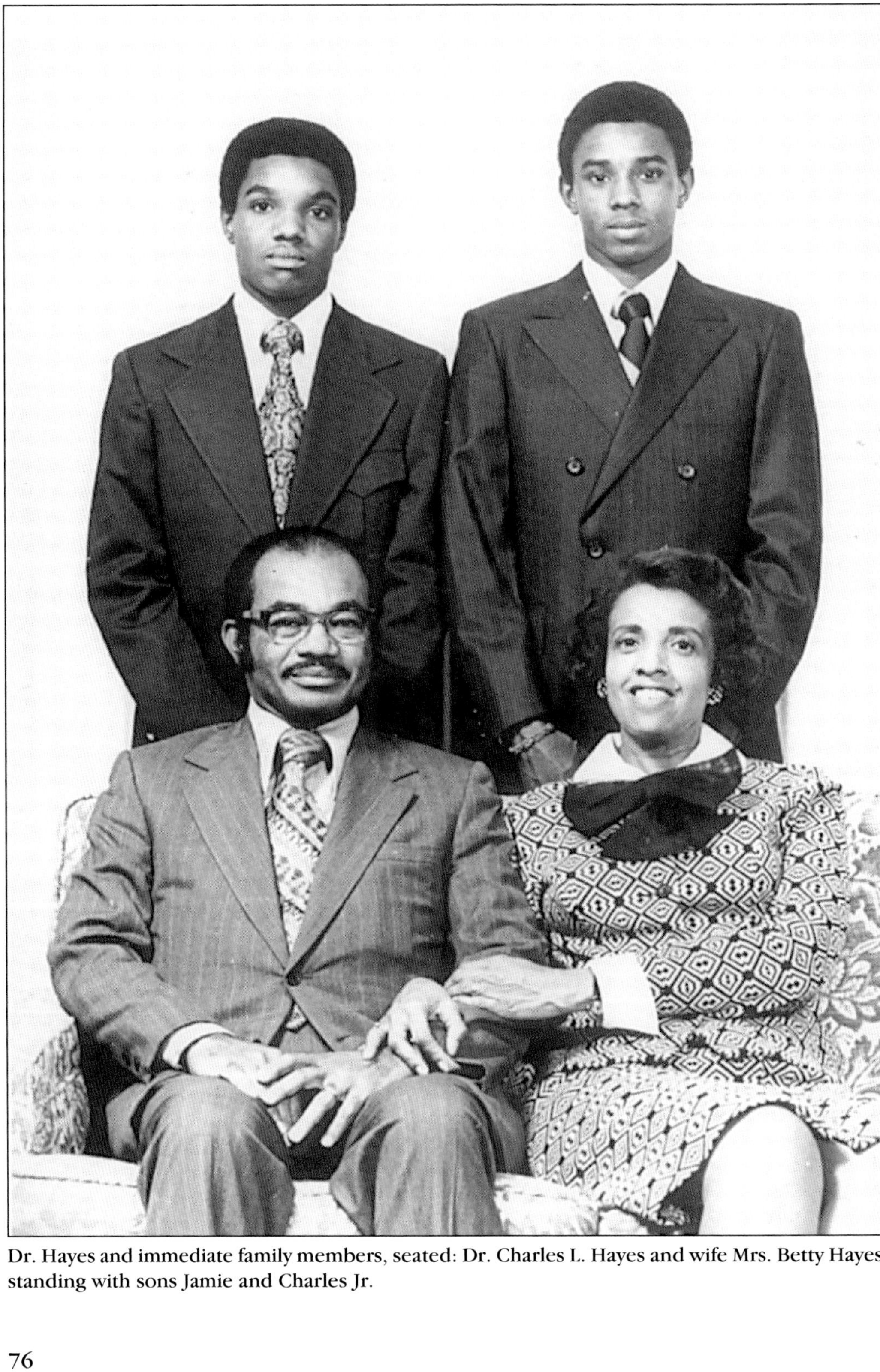

Dr. Hayes and immediate family members, seated: Dr. Charles L. Hayes and wife Mrs. Betty Hayes, standing with sons Jamie and Charles Jr.

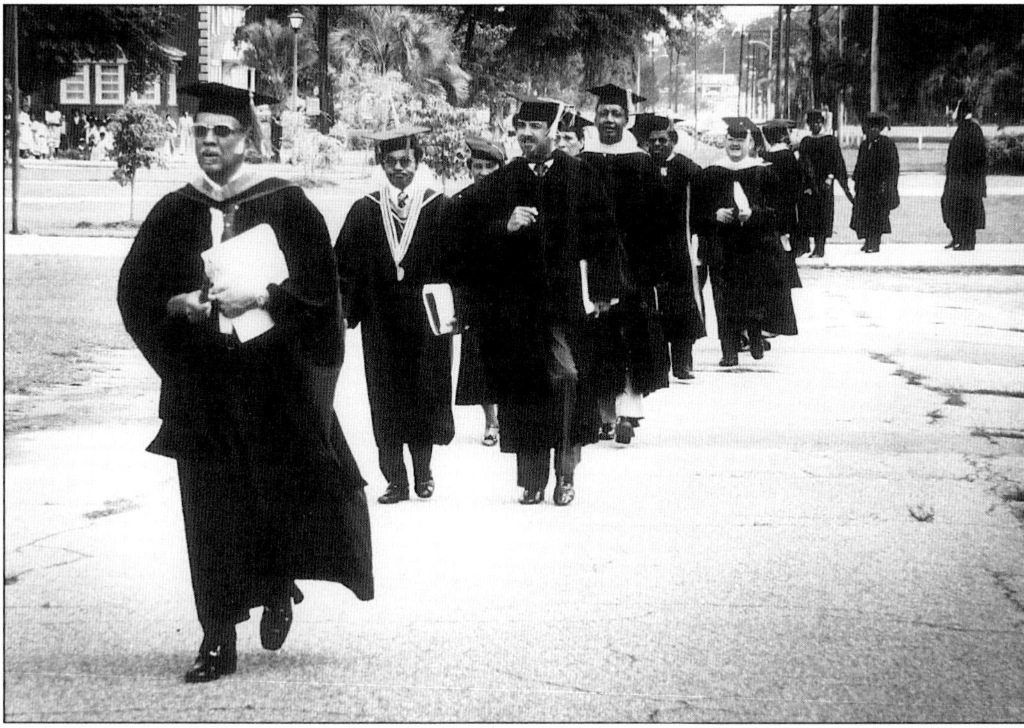

Obie W. O'Neal, professor emeritus of education, leads the graduation processional *c.* 1978. Below are members of the faculty senate. From left to right are Prof. Wiley Graydon, Dr. James Pendergrast (Dean of Academic Affairs), Prof. Willie A.R. Cochrane, Dr. Hayes (president), (standing) Dr. Bhagvat K. Joshi, Dr. Josephine Davis, Dr. Thelma D. Anderson, and unidentified.

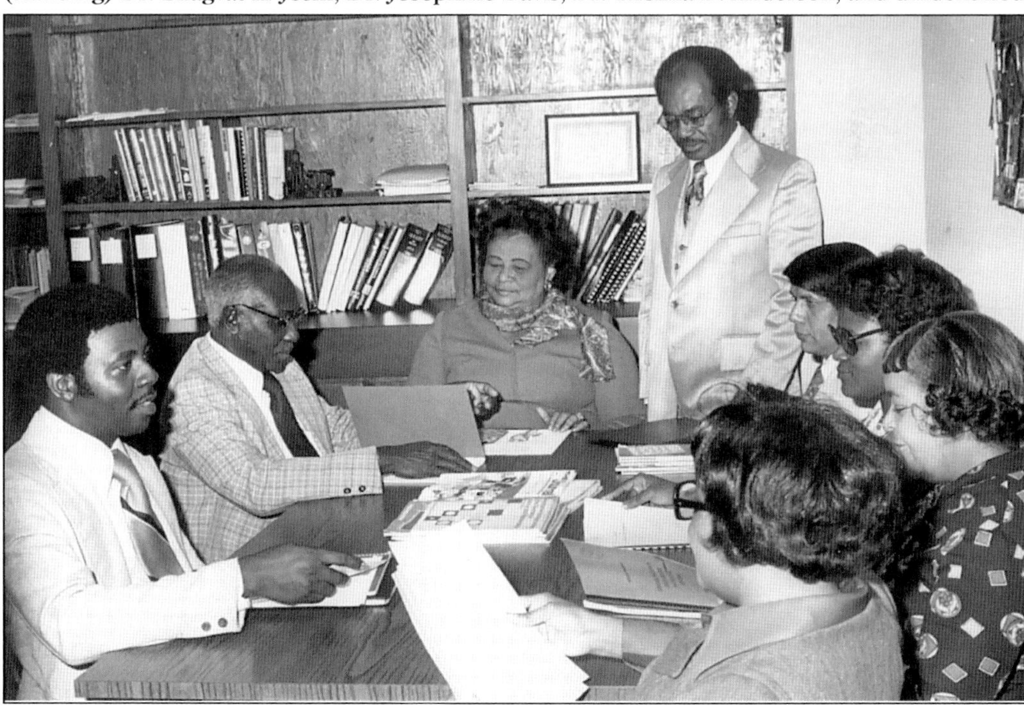

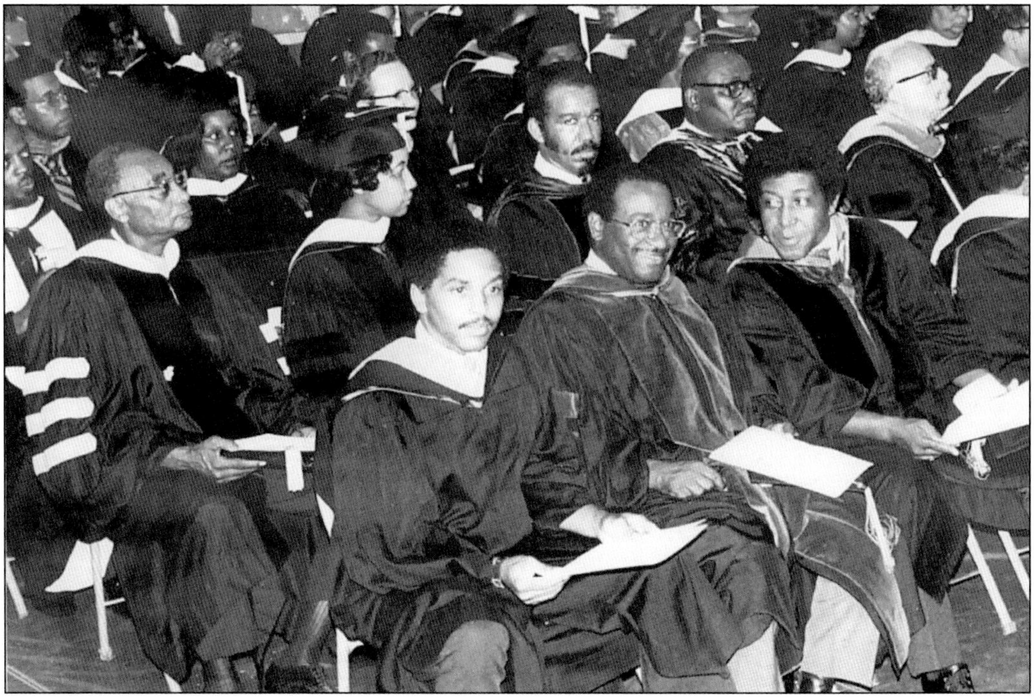

Administrators and faculty gather for commencement at Albany State. Shown in this photograph in the front row from left to right are William Johnson, Dr. C.W. Grant, and Dr. Guy C. Craft; (back row) Dr. William E. Lightfoote, Dr. Velma Grant, Dr. Robert Marshall (?), and William Rice. The picture also provides a glimpse of Dr. John E. Moore, Dr. Edward Green, Dr. Rosa Tift, and Dr. Walter Burgess, *c.* 1977.

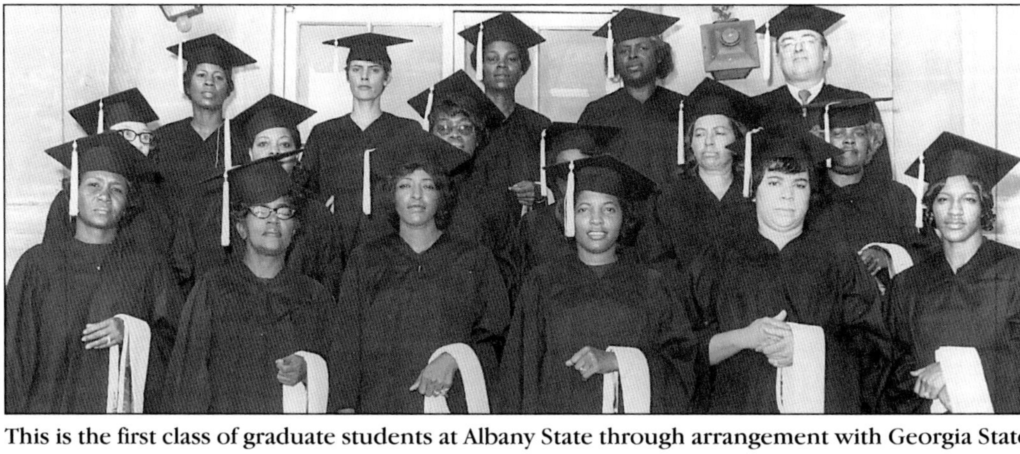

This is the first class of graduate students at Albany State through arrangement with Georgia State and Valdosta State.

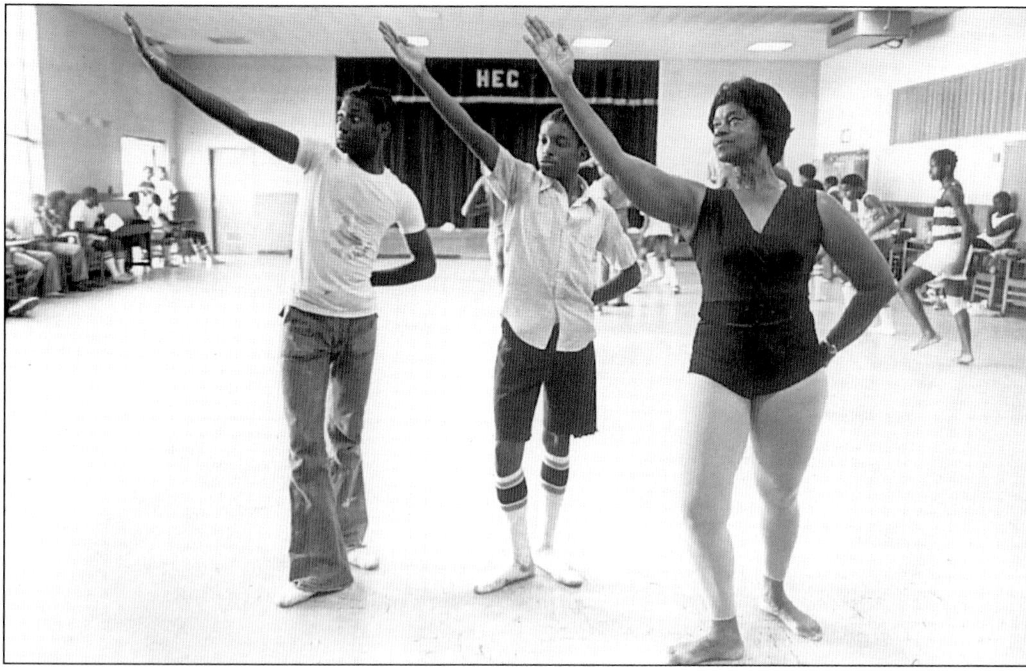

Sophronic Steele of the Department of Health and Physical Education directed classes in folk, square, and social dances. Students studied forms of folk, round, and square dance, including the national characteristics, music, and costumes of various countries. Classes exposed students to the various forms of ballroom dancing and dance etiquette.

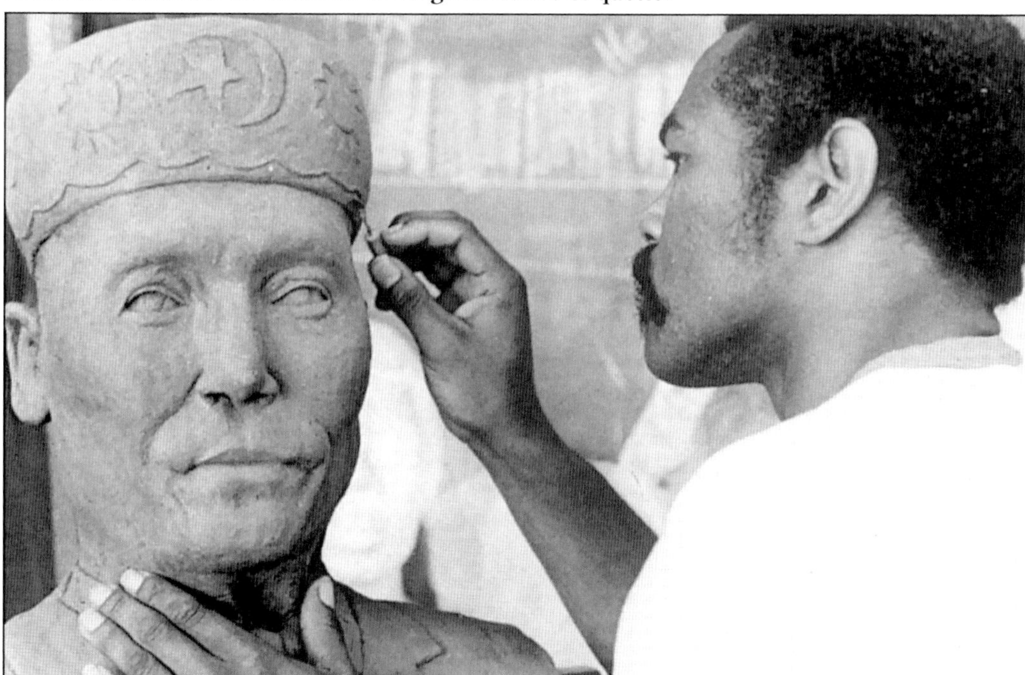

Clifford McMillan, an art major, shows his talent and love for creative expression through this amazing likeness of the Honorable Elijah Muhammad of the Nation of Islam, *c.* 1979.

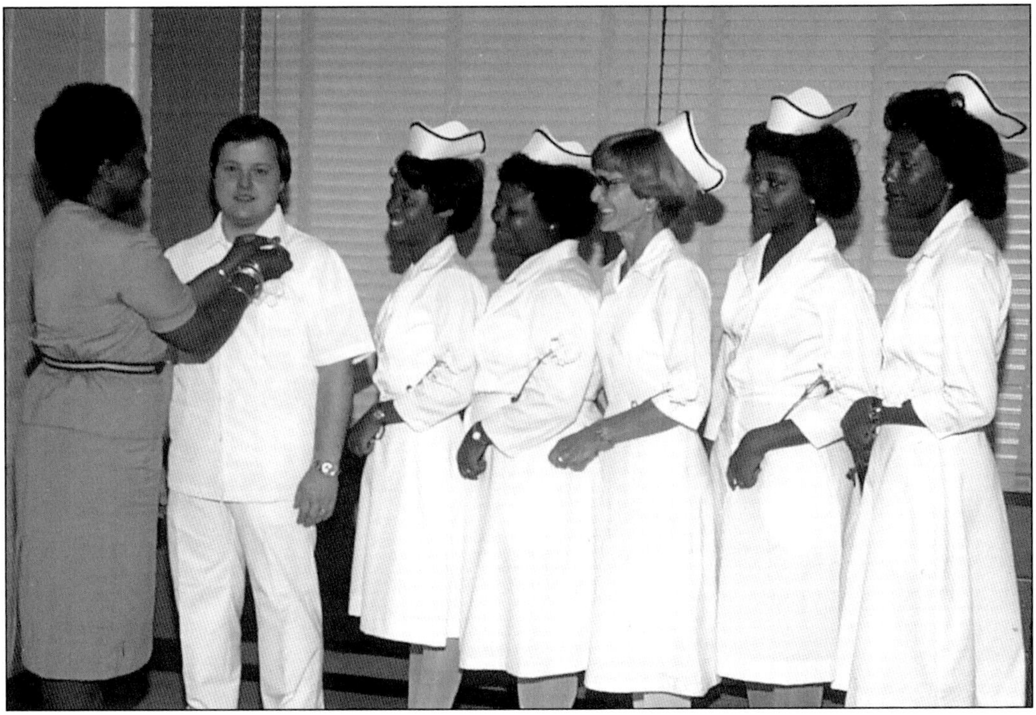

Dr. Lucille Wilson, chairperson of the Division of Nursing, congratulates students for a job well done during a pinning ceremony prior to commencement of 1981. Included in the photograph are Deborah Mobley and Brenda Holloway.

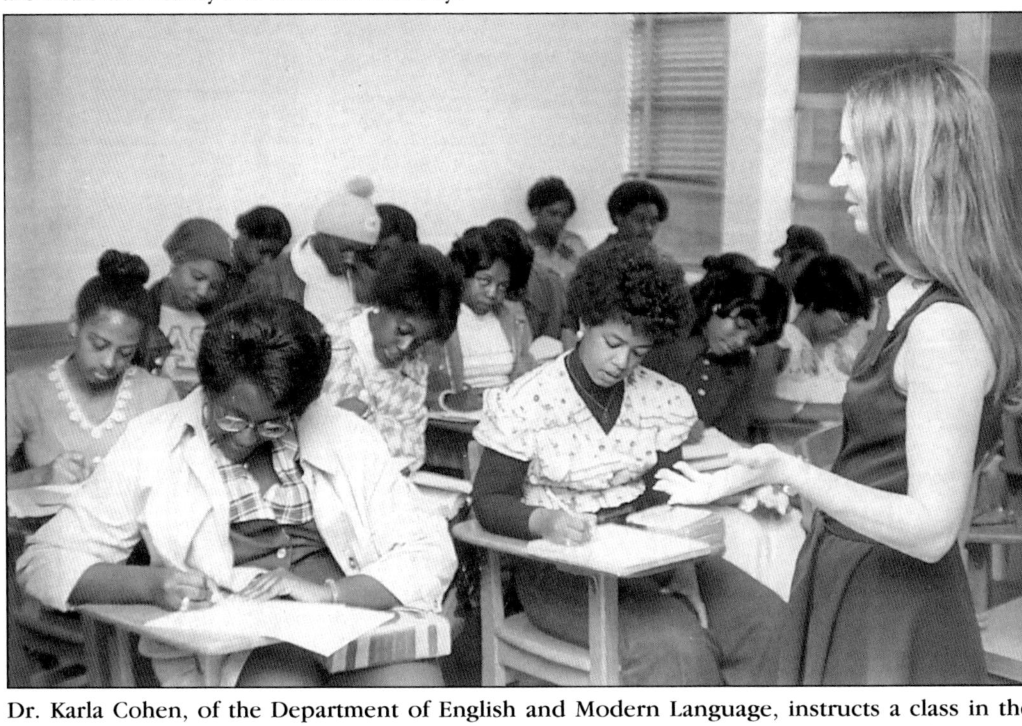

Dr. Karla Cohen, of the Department of English and Modern Language, instructs a class in the "mechanics of expression, development, and organization of ideas into paragraphs and essays."

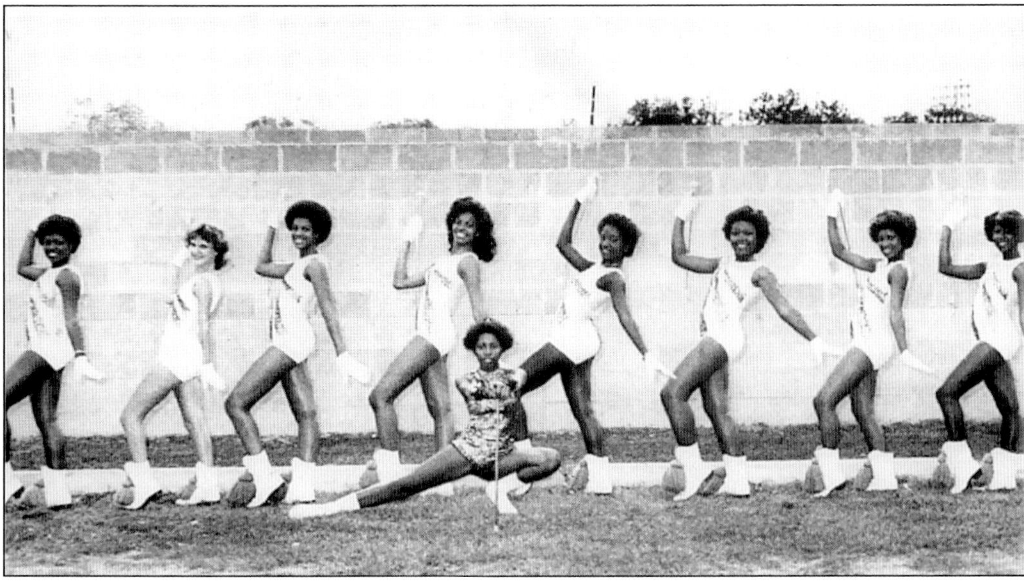

The Golden Stallions (majorettes) of the Marching Ram Band were led by Peggie Crumbley. The other majorettes are Neshanta Cunningham, Joan Roe, Judith Hampton, Debra Davis, Kimberly Casey, Gwen Cunningham, and Rolencia Shaw.

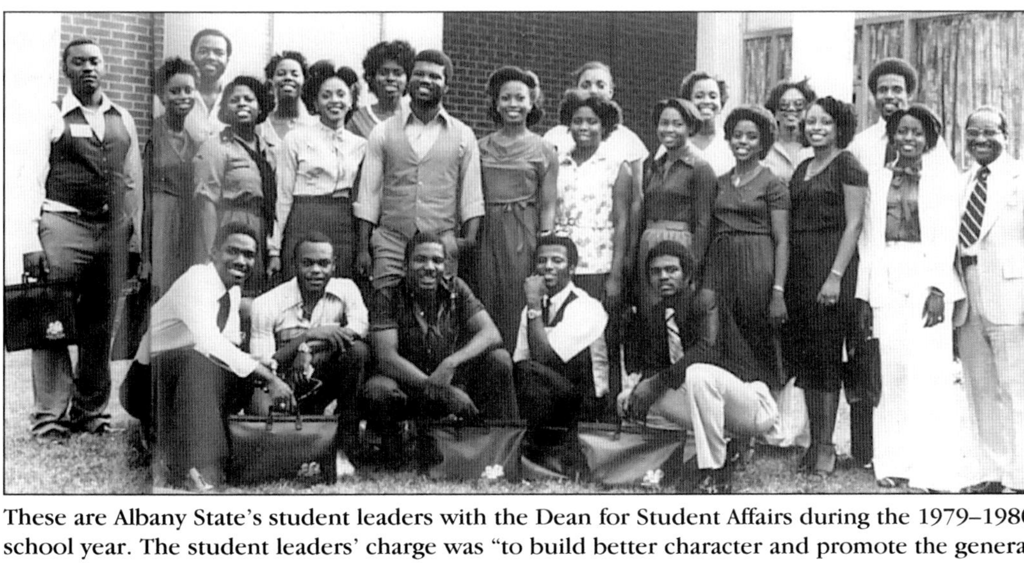

These are Albany State's student leaders with the Dean for Student Affairs during the 1979–1980 school year. The student leaders' charge was "to build better character and promote the general welfare of the school and the entire student body, while at the same time creating an opportunity for self government."

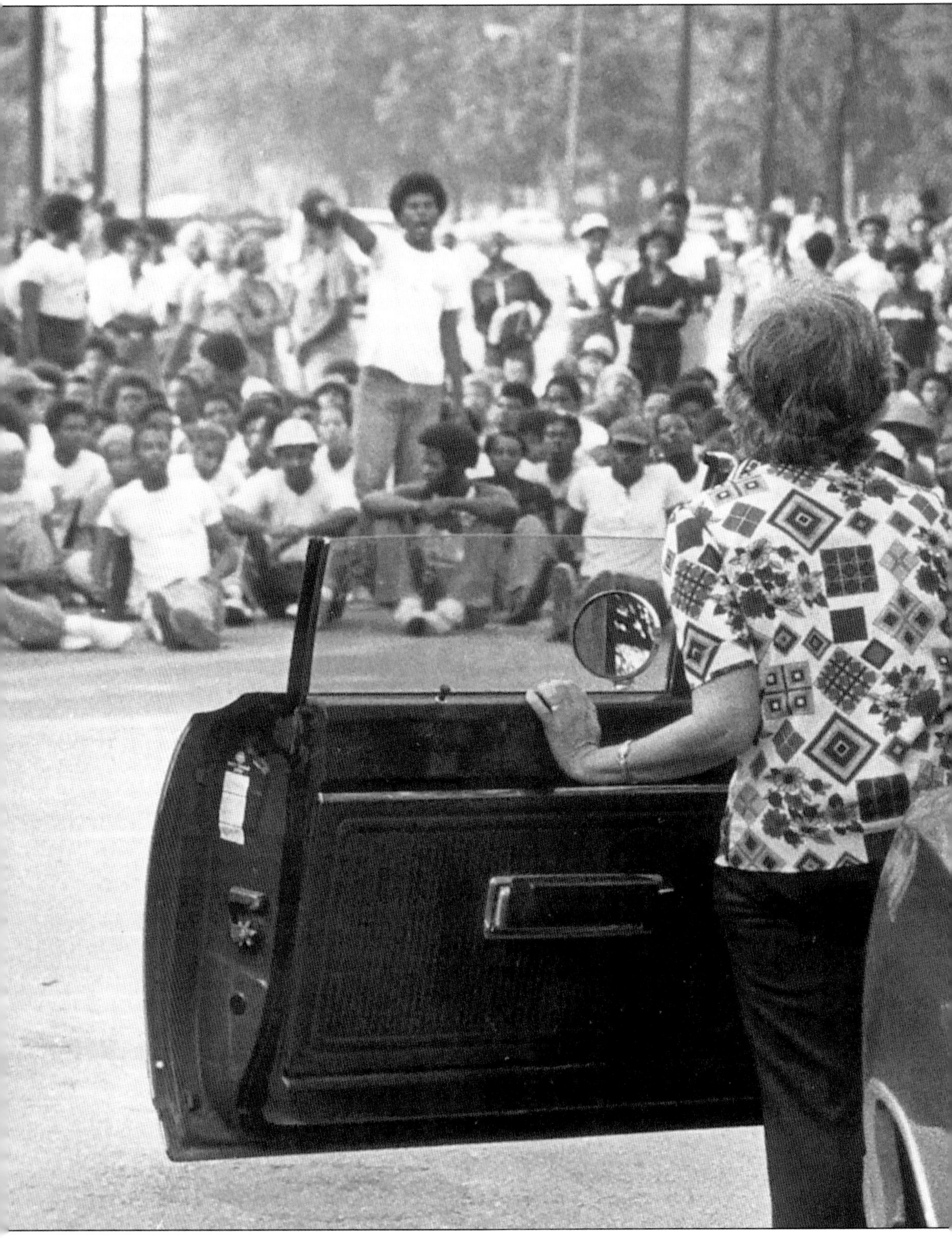

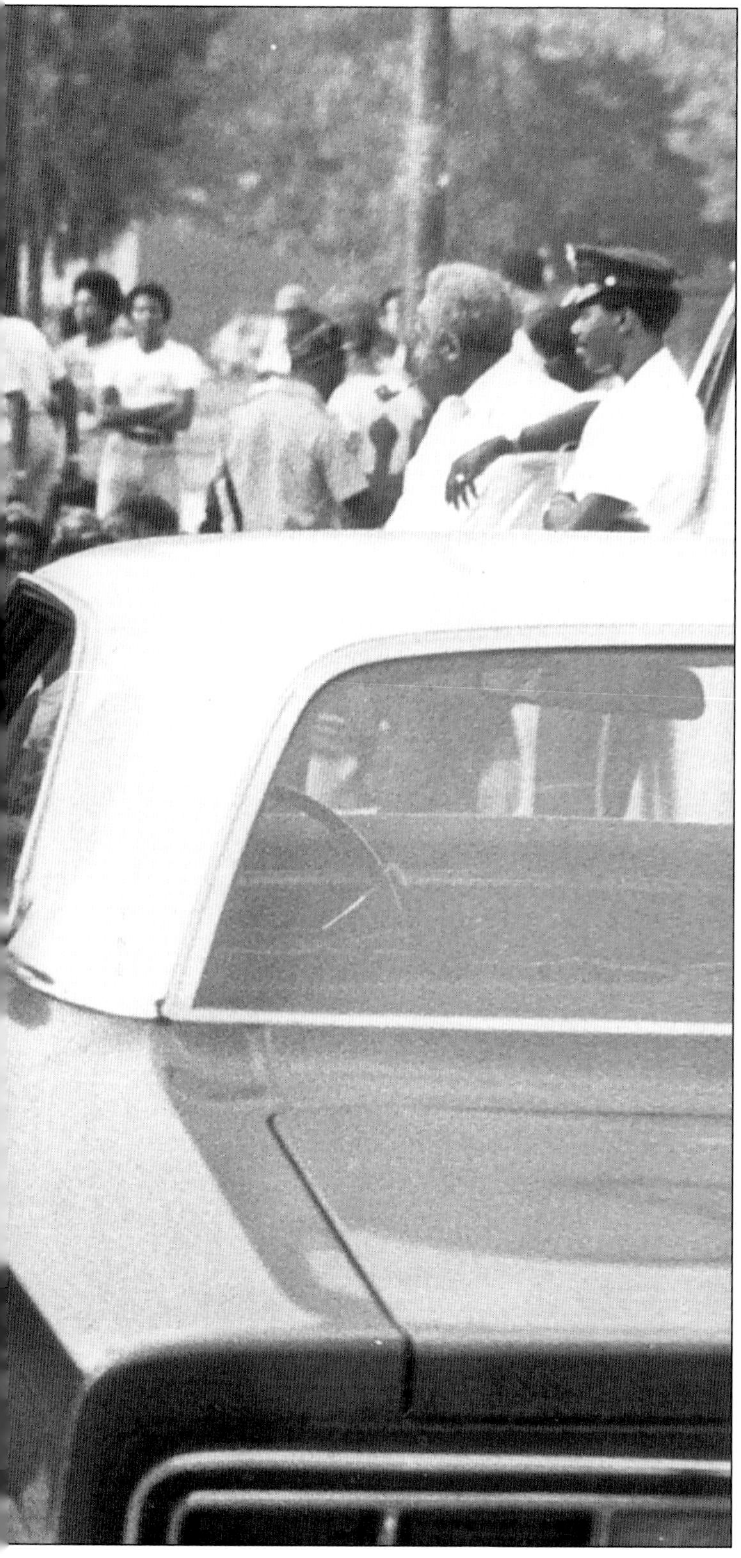

Student demonstrators took to the streets to register their protest and blocked campus entry during the spring of 1977. The protests were led by then newly elected student government association president Charles McCant. McCant and other students felt that the proposal to destroy Albany State through a merger with then Albany Junior College was not in keeping with the state-mandated mission of the historically black institution that served Georgia's black citizenry.

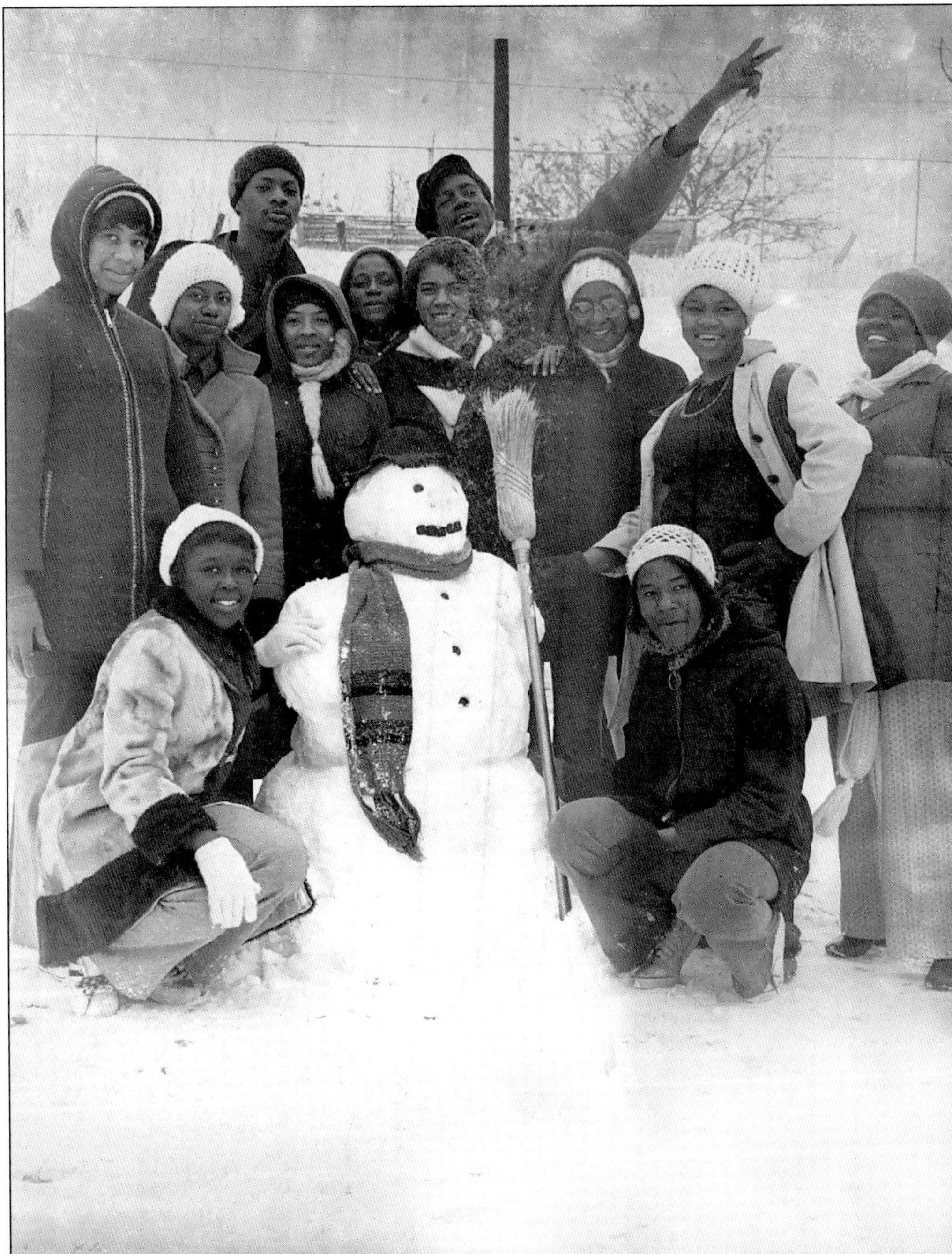

Students of Wiley Hall are joined by a few others from Albany State to build a snowman following a cold winter blast in February 1973. It is quite rare, but not impossible, for southwest Georgia to incur such a wrath from Mother Nature as this one.

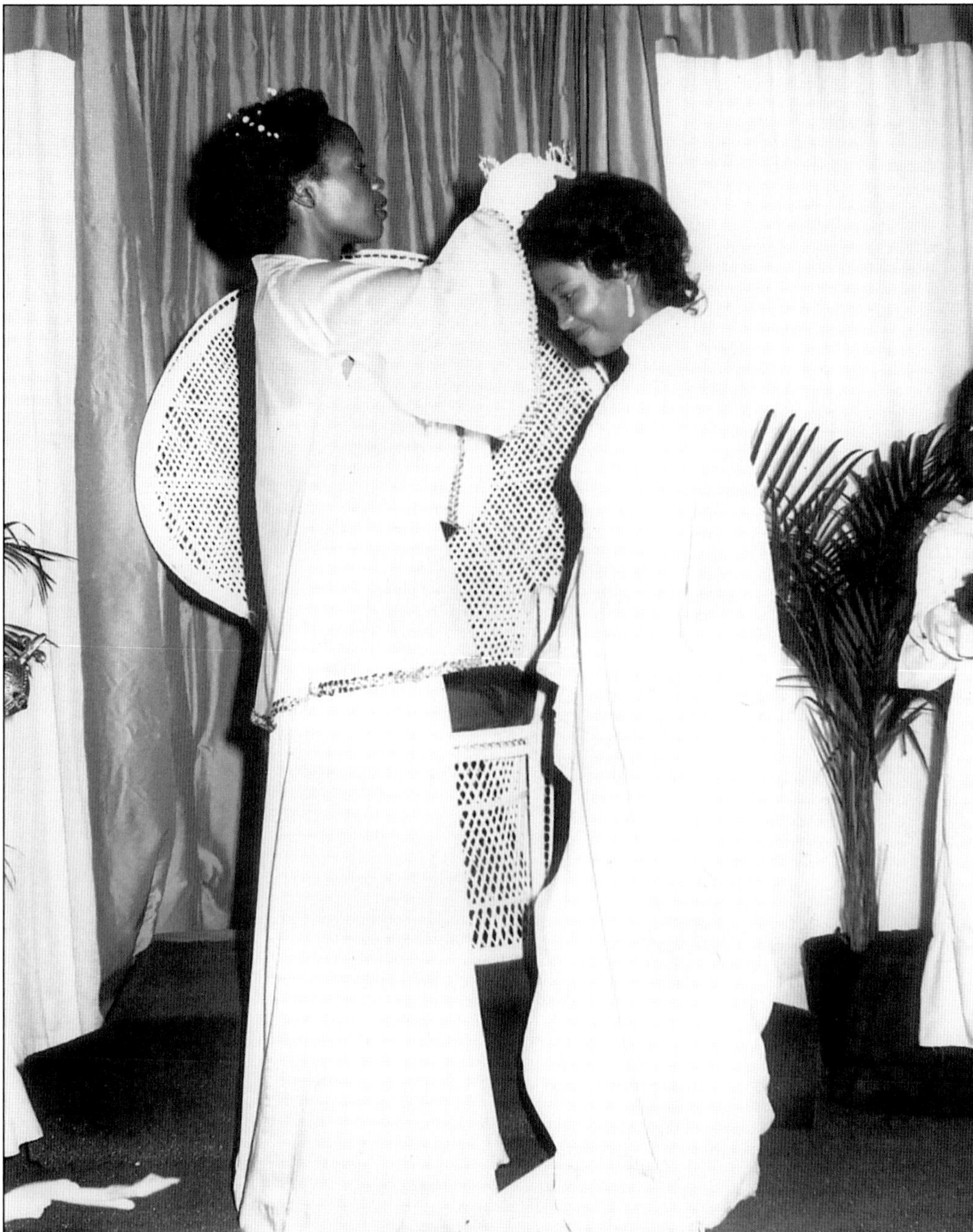

Miss Albany State 1977–1978, Phyllis Driskell, relinquishes her crown to the new queen, Patsy Farmer, Miss Albany State 1978–1979.

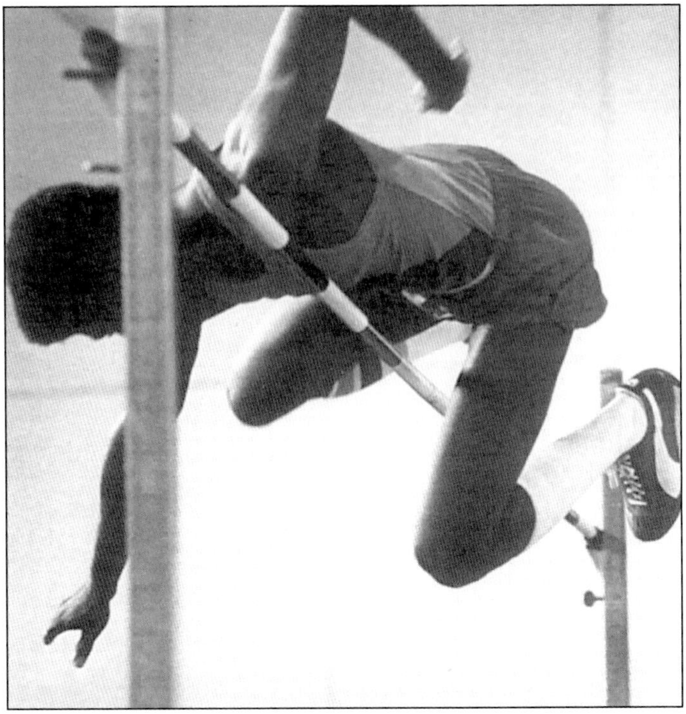

James Bruce McDaniel in 1979 was regarded as one of the America's premier high jumpers. McDaniel jumped 7 feet, 4 inches at the Florida Relays, and had 7'3" leaps at both the National AAU Indoor and Outdoor Championships.

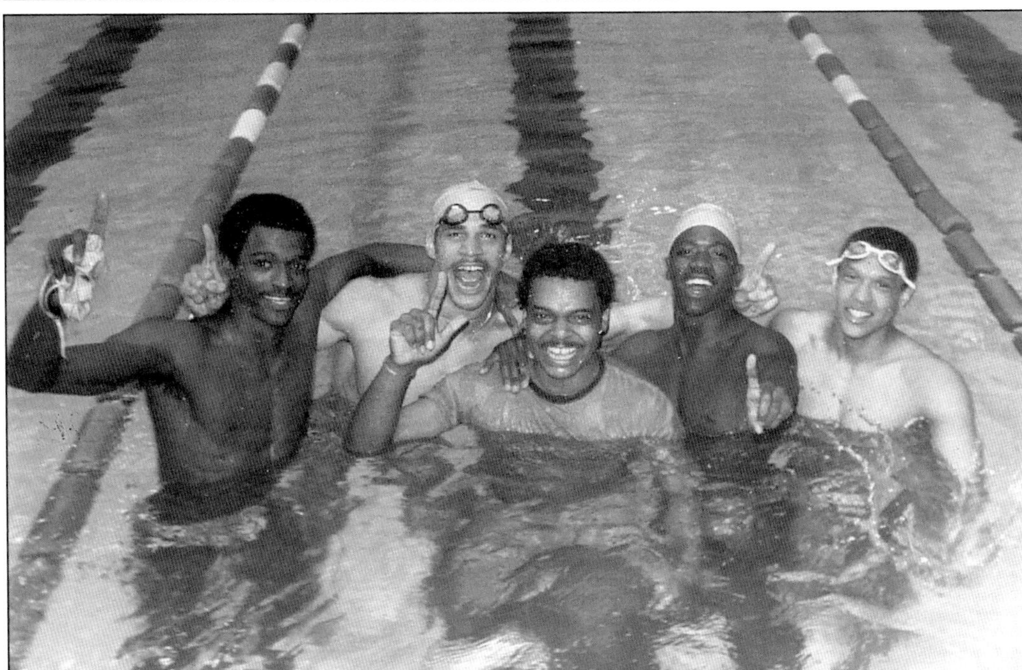

ASU Aqua-Rams were twice the National Black Collegiate Swimming and Diving champions in 1978 and 1979. Pictured from left to right are Phelan Thomas, Michael Thomas, Coach Wilburn Campbell, Ph.D., Anthony Myles, and John Pitts. En route to winning the First Black National Swimming and Diving Championship, the Albany State team posted the fastest time ever in the 400 medley relay.

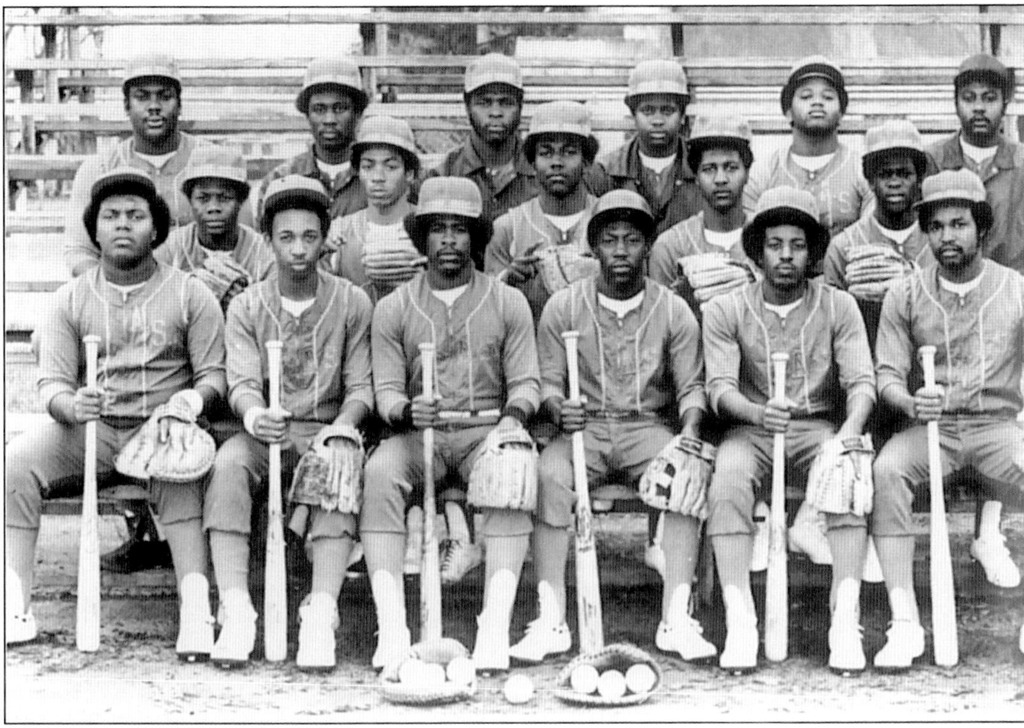

This is the baseball team, *c.* 1972. Pictured from left to right are (front row) James Harvey, Jesse Hill, John Hudson, Charles Stamper, Jackie James, and Dan James; (middle row) Billie Strober, Willie Chester, Marvin President, Charles Tift, and unidentified; (back row) Iriad Pittman, Joe Massey, Willie Boone, Dale Williams, Gregory Wells, and Coach Joe Brown.

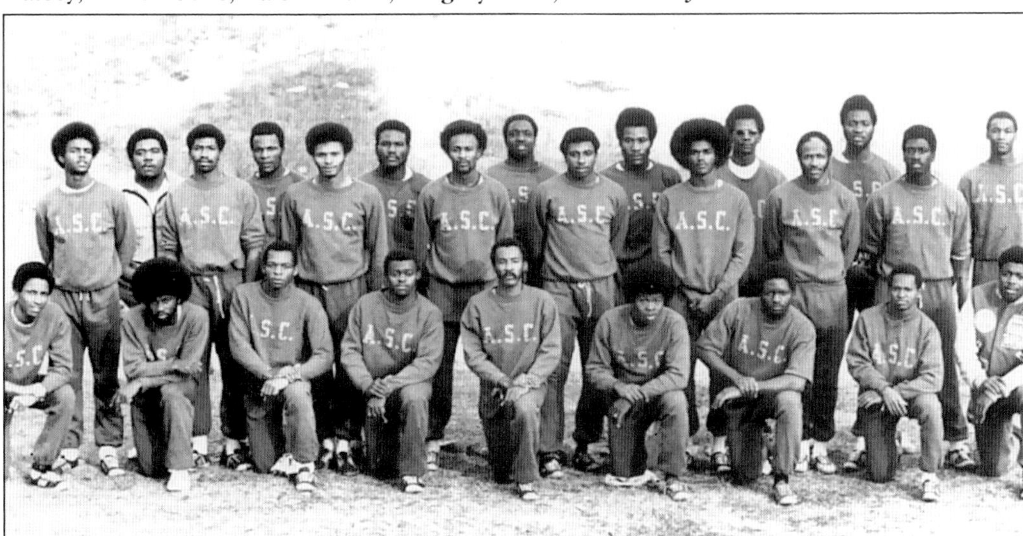

The men's track team is shown here. Pictured from left to right are (front row) Charles Cultliff, Willie Reese, Willie Colquitt, Charles Haywood, Lucious Davis, James Hall, Ruddie Nance, Mitchell Fielder, and Lester Sherman; (second row) Larry Marlins, David Barron, Johnnie Scott, Eddie Wilson, Earl Gibbs, Angelo Taylor, and Johnnie Seabrooks; (third row) Larry Brooks, Myron Jackson, John Lester, David Woodward, Xavier Smith, Larry Moore, and Harold Little.

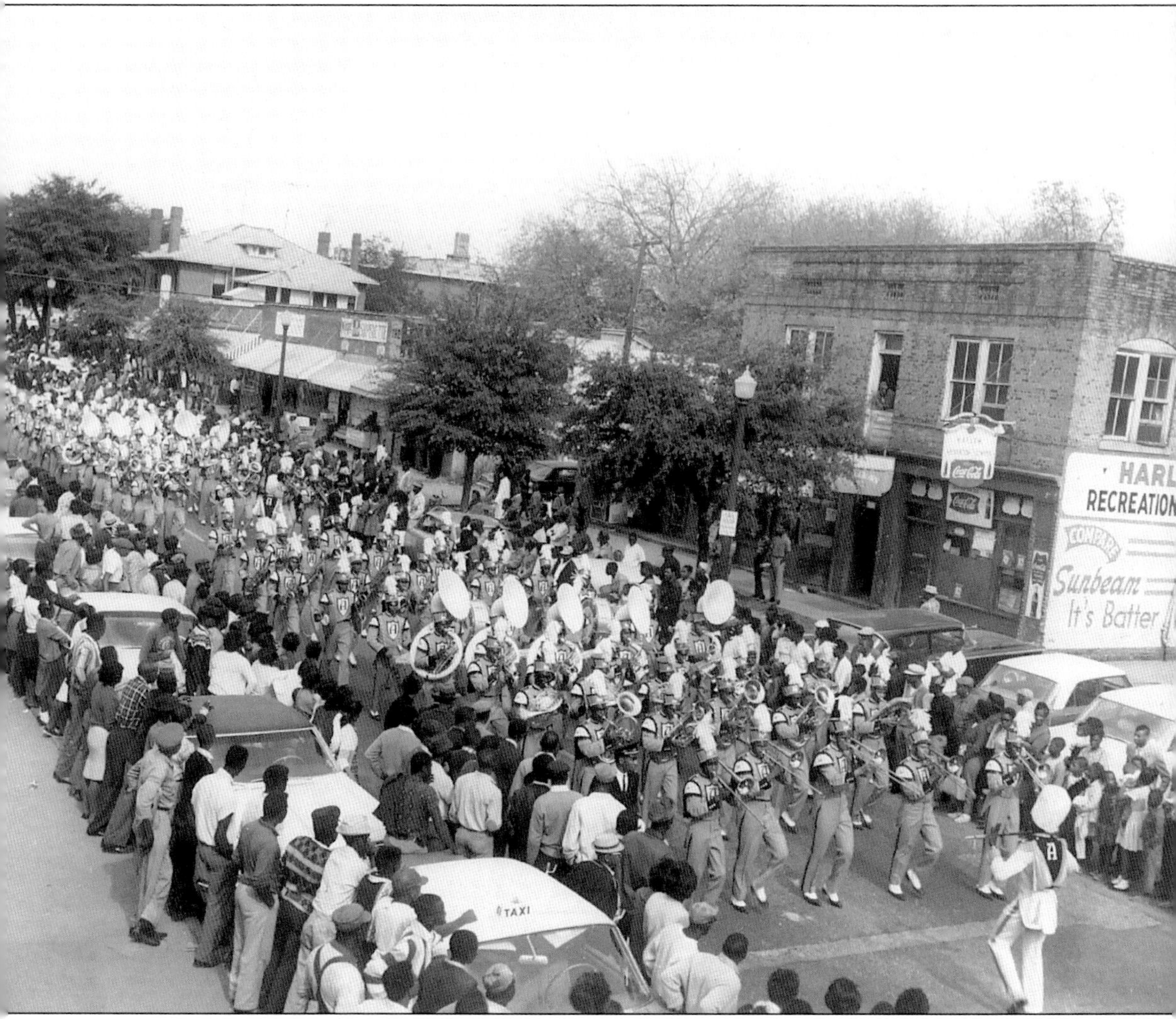

Members of the Marching Rams proceed on the parade route in downtown Albany to the delight of onlooking alumni, family, friends, and the Albany community for Homecoming *c.* 1977.

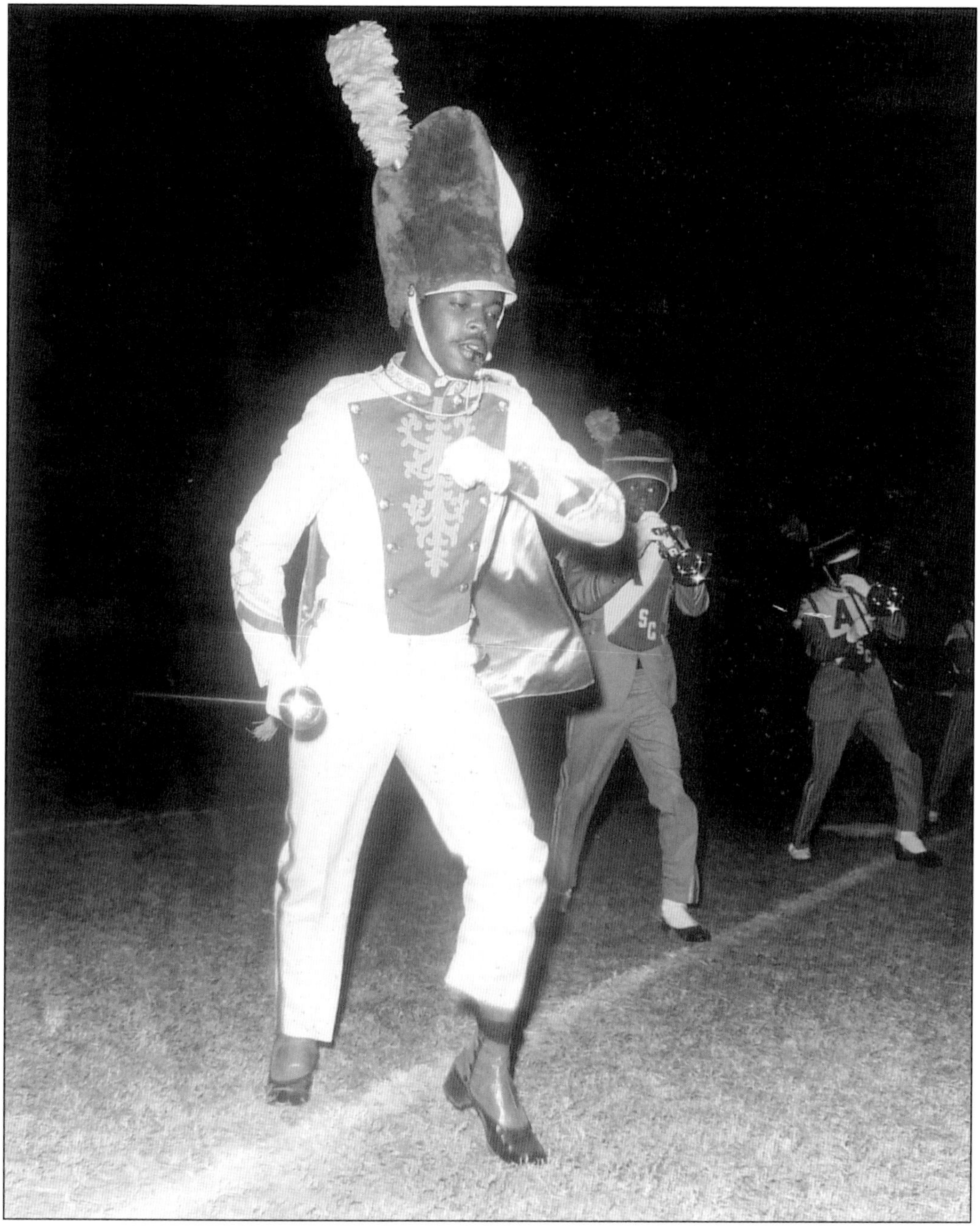

This drum major leads the Marching Rams *c.* 1975. Under the direction of Dr. Lamar Smith, the Marching Rams have been the pride of ASU for over three decades.

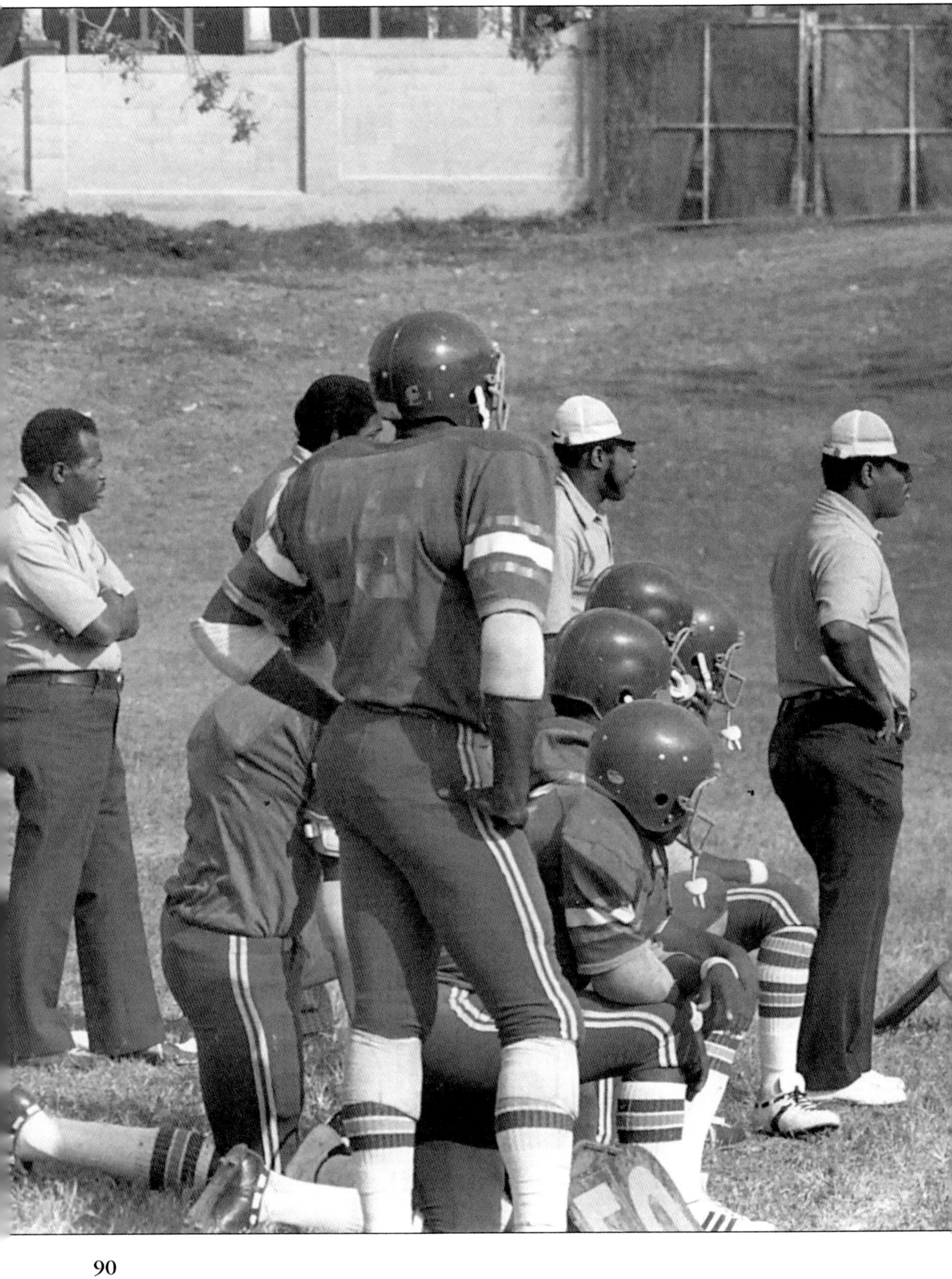

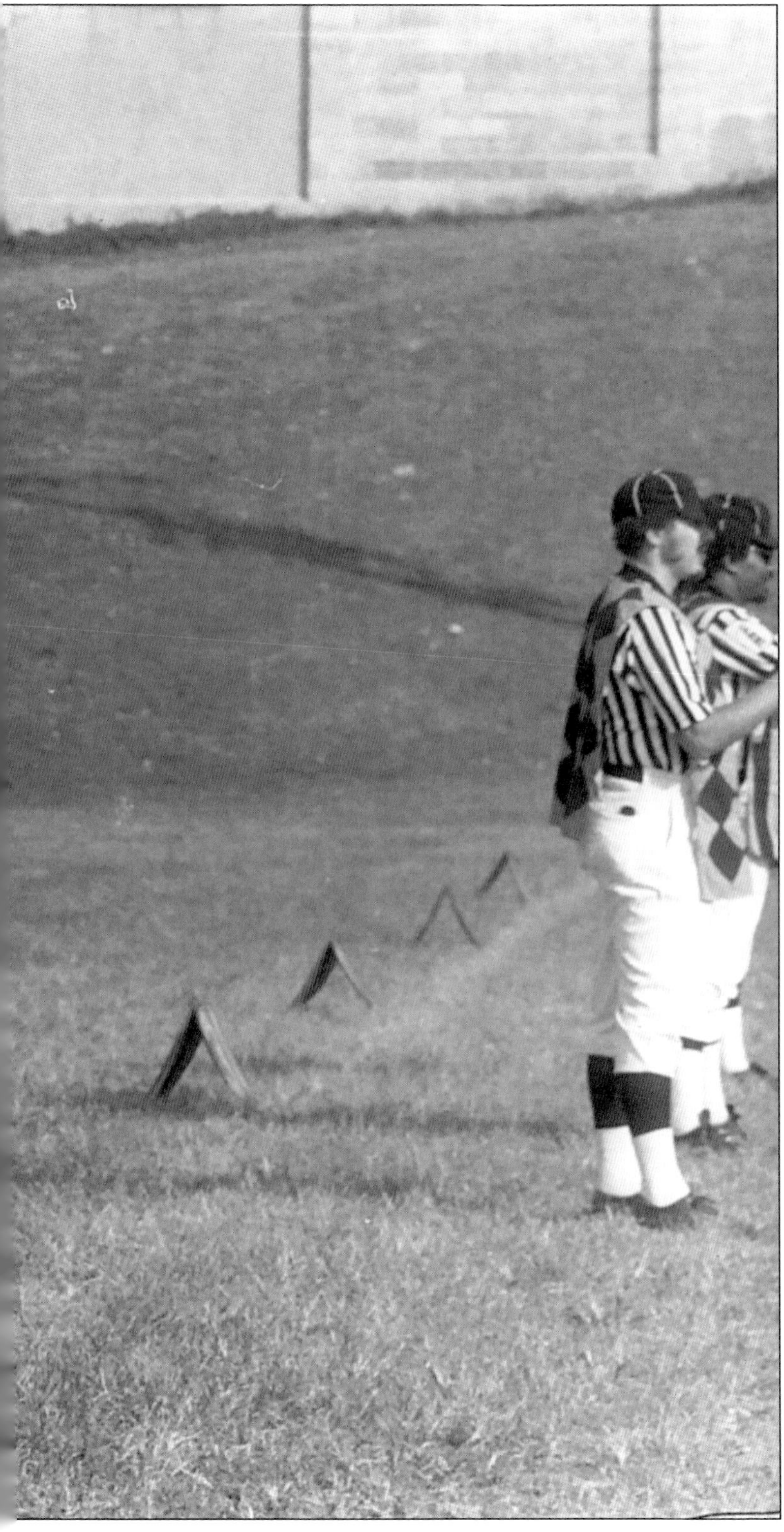

Coach Smith is shown en route to his first SIAC championship in 1972 during his second year as coach at Albany State. Coach Hampton "Hamp" Smith, a 1958 graduate of Mississippi Valley State University, started his coaching career at Albany State in 1971 and ended in 1976 with a winning record. His second stint at ASU was begun in 1982. Smith has guided the Golden Rams to seven Southern Intercollegiate Athletic Conference (SIAC) championships. Smith is the only coach in SIAC history to lead a team to three straight appearances in the NCAA Division II Playoffs.

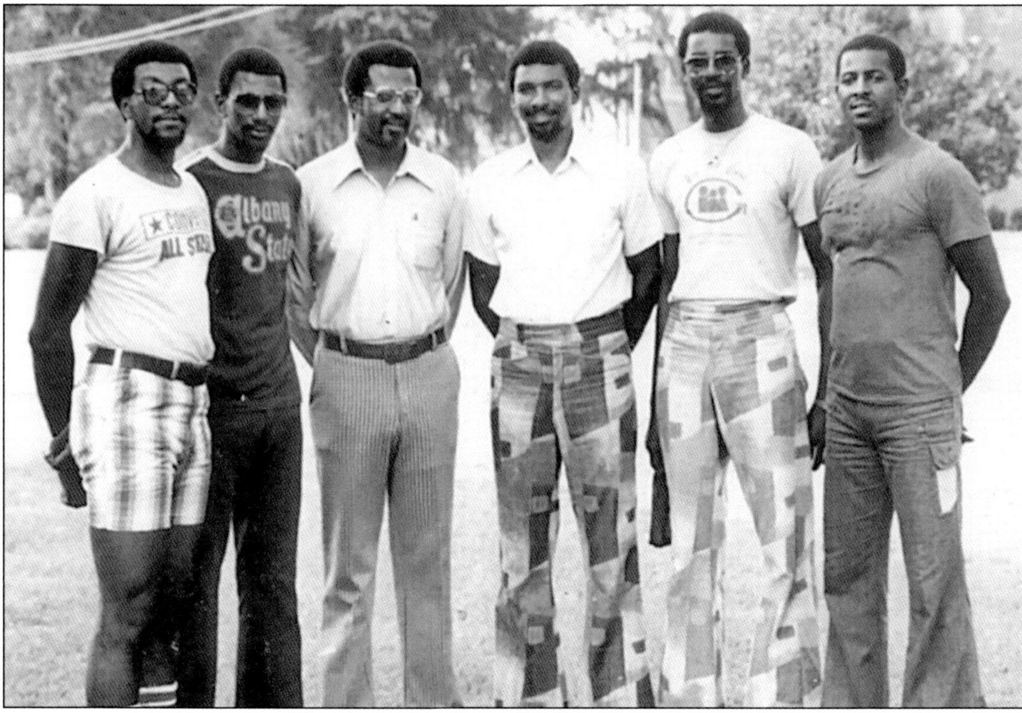

For nearly two decades the Jones brothers made a strong appearance in intercollegiate, ABA, and NBA basketball competitions. They are (from left to right) Major (1972–1976), Charles (1975–1979), Oliver (1961–1965), Melvin (1964–1968), Caldwell (1969–1973), and Wilbert (1965–1969).

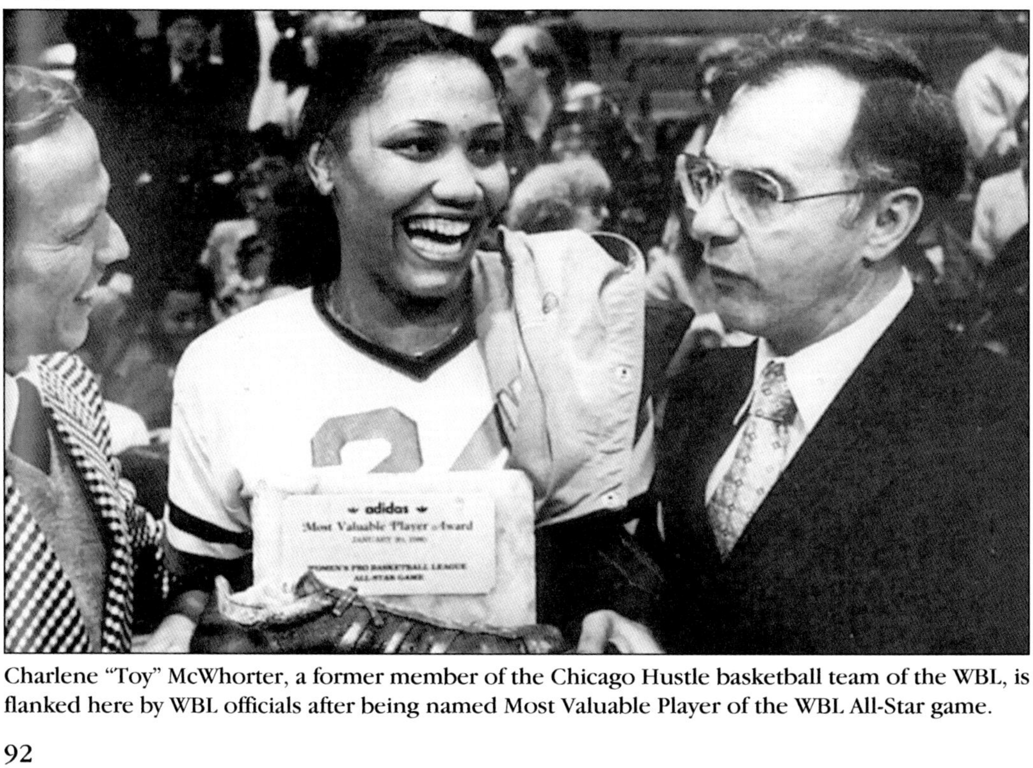

Charlene "Toy" McWhorter, a former member of the Chicago Hustle basketball team of the WBL, is flanked here by WBL officials after being named Most Valuable Player of the WBL All-Star game.

Six

Dr. Billy C. Black 1980–1996

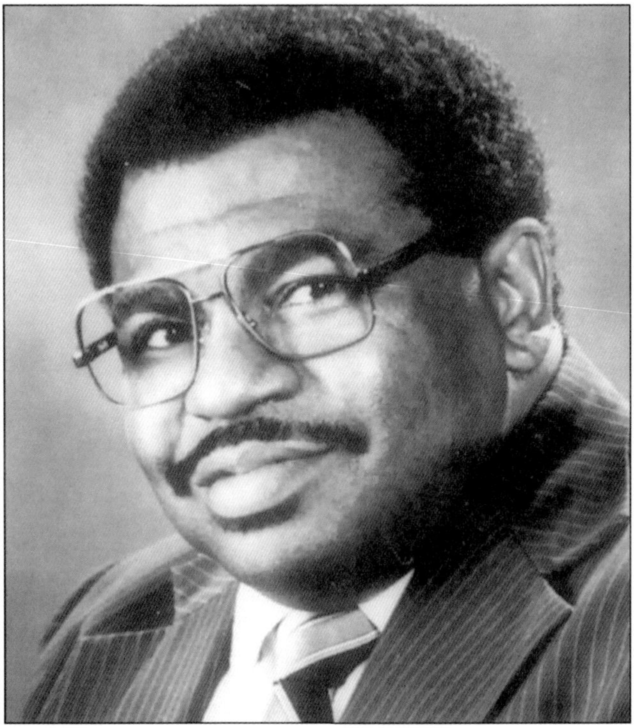

Dr. Billy C. Black, the sixth president, is a native of Beatrice, Alabama. Dr. Black earned a B.S. degree from Tuskegee Institute (now University), and M.S. and Ph.D. degrees from Iowa State University in Ames. In June 1996, the Board of Regents conferred upon Dr. Black the title "President Emeritus." Dr. Black came to the college in 1964 as a professor of chemistry. Later he served as chairman of the Division of Arts and Sciences and as interim assistant to the Dean for Academic Affairs. Following the tragic flooding of the campus by Hurricane Alberto in July 1994, Dr. Black declared the college "unsinkable" and worked with pre-eminent planners to design a "new" Albany State College that would be "bigger, stronger, and better." Dr. Black's tenure was marked by dramatic growth in enrollment, an increase in the percentage of faculty holding terminal degrees, an aggressive expansion of programming, and improvements in the physical plant. Under his visionary leadership, Albany State achieved university status and adopted a bold strategic plan and a vision for expansion that targeted the needs of the citizens in the 24-county area served by the institution. He urged aggressive goal setting in every school and department, and was involved in state and national projects to improve educational opportunities and access, especially in science and mathematics.

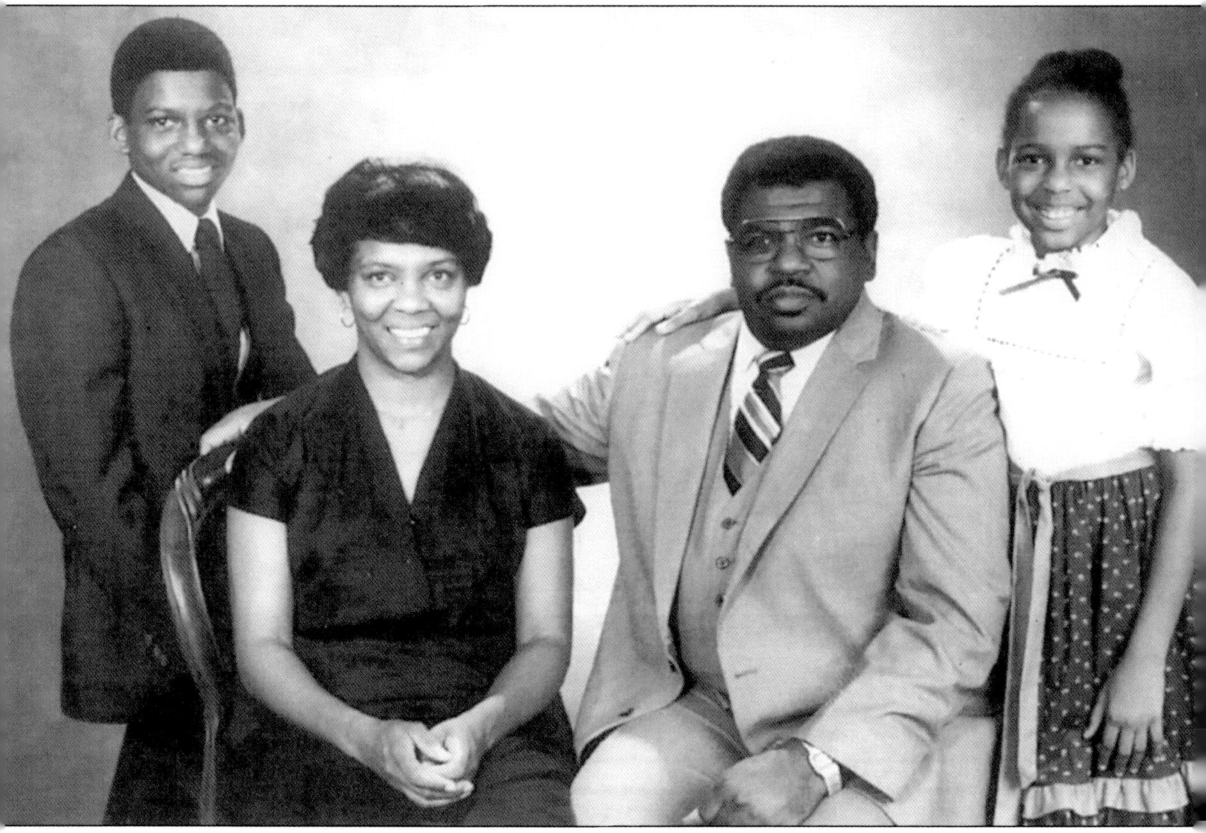

President Black and his wife Mrs. Helen Black with son Eddie and daughter Marla are pictured here. Mrs. Black, a member of the Albany State "family" since 1964, worked in school departments on campus, including the Nursing Division, Institutional Research and Academic Affairs, and as the assistant director of the Word Processing Department.

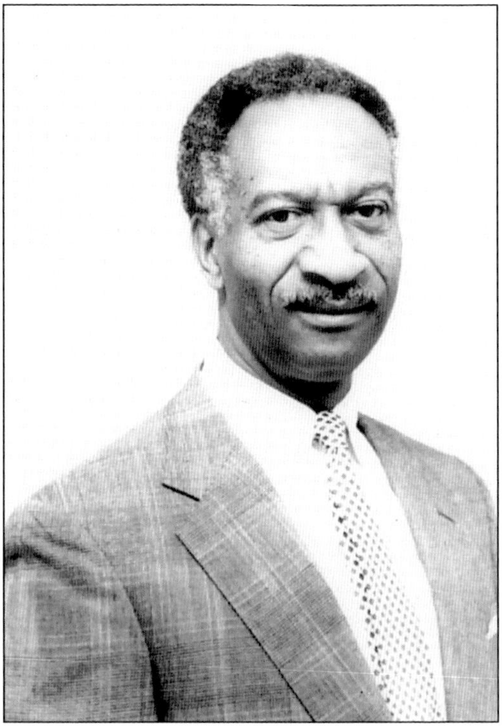

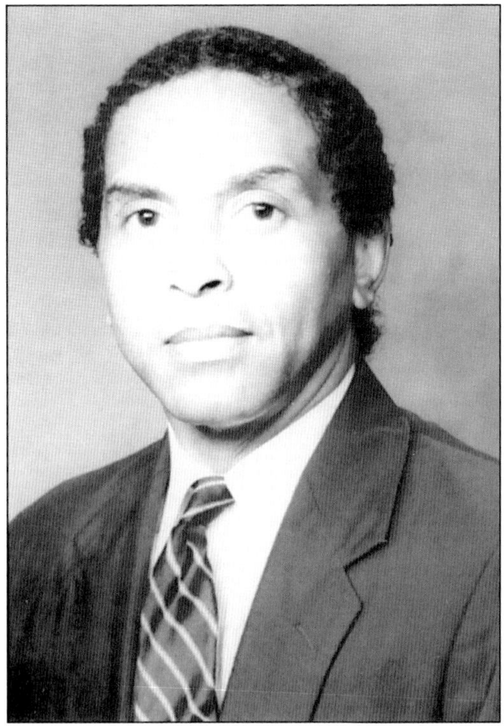

(above, left) This is Dr. Ernest Benson, vice president for academic affairs. *(above, right)* Pictured here is Mr. William Johnson, vice president of fiscal affairs.

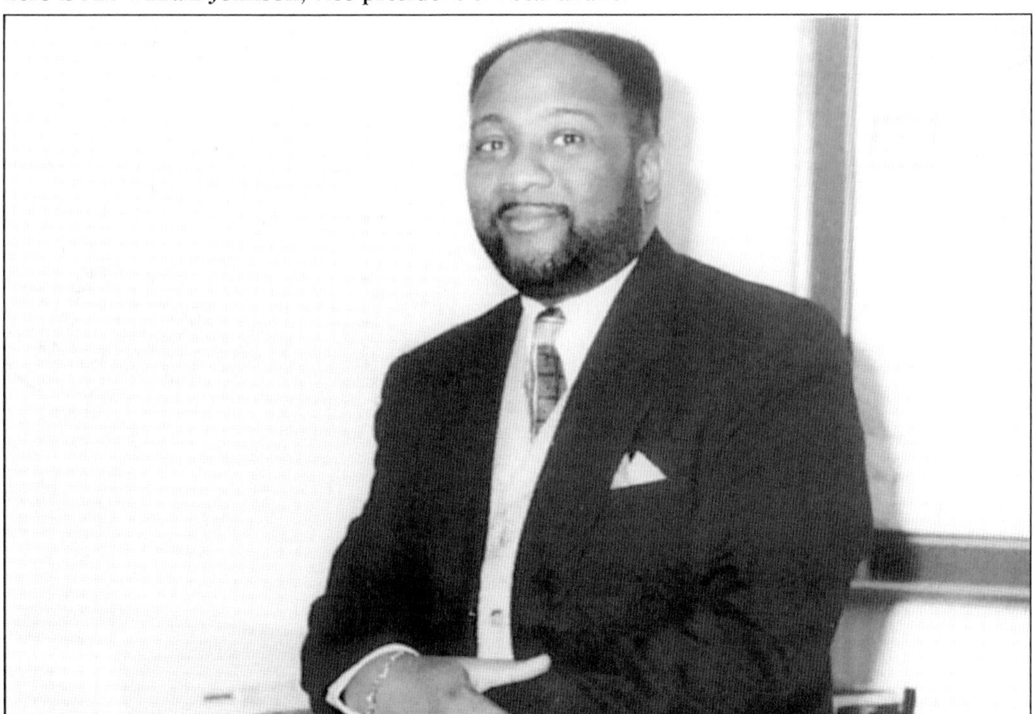

Dr. Robert R. Jennings, vice president of institutional advancement, is shown here.

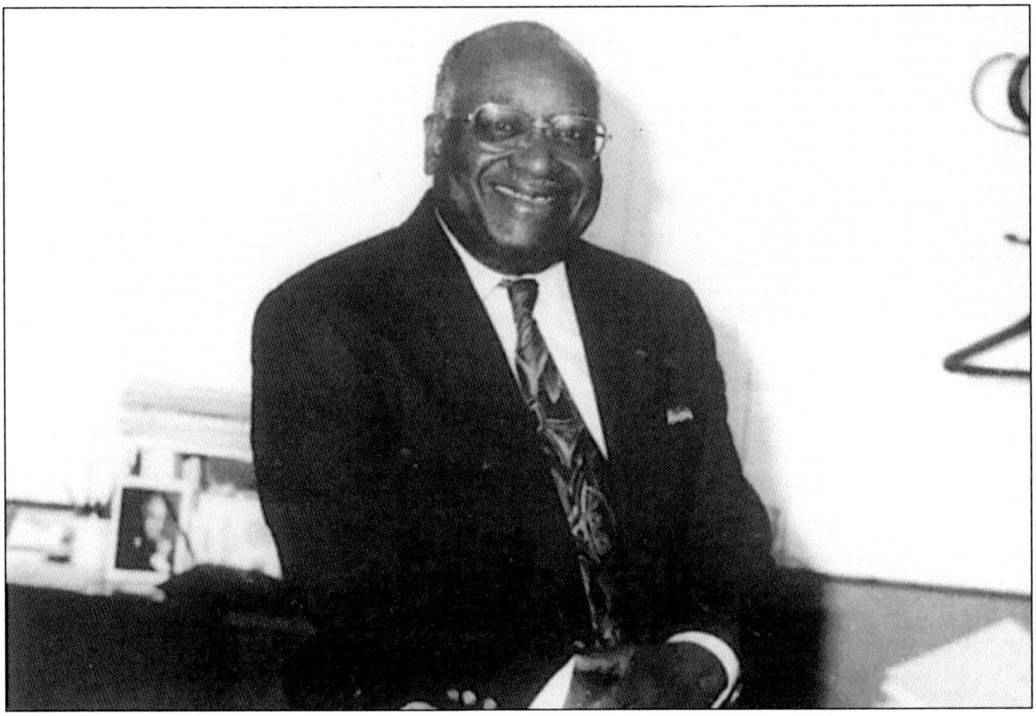

Here is Dr. C.W. Grant, vice president of student affairs.

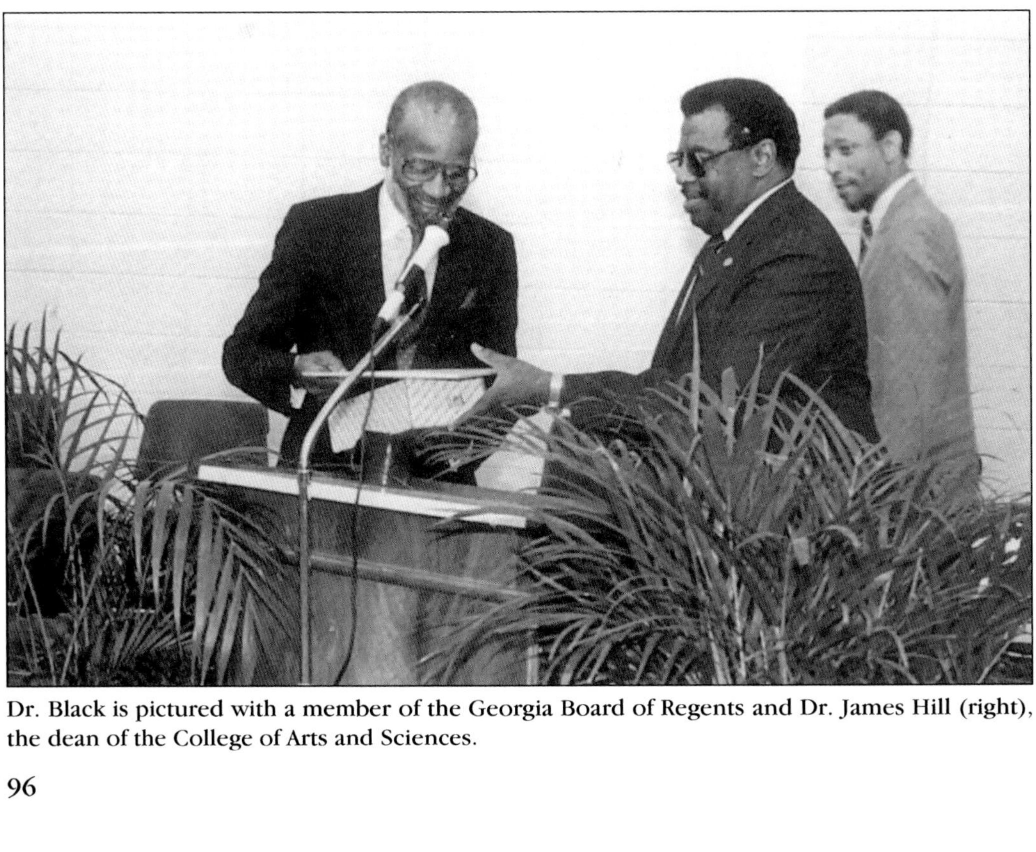

Dr. Black is pictured with a member of the Georgia Board of Regents and Dr. James Hill (right), the dean of the College of Arts and Sciences.

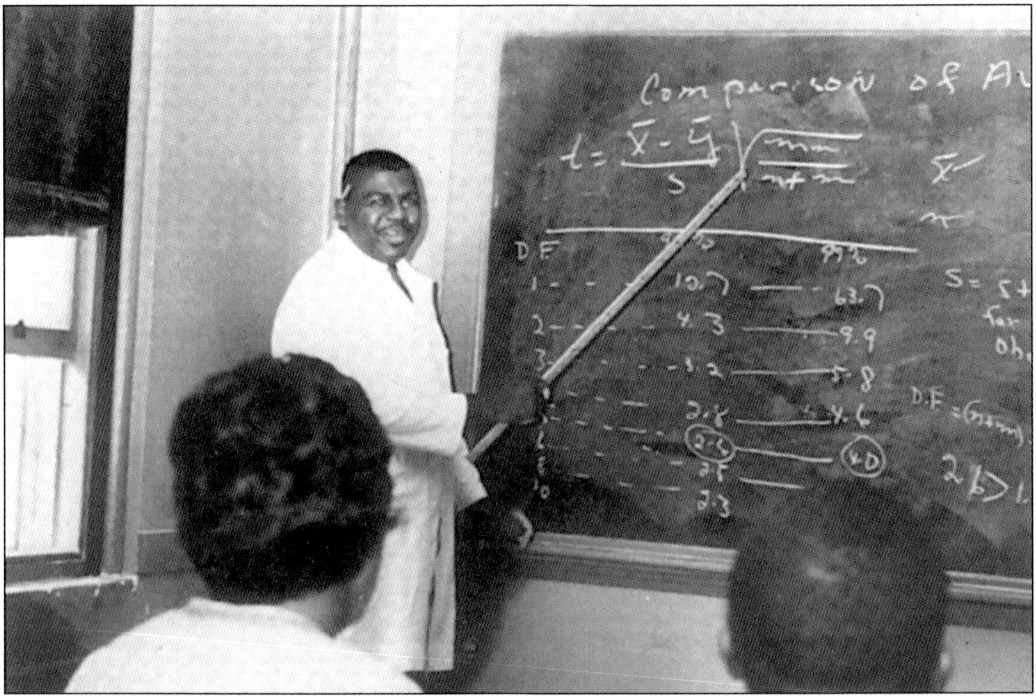

As a professor, Dr. Black molded students into adept thinkers, organizers, researchers, and scholars in the fields of science and medicine. Below young Dr. Black demonstrates the use of a potentiometer.

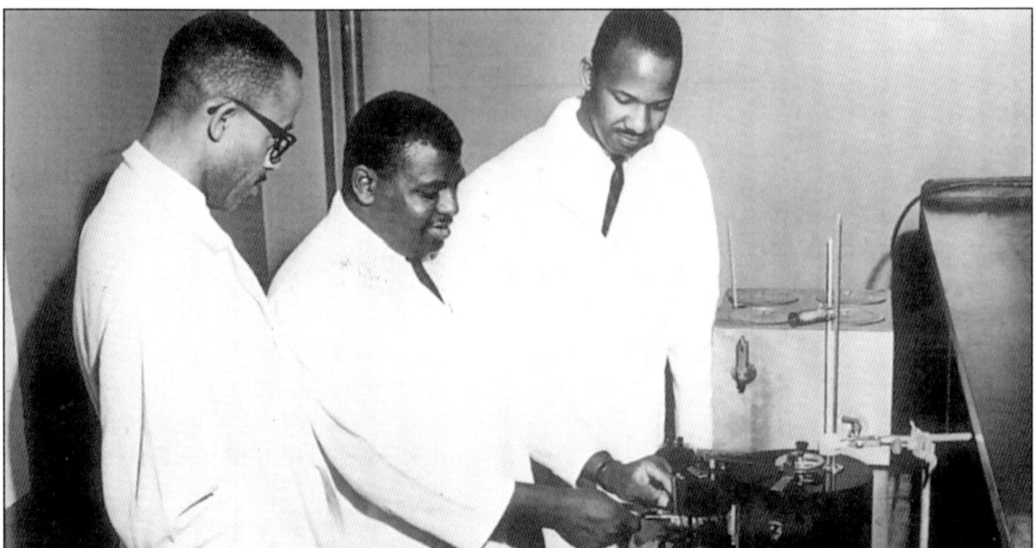

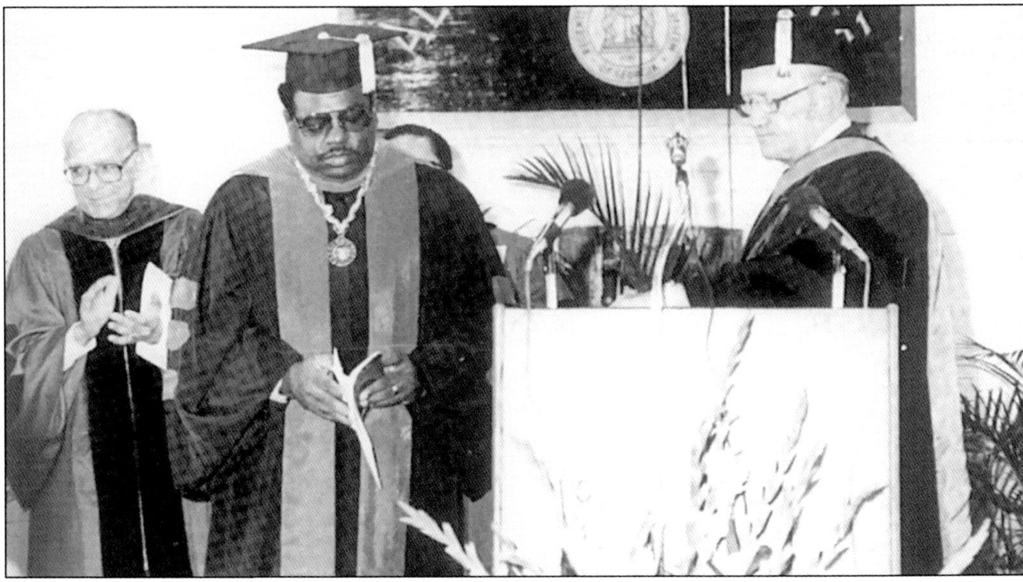

The inaugural ceremonies, presided over by Dr. Vernon Crawford, chancellor of the University System of Georgia, culminated in a week of festivities commemorating the investiture of Dr. Billy Charleston Black as the sixth president of Albany State. Below, Hon. Jackie M. Ward, chairperson of the Georgia Board of Regents and Dr. Billy Black are pictured following commencement, *c*. 1988.

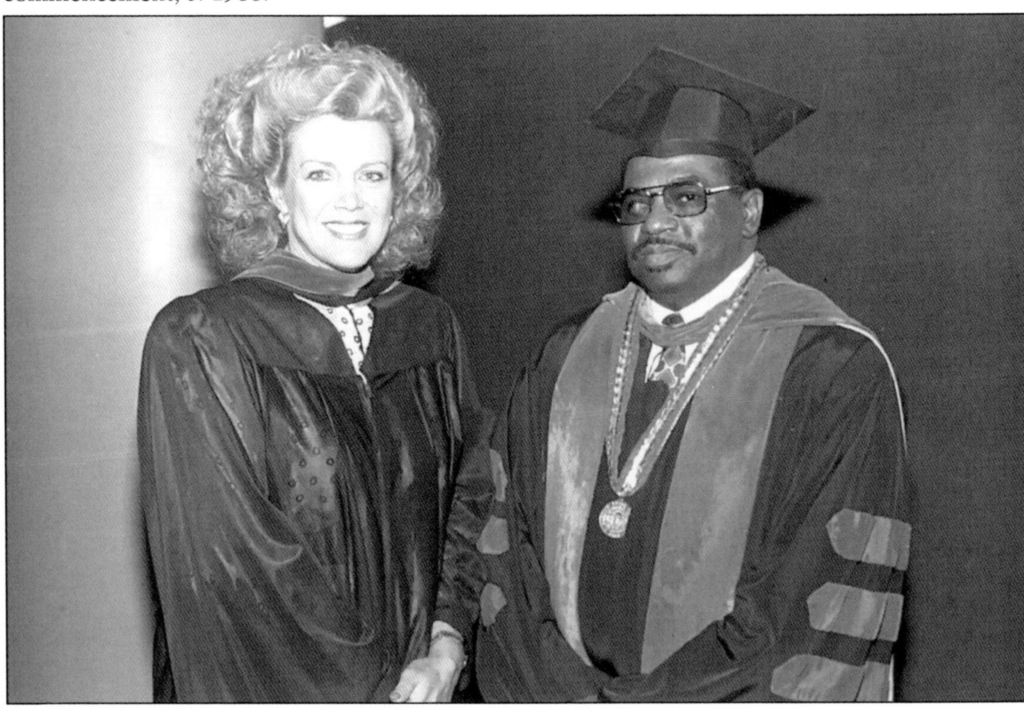

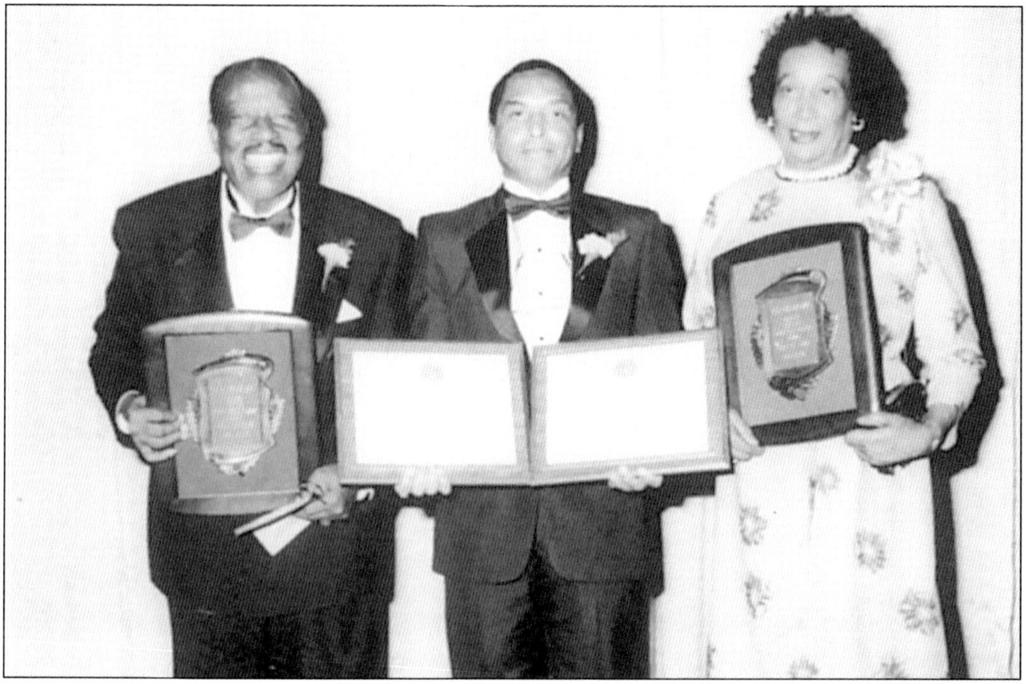

The following are inductees into the ASU National Alumni Hall of Fame: (from left to right) A.O. Shields `42, William Johnson (National Alumni president), and 1948 Olympic High Jump Gold medalist Alice Coachman Davis `49.

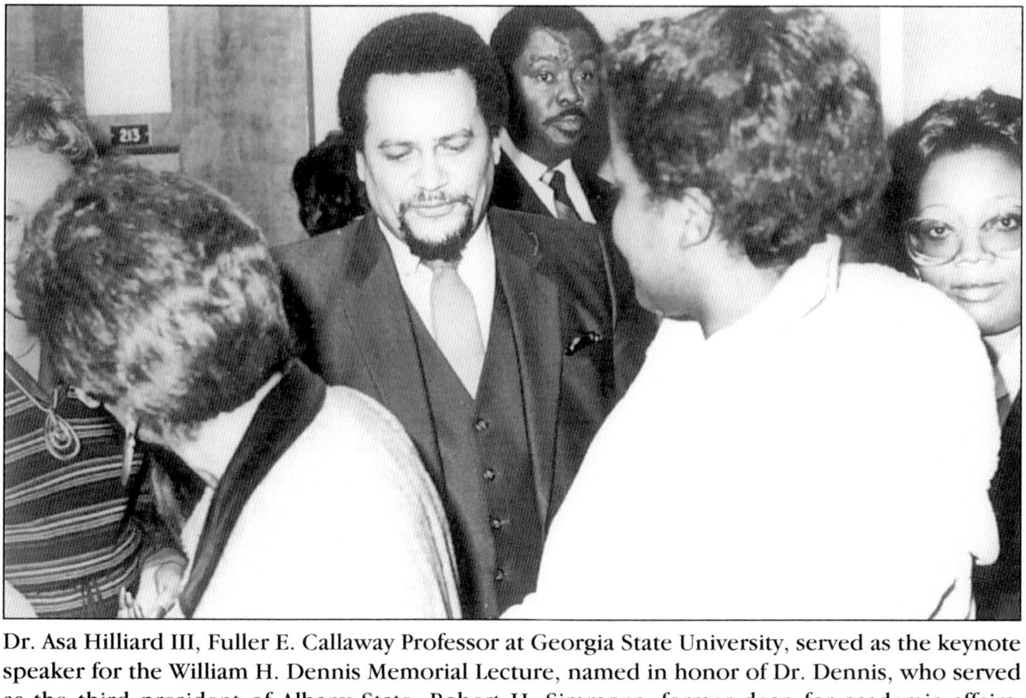

Dr. Asa Hilliard III, Fuller E. Callaway Professor at Georgia State University, served as the keynote speaker for the William H. Dennis Memorial Lecture, named in honor of Dr. Dennis, who served as the third president of Albany State. Robert H. Simmons, former dean for academic affairs, initiated the lecture series in 1970. The above photograph shows Dr. Hilliard interacting with Albany State students following his lecture.

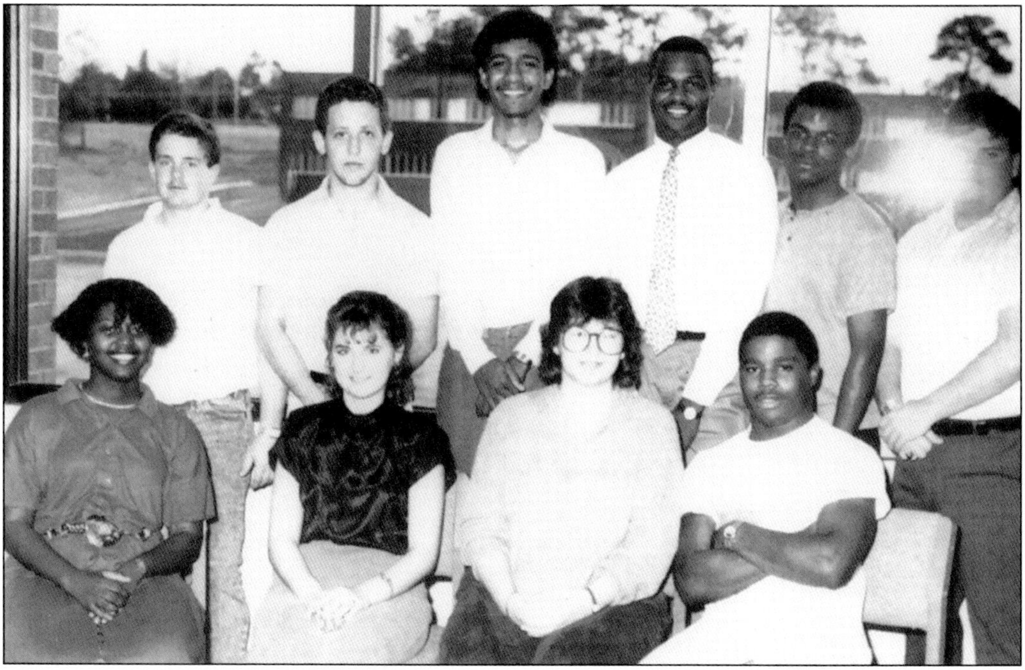

The Presidential Scholars Program was initiated in 1987 to award scholarships to students in each entering class. Scholarship recipients must rank in the upper five percent of his graduating high school class. The 1989 scholars from left to right are (front row) Cheryl Griffin, Mechelle Knight, Amy Davis, and Richard Simpkins. In the second row are Kip Rines, Dewain Autrey, Sean Owens, Stephen Bruce, Terry Shoemaker, and Robert VonMendenhall.

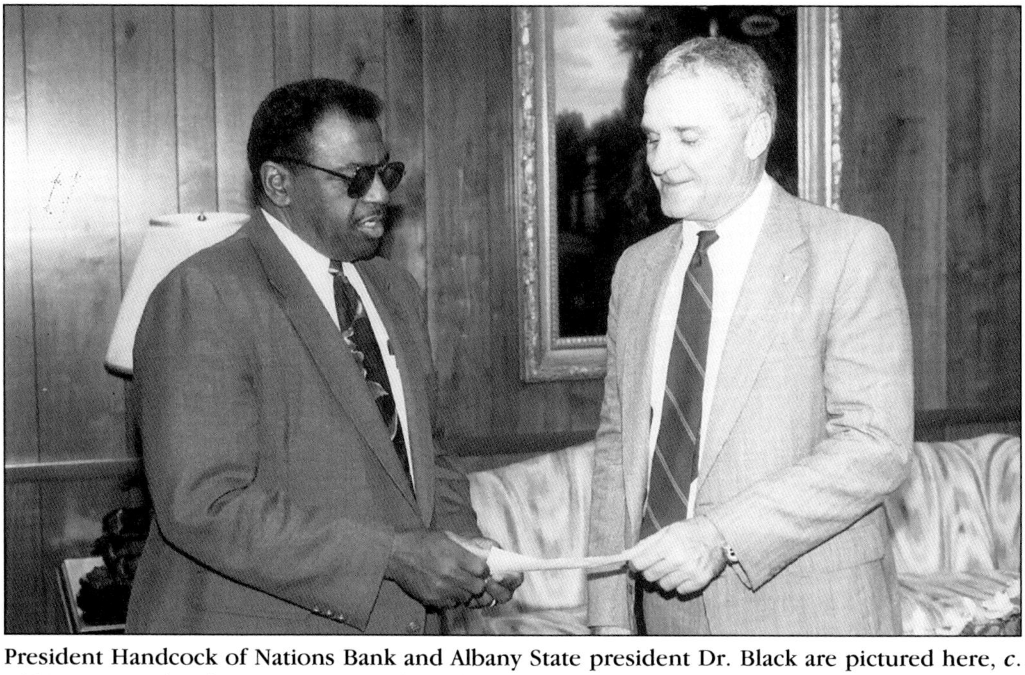

President Handcock of Nations Bank and Albany State president Dr. Black are pictured here, *c.* 1992. Mr. Handcock is presenting a check for $5,000 to the Albany State Foundation to support the Center for the Study of the Black Male, now the Center for the African American Male.

Jazz singer Liz Spraggins is a frequent visitor to Albany State. Spraggins has performed for former President Jimmy Carter, Secretary of State Gen. Colin Powell, former Gov. Joe Frank Harris, and countless others. She has shared the stage with Aretha Franklin, Gladys Knight, Daryl Coley, Marvin Gaye, Dionne Warwick, Lou Rawls, and many others.

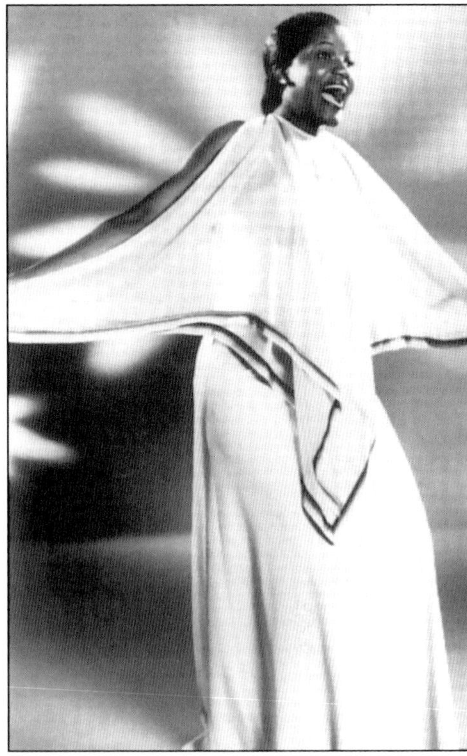

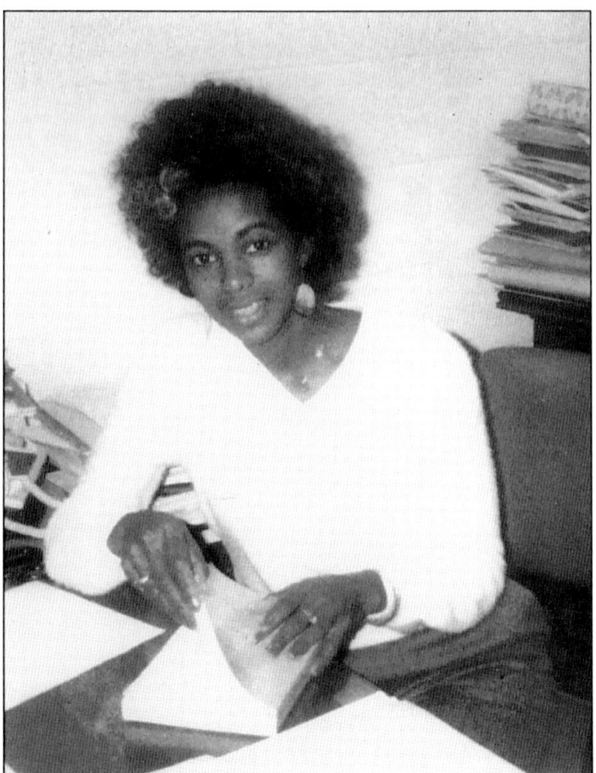

Saundra Sharp served as writer-in-residence in the Department of English and Modern Languages for the 1988–1989 school year. Sharp, a distinguished actress and producer, has appeared in many stage productions such as *Black Girl*, and *Hello Dolly*, and has played major roles in television shows such as *Knots Landing*, *St. Elsewhere*, *All About Us*, and *Wonder Woman*. She has made appearances as a guest star in *Benson*, *Barnaby Jones*, *The Jeffersons*, *T.J. Hooker*, and *Lou Grant*.

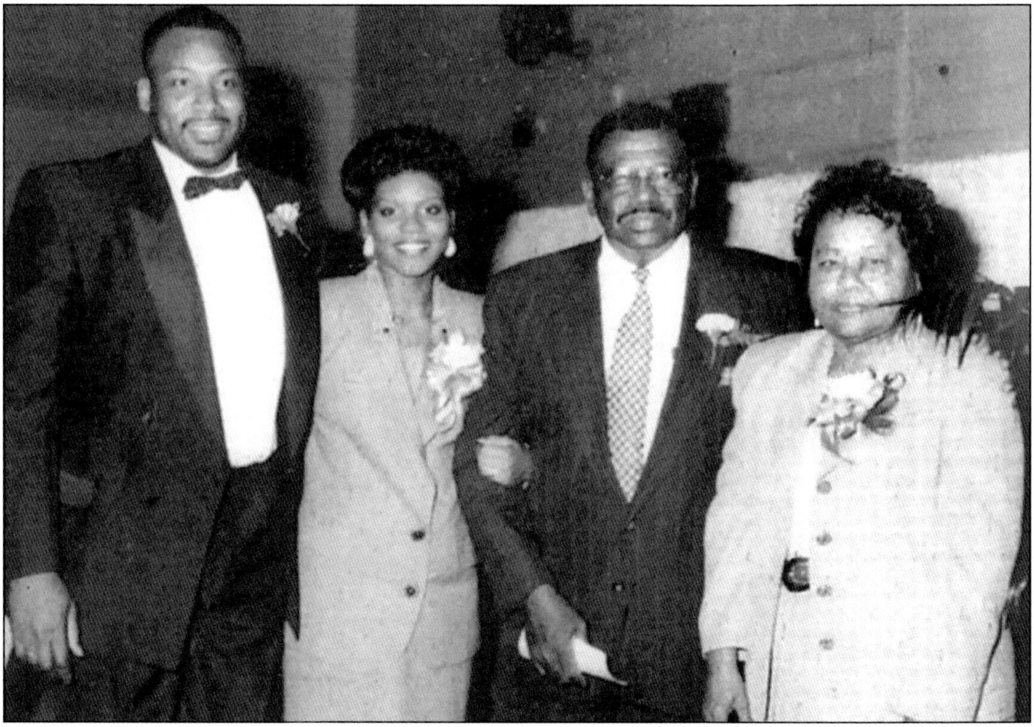

From left to right, Hon. Kenderson Hill ('83) and Semora Johns ('91) (emcees) join President Black and his former administrative assistant, Mrs. Mary Crawford.

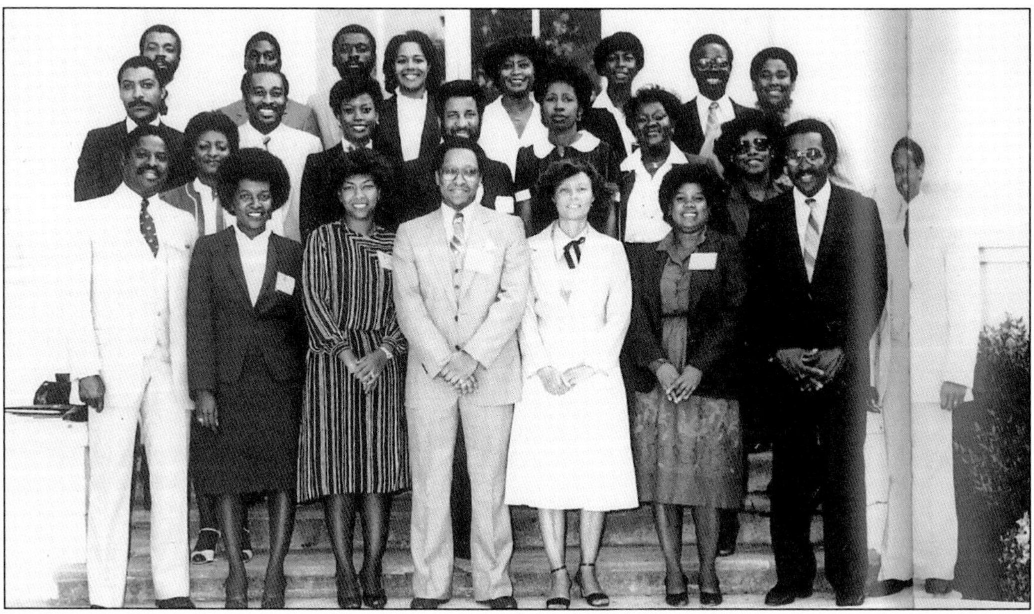

A Youth Motivation Task Force conference was organized in 1983 and coordinated by Albany State. The office of career development showcases a team of professionals each year from the business and industrial community. Students have the opportunity to interact for two and a half days with ASU alumni and others about expectations in the workforce through a series of classroom visitations, group seminars, etc.

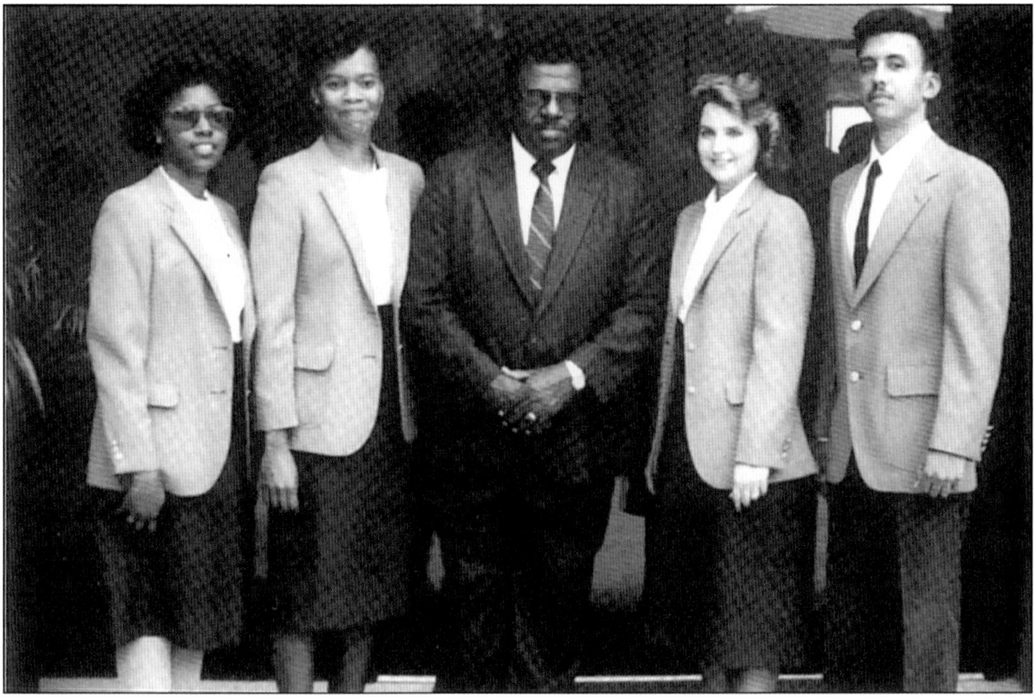

The Golden Ambassadors of Albany State in 1989 are, from left to right, Tracey Cotton, Ingrid Driskell, President Black, Mechelle Knight, and Oscar King.

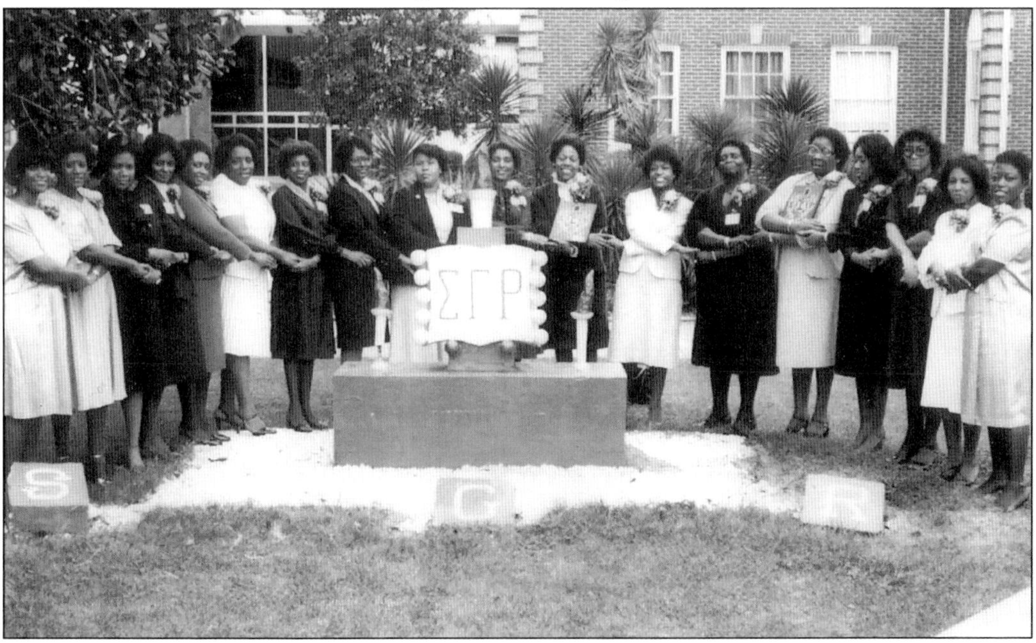

Sigma Gamma Rho sorority, Zeta Phi Chapter, was chartered on the Albany State campus on November 28, 1975. Pictured from left to right, *c*. 1989, are Tommie Wimberly, Polly Roberts, Mary Frances Williams, Mable Rockwell, Mattie Hill, Josephine Farrell, Sandy Pointer, Doris Emerson, Yvette Battle, Diane P. Frink, Katie K. White, Dorothy Hubbard, B. Elizabeth Davis, Catherine Thomas, Deborah Battle, Brenda Jones, Joanne Aldridge, and Gloria Powell.

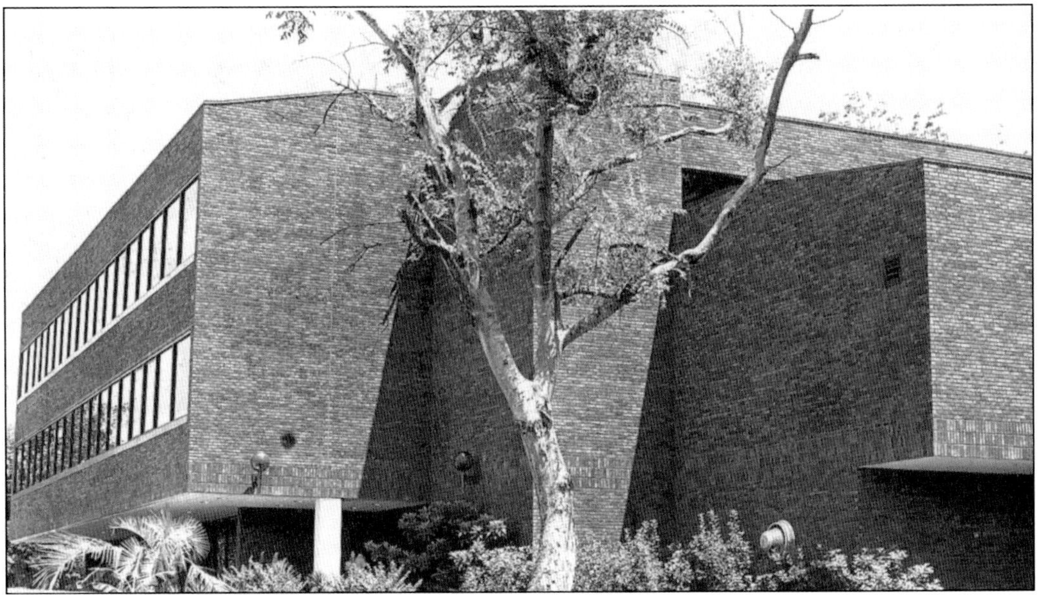

Robert H. Simmons Hall, constructed in 1975, serves as a classroom building and an office building. The building was named for former dean of academic affairs, Robert H. Simmons.

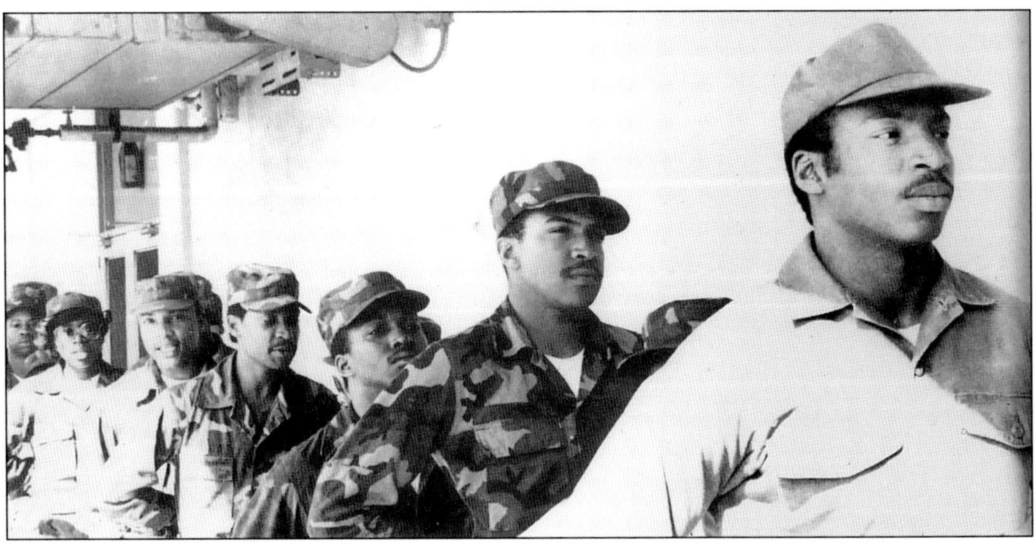

Albany State University's United States Army Reserve Officers Training Corps (ROTC) was established in 1976 in conjunction with Fort Valley State University. This photograph depicts cadets taking weekend classes and field training exercises. Programs were designed to prepare the MS III cadets for excellence during advance camp and offer the opportunity for a commission in the United States Army.

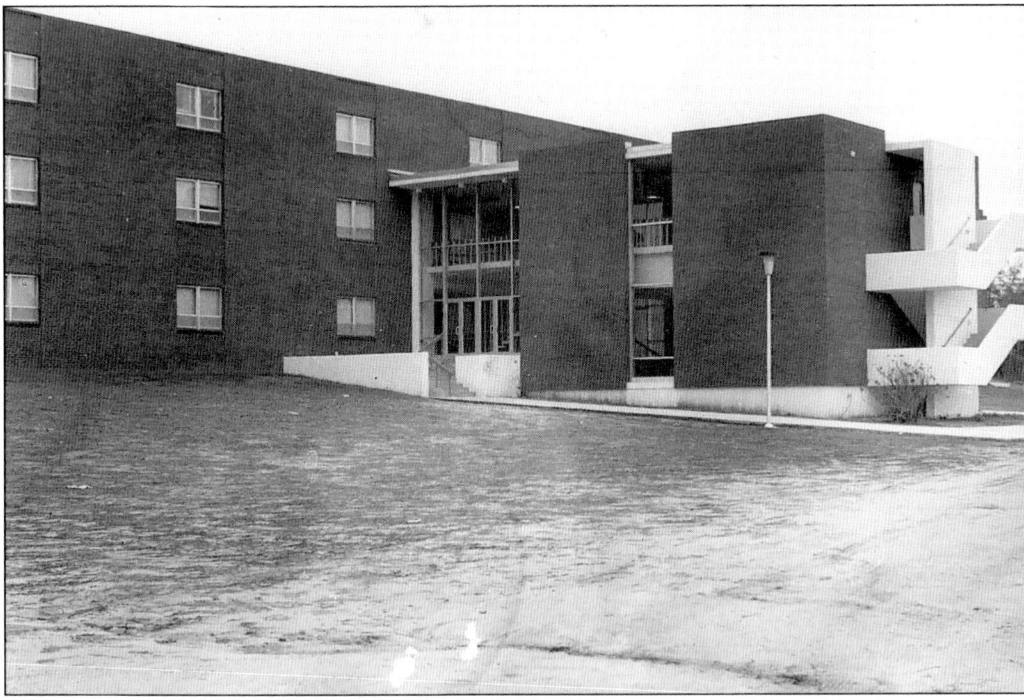

Ophelia G. Andrews Hall, a three-level building, was designed to accommodate 192 students. The facility consists of lounges, study areas, and a kitchen and has housed both female and male students throughout its history. The dormitory is named for Professor Andrews, who served on Albany State faculty from 1941 to 1953.

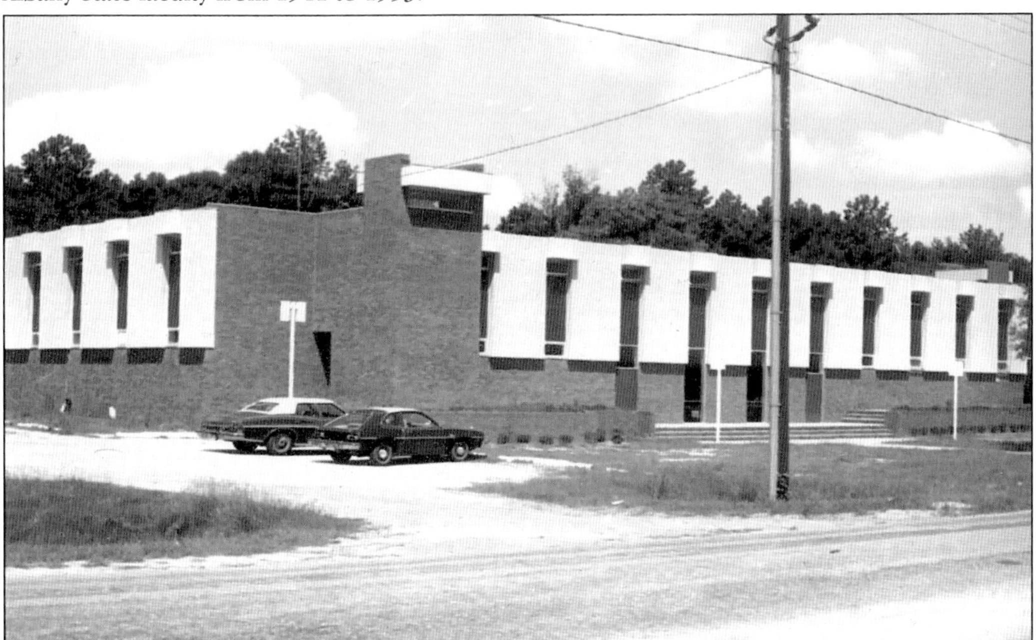

Richard Blaylock Hall, which served as a men's dormitory, was named for the director of plant operations during the 1960s.

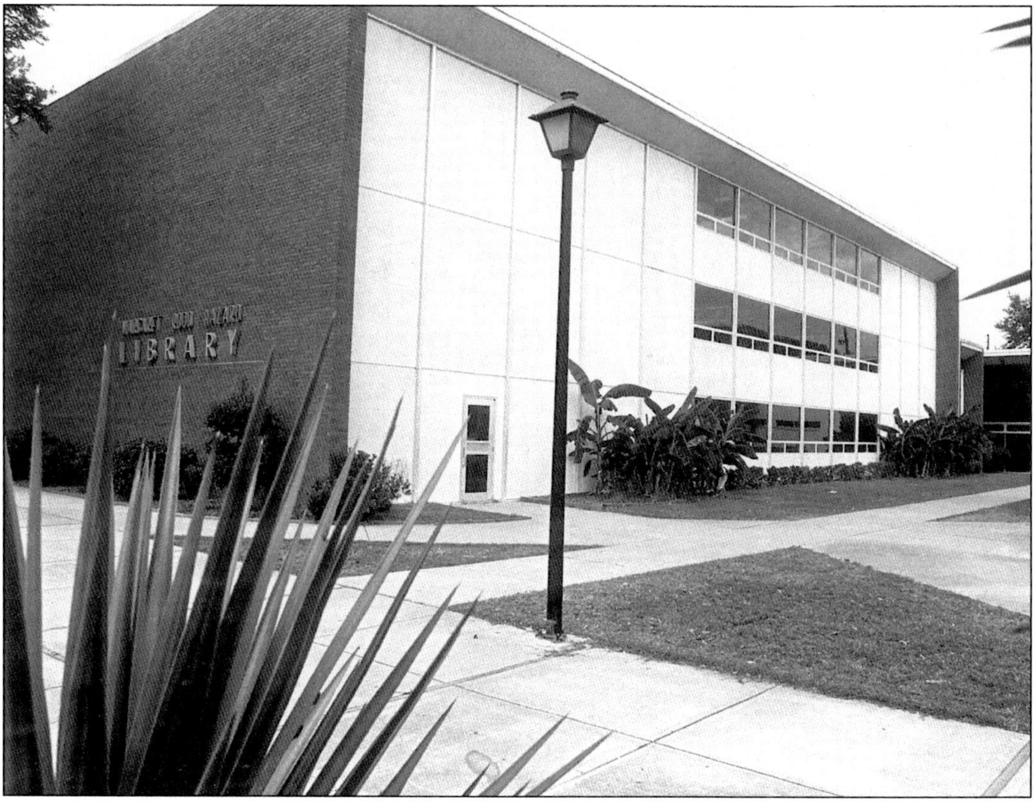

This photograph shows Margaret Rood Hazard Library.

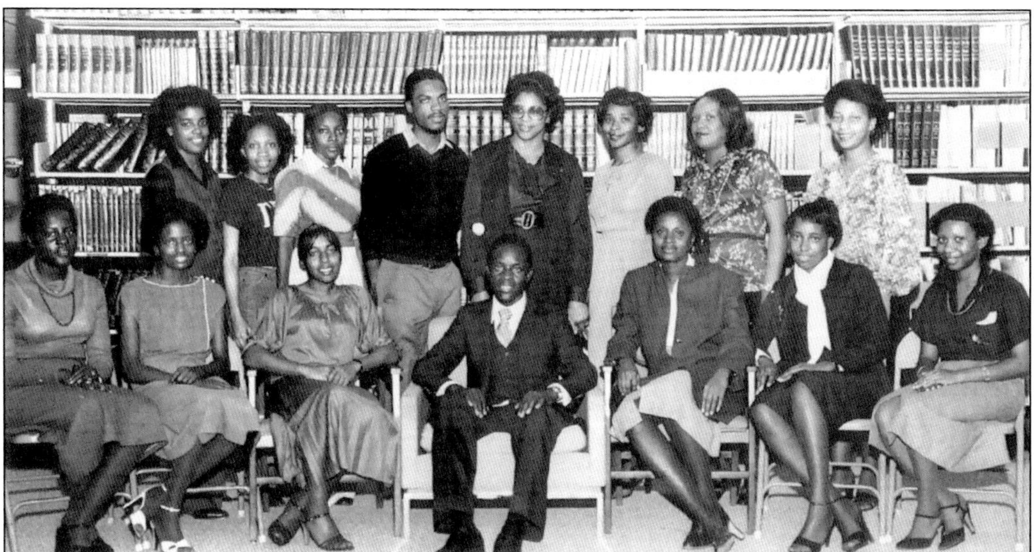

Pictured here is the library club in 1979, with Betty Frazier (center), club advisor and acquisitions librarian. Staff members in the picture include Nettie Broadway, Annie McFarland, and Ruth Wagner, and club president Gilbert Udoto..

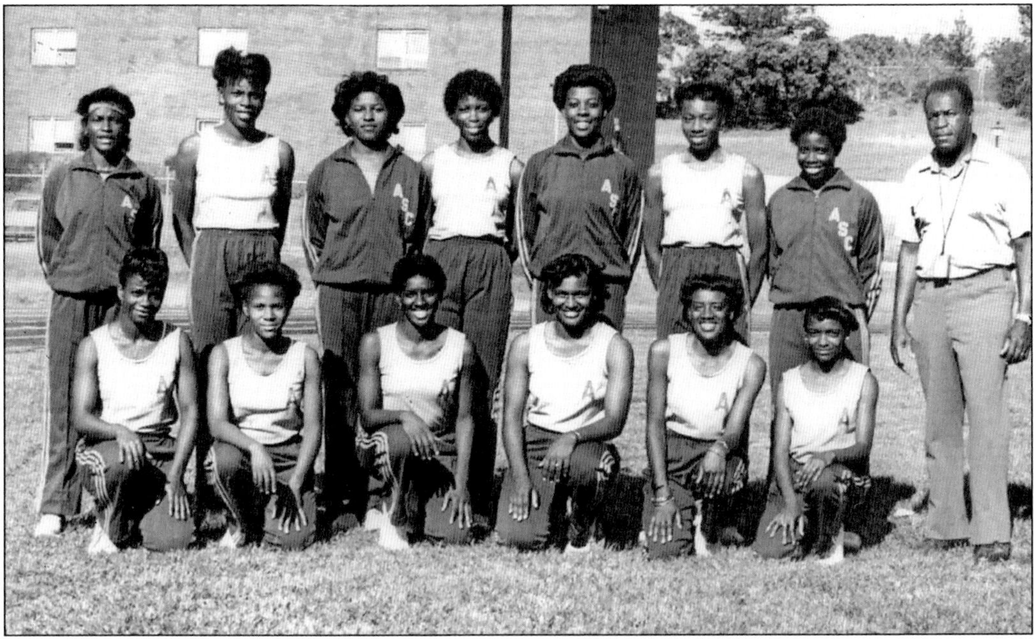

Here is the 1984 Albany State women's track team. Standing from left to right are Priscilla Williams, Linda Nix, Brenda Nelson, Lorrye Kingdom, Alga Turner, Xavine Copeland, Elaine McCain, and Robert Cross, coach. Kneeling are Betty Mitchell, Jackie Brown, Stephanie Collier, Debra White, Valerie Bell, and Delois Stanton.

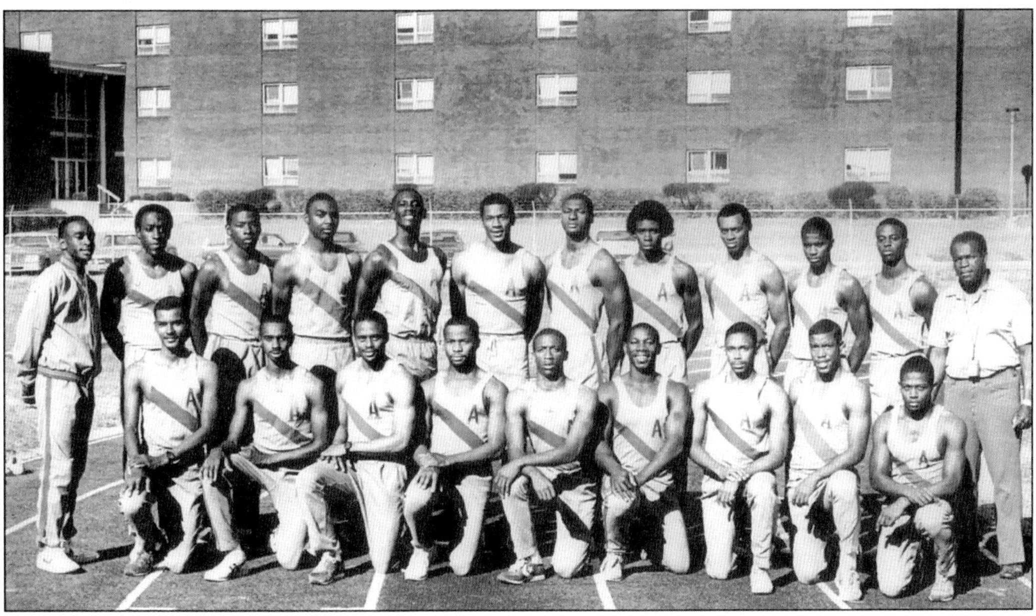

The 1984 Albany State Rams men's team won the Southern Intercollegiate Athletic Conference (SIAC) for the twelfth time since 1972. Standing from left to right are Kenneth Davis, Robert Wilburn, Fred Thomas, Ricky Phelps, Anthony Mason, Calvin Studdemeire, John James, Ervin Dailey, Cedric Randolph, Todd Gamble, Derrick Wilson, and Robert Cross, track coach. Kneeling are Medgar Cooks, Ernest Lawrence, Kenneth Stewart, Edward Mays, Thomas Sylvester, Clifford Cook, Kerry Roberts Harry Whitt, and Marcus Browning.

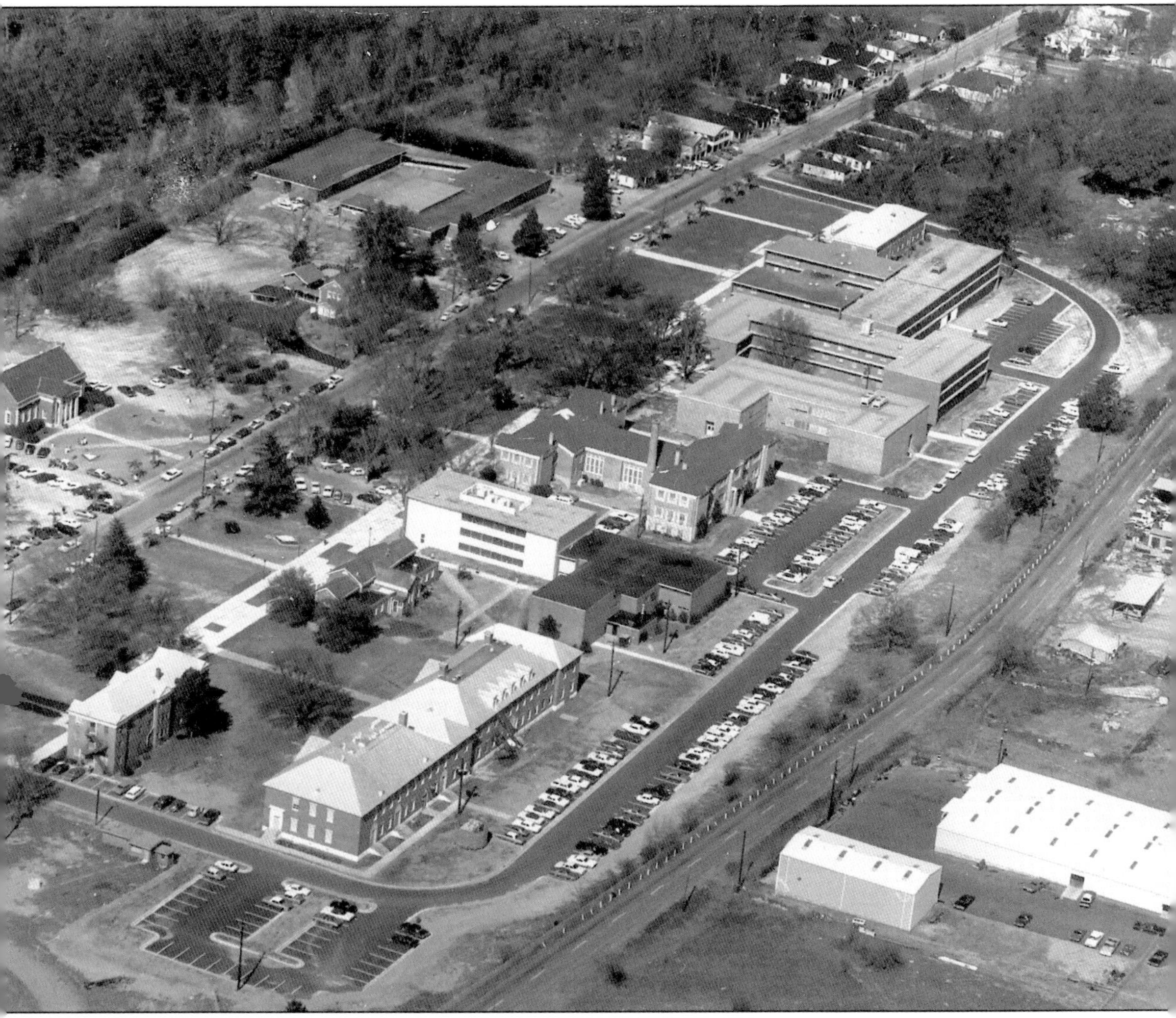

This is an aerial view of Albany State campus before the flood, *c*. 1979.

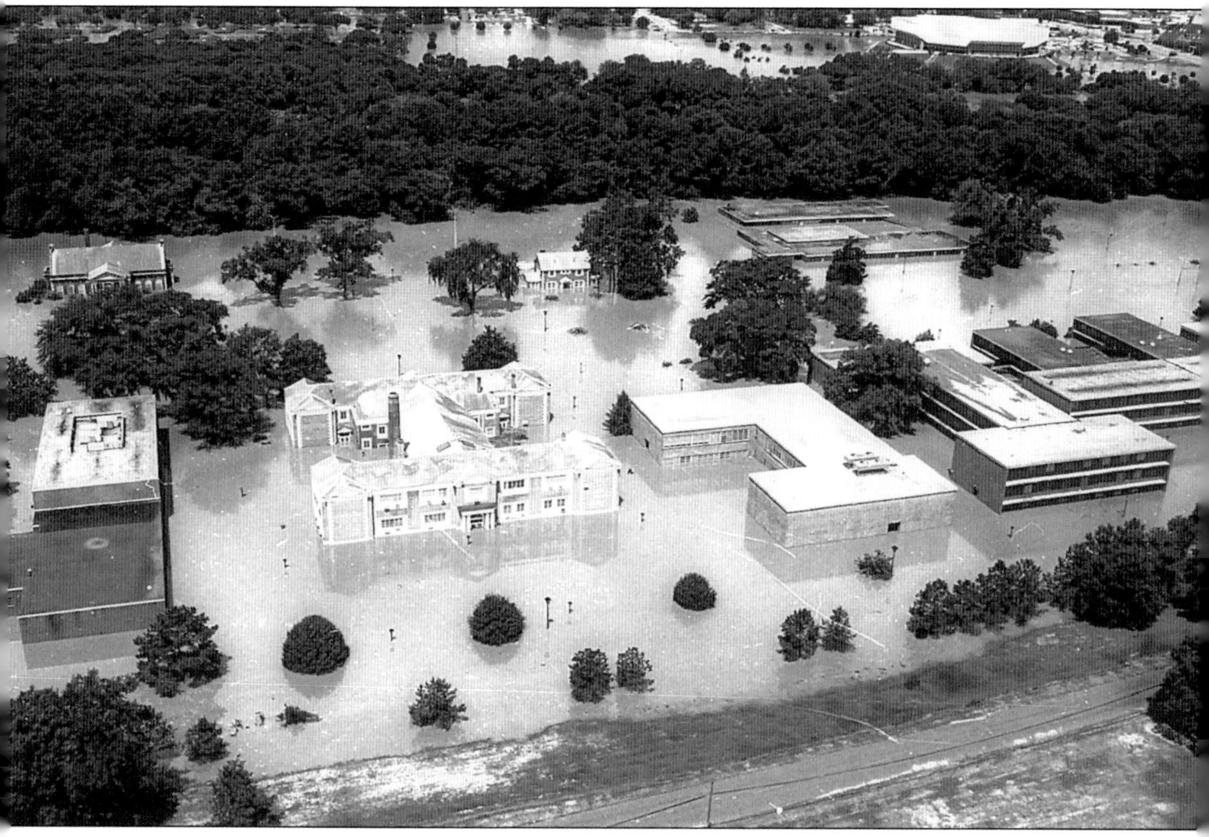

On July 7, 1994, Albany State experienced the worst disaster in its 93-year history when the Flint River, which runs along the west side of campus, flooded. All but 3 of the 31 buildings on campus were damaged, including the first floor of the recently completed James Pendergast Memorial Library. Sixteen buildings subsequently had to be demolished. Damage was estimated at more than $112 million. When word came on July 5 that flooding was imminent, President Black ordered the evacuation of students, while faculty and staff worked valiantly to pack records, secure computers, and move other items of value and importance to upper floors. Volunteers from the school and the community constructed a temporary levee on the east bank of the river, hoping to hold back the water. Two days later, however, the Flint River crested at 44 feet, sending flood waters to inundate the campus—10 feet of water stood stagnant for more than a week before receding. President Black immediately began planning for rebuilding, including setting up a temporary campus with modular units for classes, administration, and student housing, so that fall classes could commence.

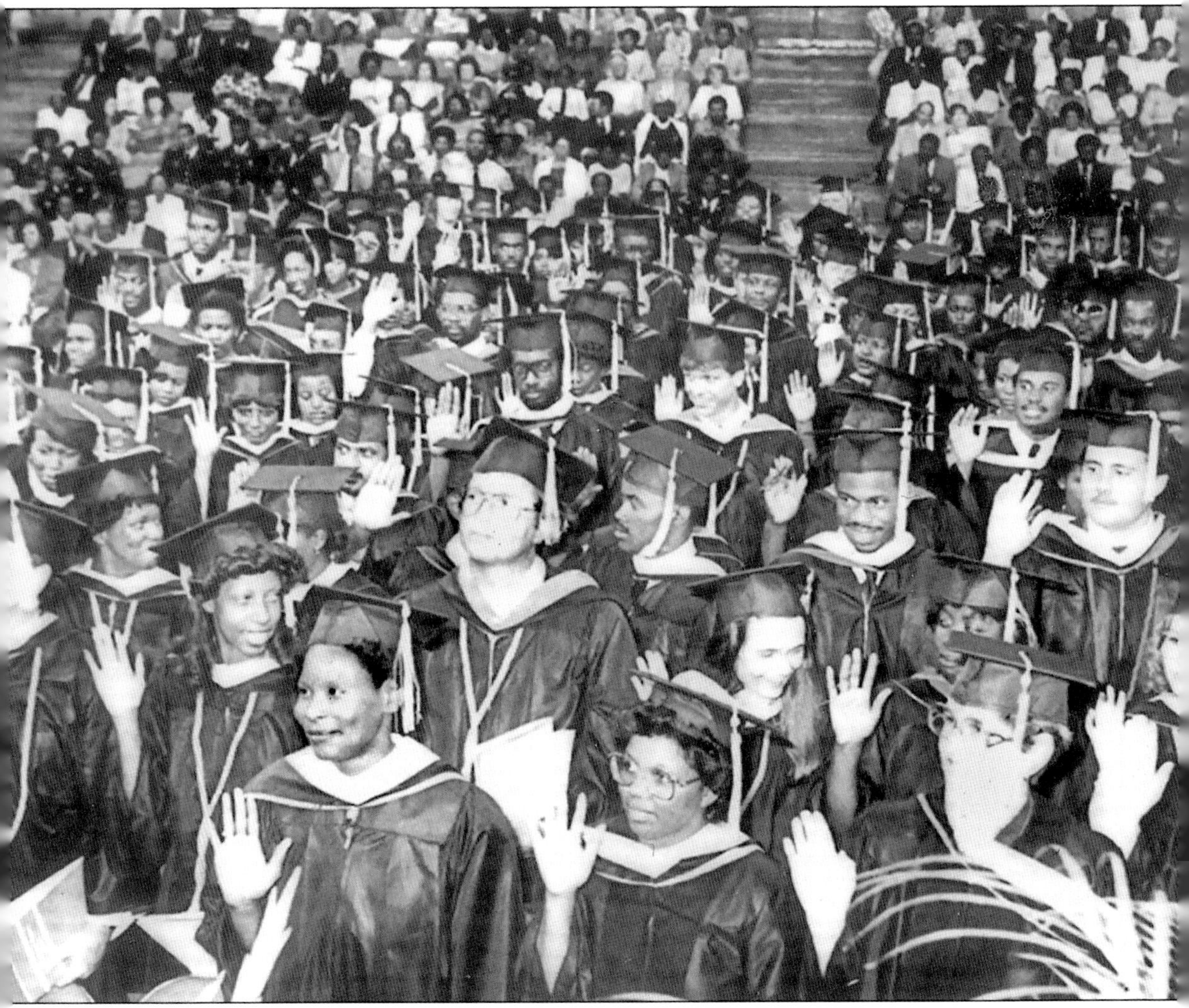

During the 65th annual commencement at Albany State, 214 students received degrees. Dr. Luther Burse, president of Fort Valley State, delivered the commencement address. According to

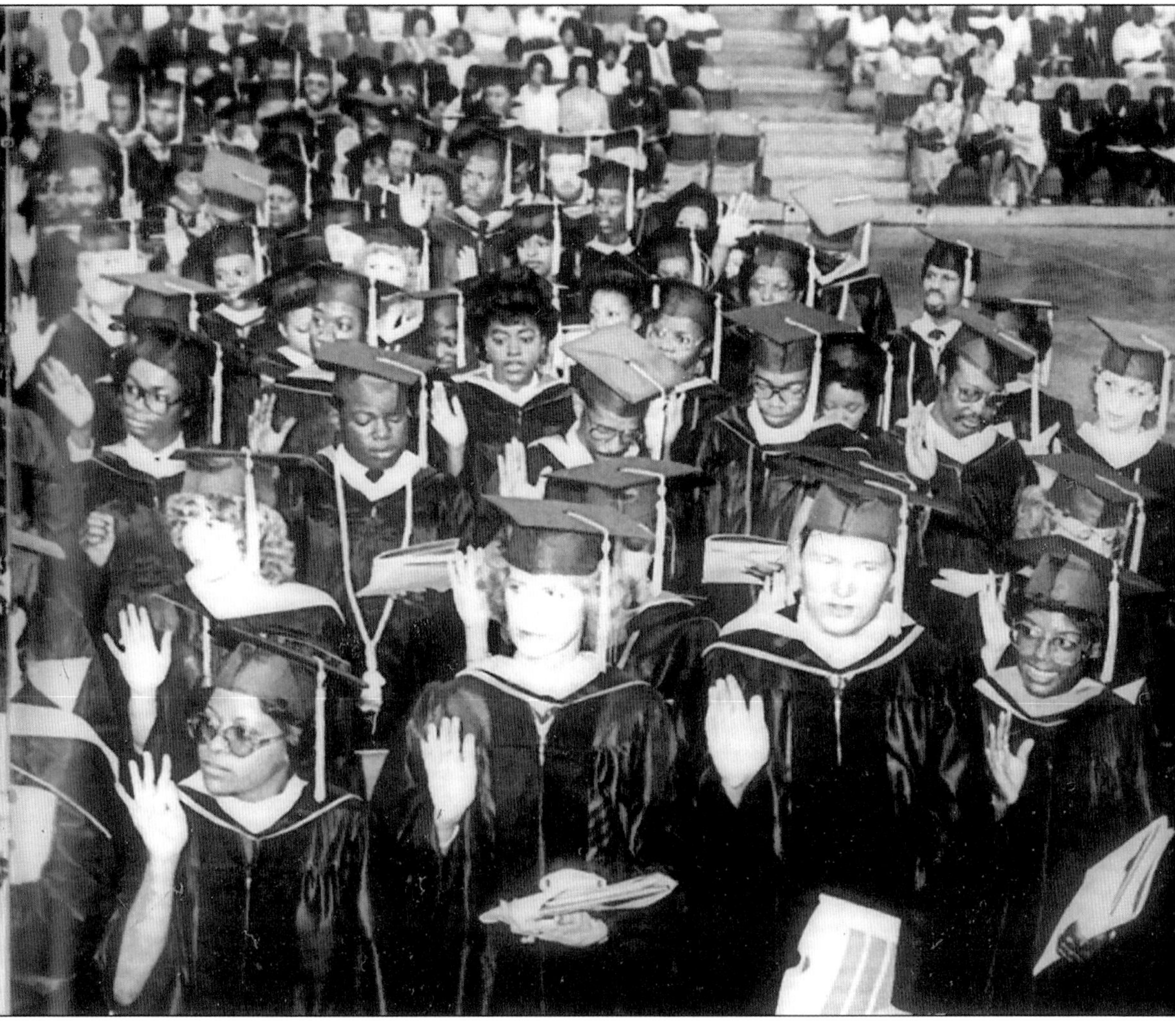

Burse, "Education cannot be viewed in isolation from the political, economic, and social structures of our society."

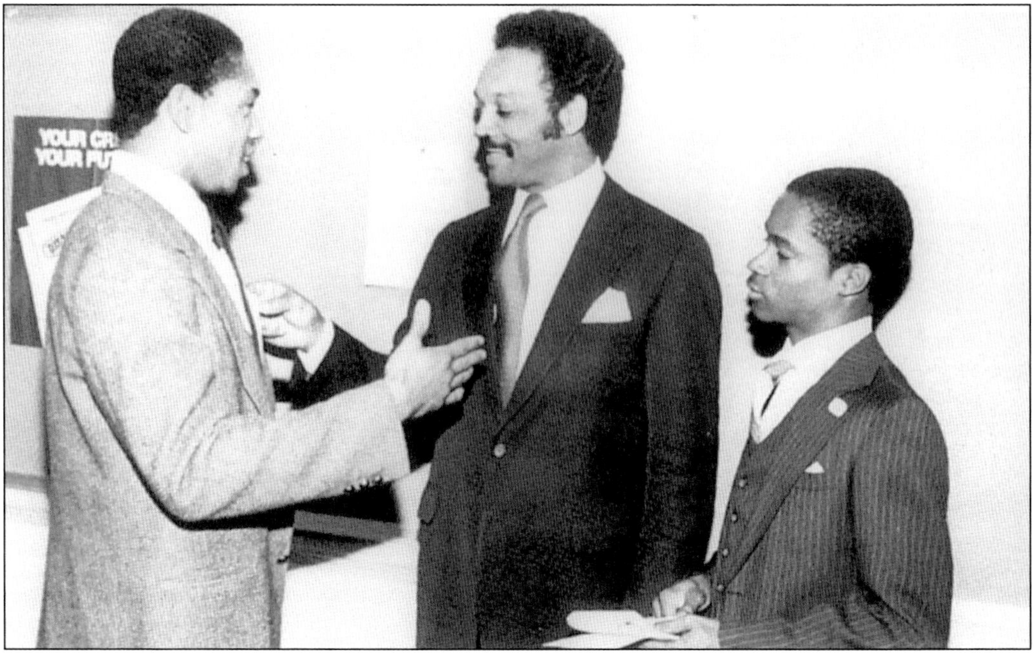

Rev. Jesse Jackson campaigned on Albany State's campus during his 1984 bid for the United States Presidency. From left to right are Virgil Adams (alumnus and supporter), Presidential candidate Rev. Jesse Jackson, and an unidentified ASU student.

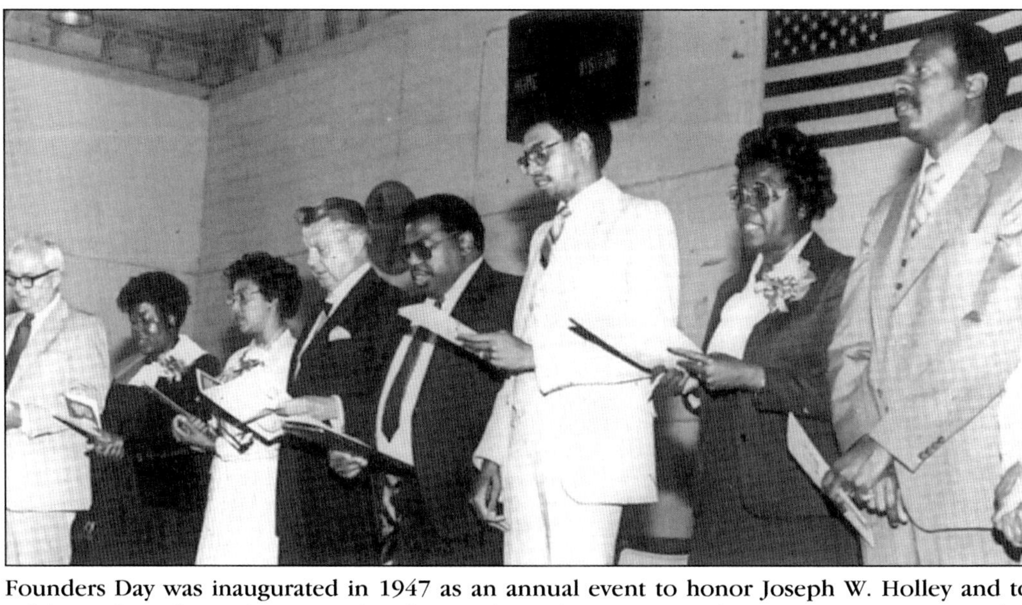

Founders Day was inaugurated in 1947 as an annual event to honor Joseph W. Holley and to celebrate the college's history and tradition. Shown here is a Founder's Day ceremony *c.* 1984.

Seven

Dr. Portia Holmes Shields 1996–

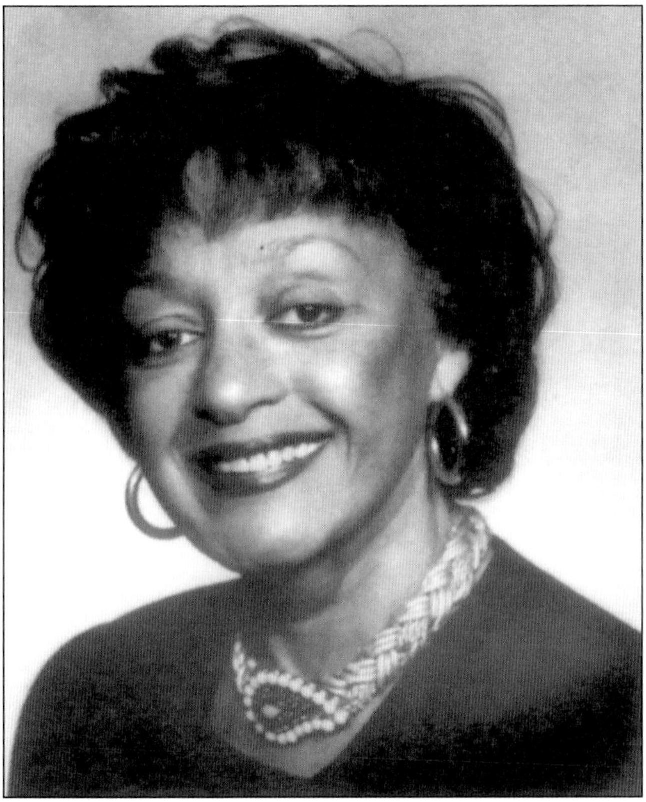

On September 1, 1996, Dr. Portia Holmes Shields, former dean of the School of Education at Howard University, Washington, D.C., became the first female and seventh president of ASU. Having received graduate degrees from the University of Maryland in early childhood/elementary education, Dr. Shields worked in the field of education as a teacher and in many other capacities. Dr. Shields's first project as president was to spearhead an aggressive $153 million rebuilding plan following the 1994 flood. Besides overseeing the university's rebuilding, she has brought national and international recognition to ASU through her professional activities and has demonstrated the university's commitment to community service. Under President Shields's leadership, community development and outreach initiatives have grown to include special programs such as Academic Boot Camp, The Holley Institute, Post Secondary Readiness Enrichment Program (PREP), the academic component to the National Youth Sports Program, and special training and resources for small businesses. She is married to William H. Lewis, an attorney, and has grown children and is a proud grandmother.

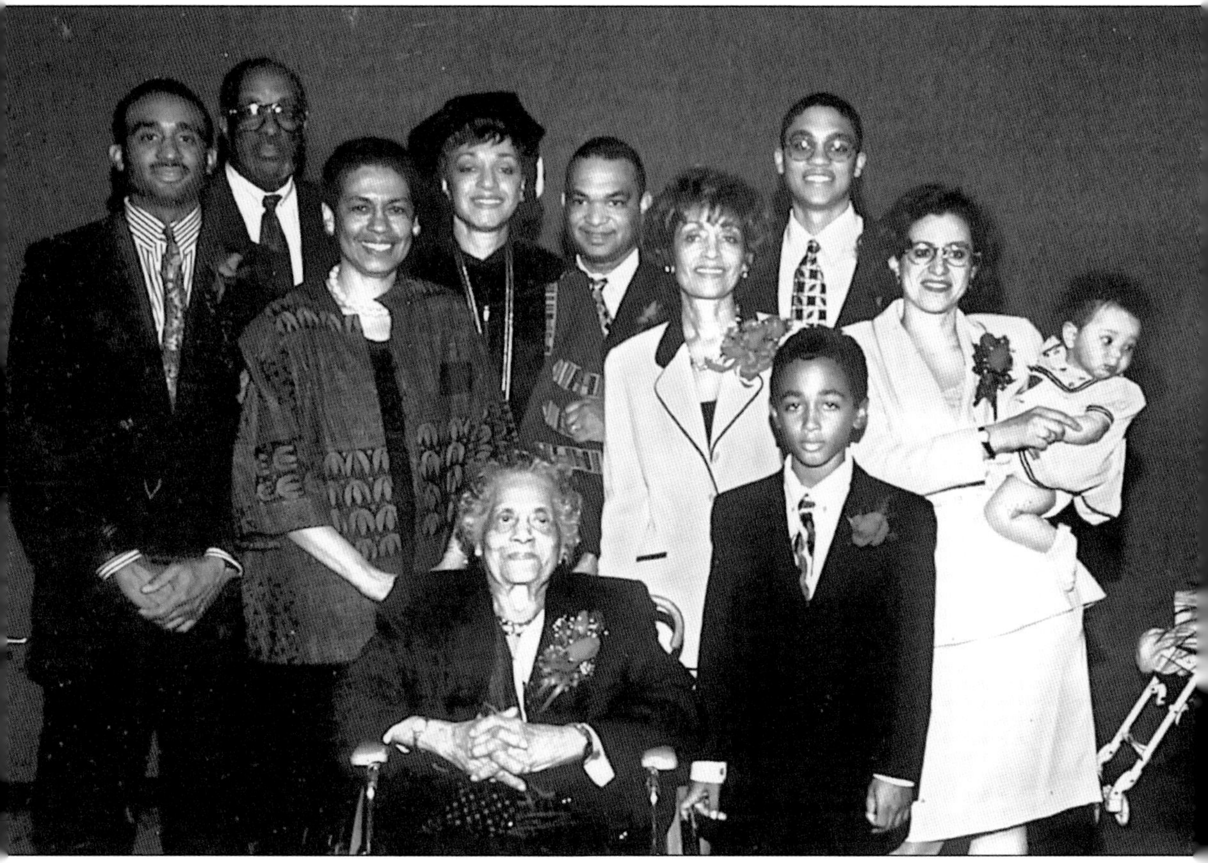

President Shields and her family are seen at the inaugural ceremonies. From left to right in the front row are Vela Holmes (mother) and Aaron Shields (grandson). Also surrounding Dr. Shields are Joseph Shields (son), William Lewis (husband), Craig Shields (son), Rep. Eleanor Holmes Norton (sister), Kyle Shields (son), and Nellie Holmes Hollomand (sister).

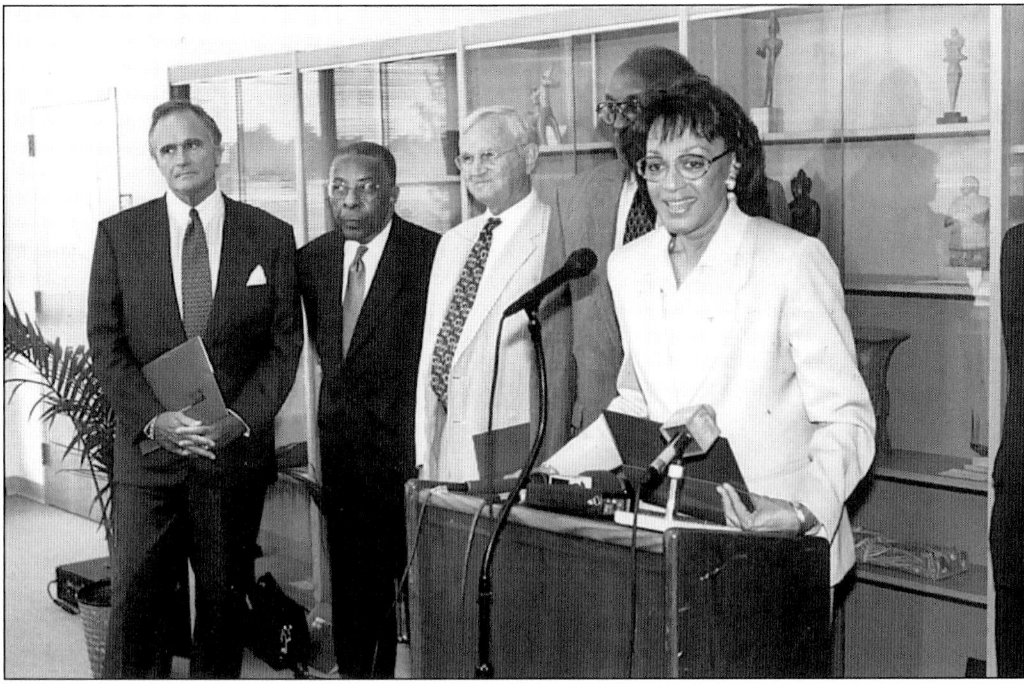

Members of the Board of Regents in 1996 Don Leebern Jr., Eldridge McMillan, and Thomas F. Allgood Sr. appear with William Lewis, and President Portia Shields.

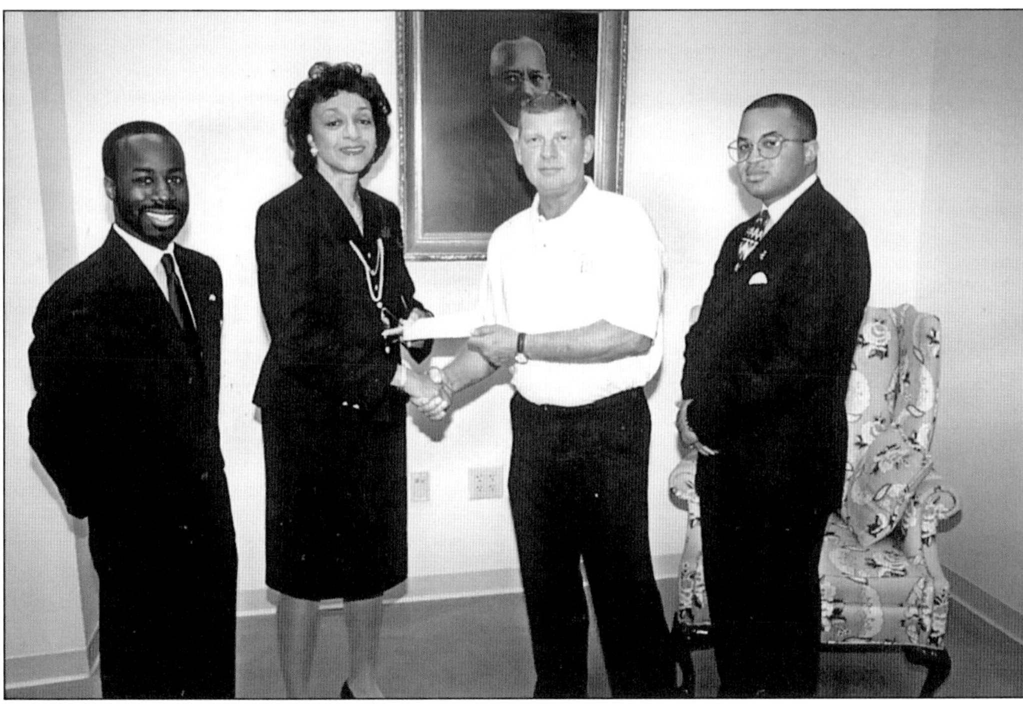

From left to right are Clifford Porter, director of the ASU Foundation; President Portia Holmes Shields; William ? of Georgia Emergency Management Association (GEMA); and Kenneth Dyer, vice president for fiscal affairs.

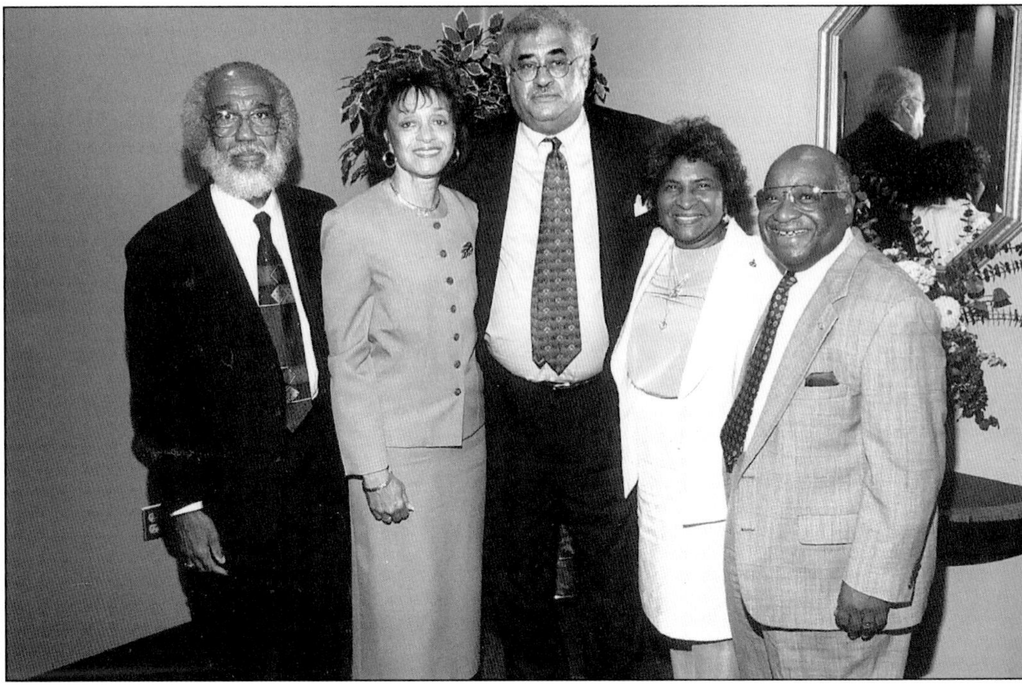

Starting on the left, Dr. Eugene Sherman, Professor Emeritus of sociology; Portia Holmes Shields, president of ASU; Frederick Humphries, President Emeritus of Florida A&M University; Lucille Wilson, Dean of the School of Nursing and Allied Health Sciences; and Cornelius "C.W" Grant, Dean Emeritus of student affairs, happily pose for a photograph following a graduate school symposium.

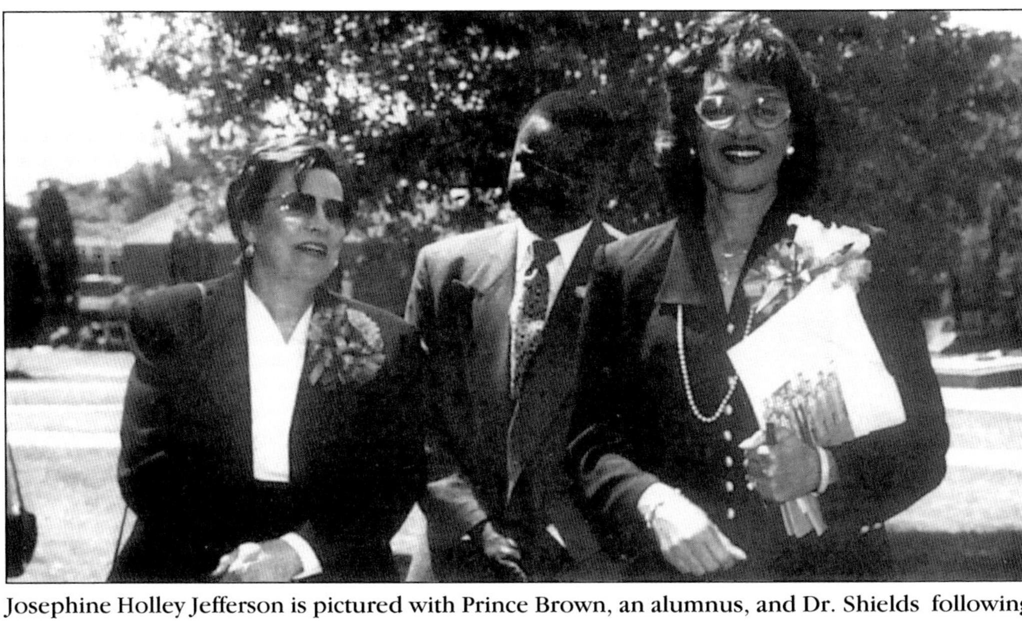

Josephine Holley Jefferson is pictured with Prince Brown, an alumnus, and Dr. Shields following a Founders Day ceremony, established in honor of Mrs. Jefferson's father, Joseph W. Holley.

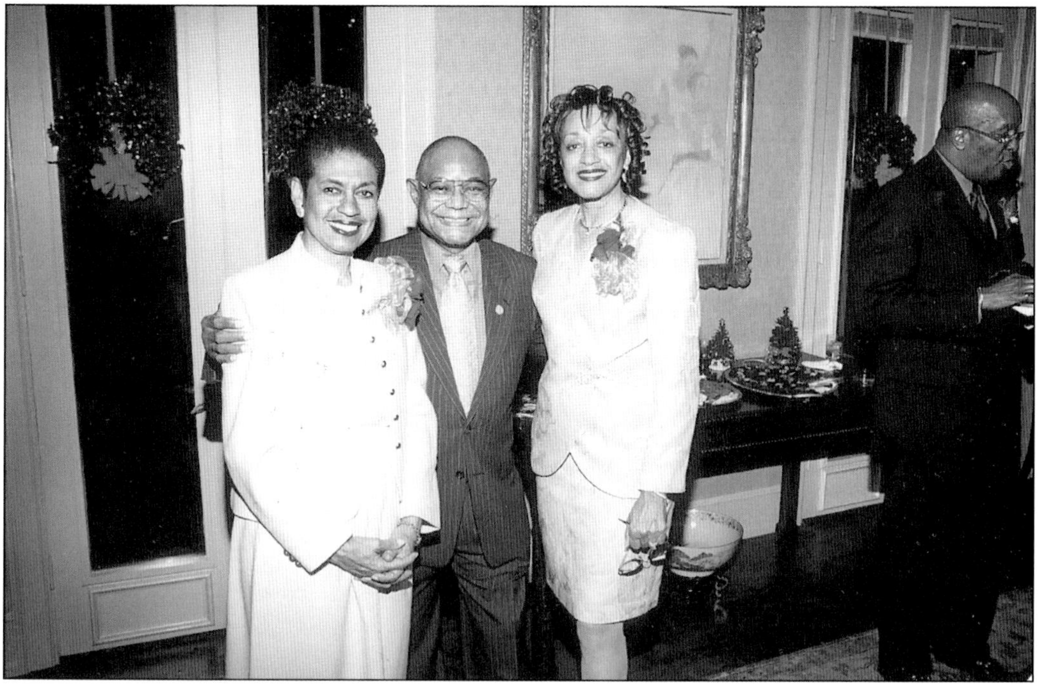

From left to right, Hon. Eleanor Holmes Norton, Dr. Walter Carl Gordon (local physician), an ASU supporter, and President Shields pose for a photograph.

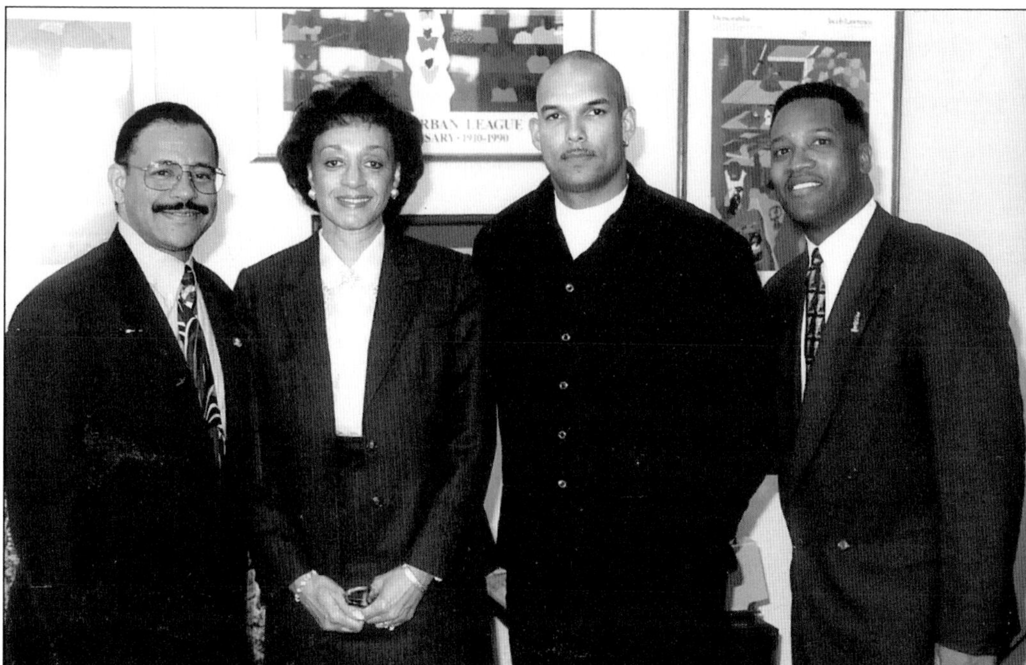

Congressman Sanford Bishop, Dr. Shields, David Justice of the 1998 World Champion Atlanta Braves, and Steven Belk of Coca Cola are pictured from left to right.

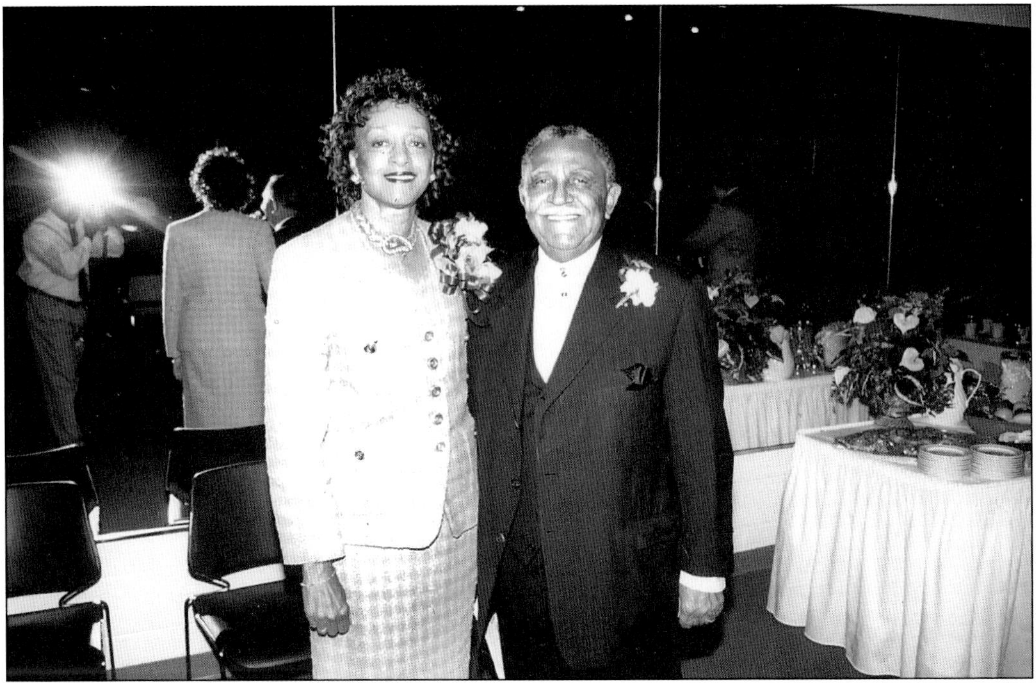

Pictured here is President Shields with Rev. Joseph Lowery of the Southern Christian Leadership Conference (SCLC). Reverend Lowery served as speaker for Honors Day Convocation.

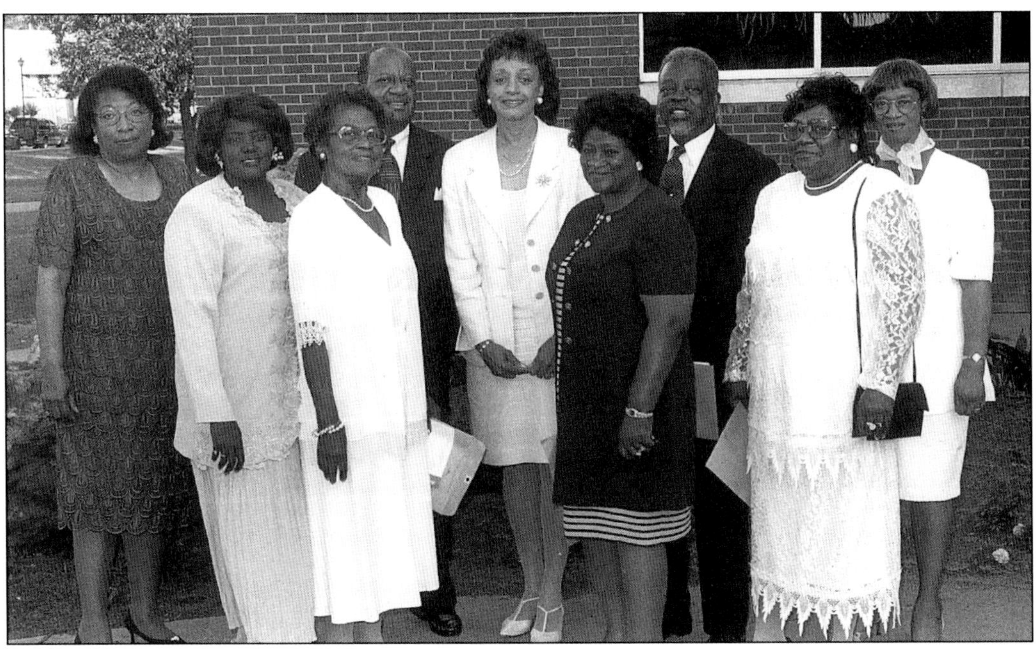

Here are some ASU retirees in 1997. They are (front row left to right) Ocie W. Troutman of developmental studies; Gladys Wilson, housing; Mattie Gulley, university post office; and DeHazel Fowler. In the back row are Dr. Helen Foster, Professor Emeritus of business; Dr. Egbert Bacon, Professor Emeritus of music; Dr. Shields; George I. Hill, natural sciences; and Marion Peterson, fiscal affairs.

President Shields and Former Ambassador Andrew Young are seen at the dedication of the Flint River Water Planning Policy Center and the launching of a new graduate concentration in water resources management and policy studies at ASU.

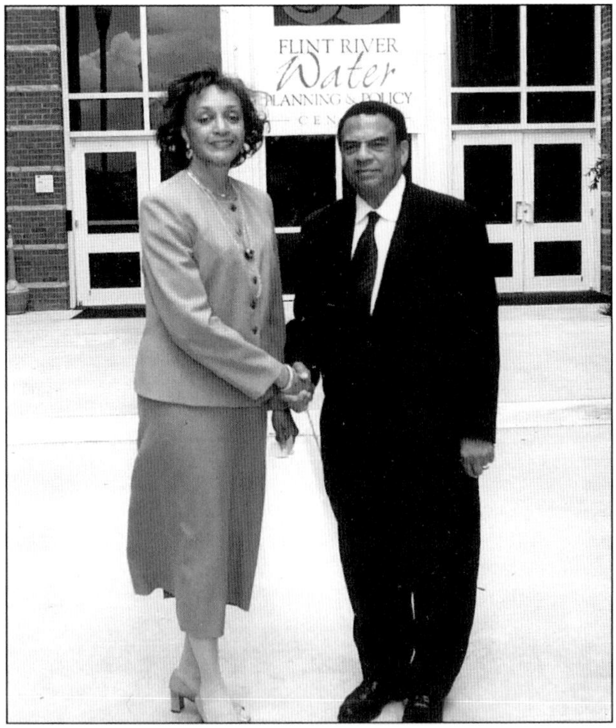

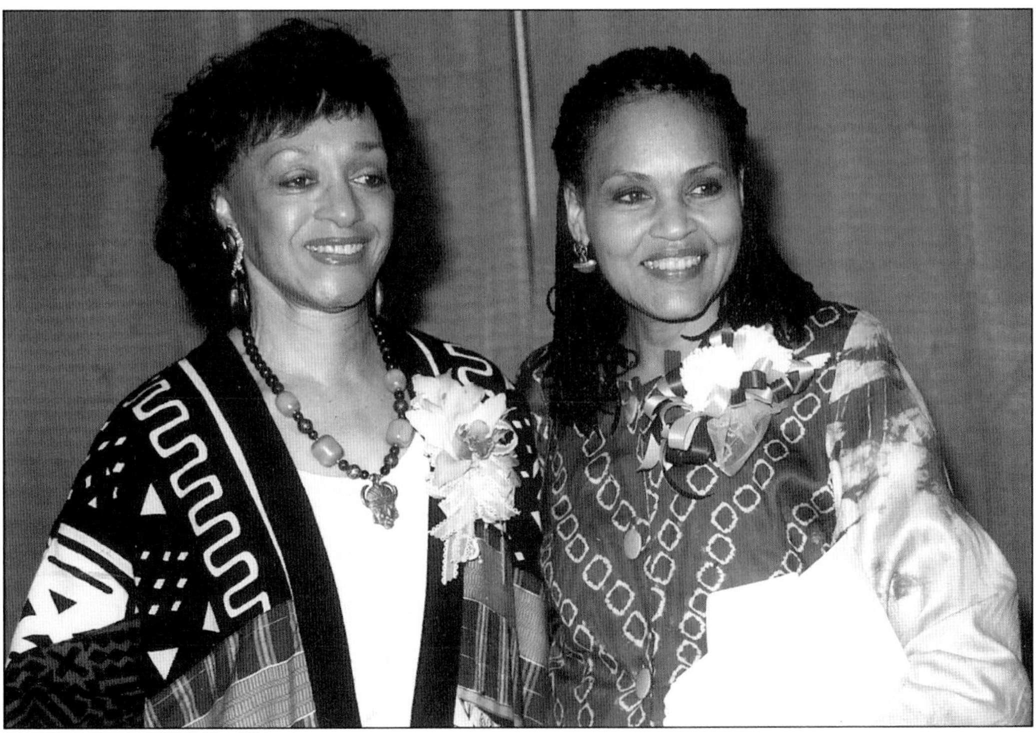

Dr. Shields and Charlayne Hunter-Gault, a national correspondent for the *Jim Lehrer News Hour*, pose together. Hunter-Gault served as moderator for a general session as part of the inaugural ceremonies.

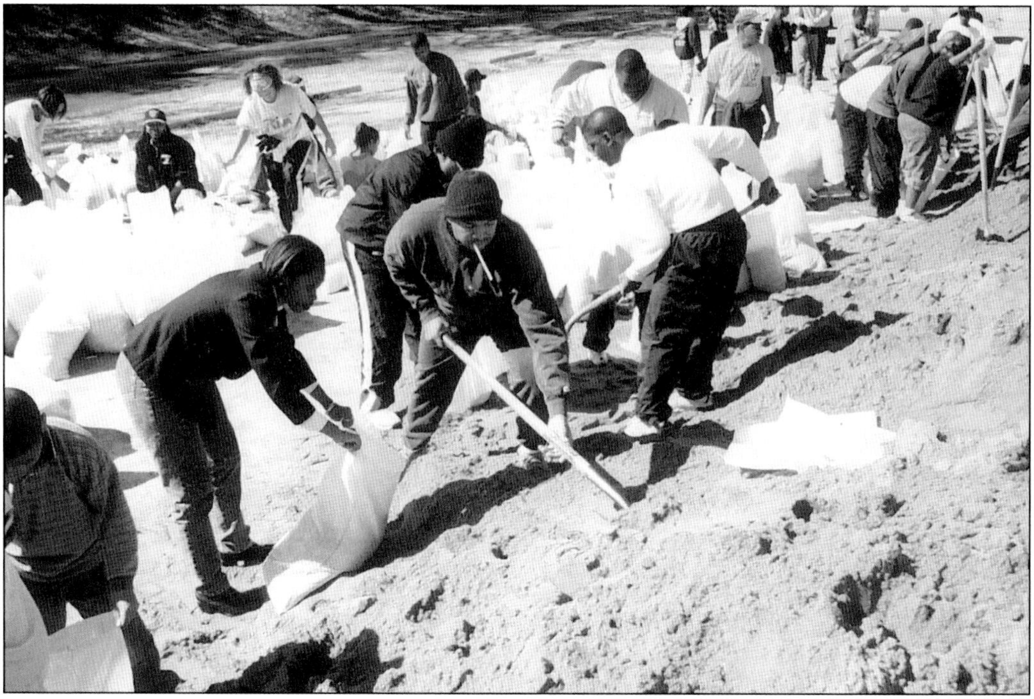

Students, the Albany community, and President Shields brace themselves for the oncoming flood of 1998 by placing sandbags throughout vulnerable spots surrounding campus.

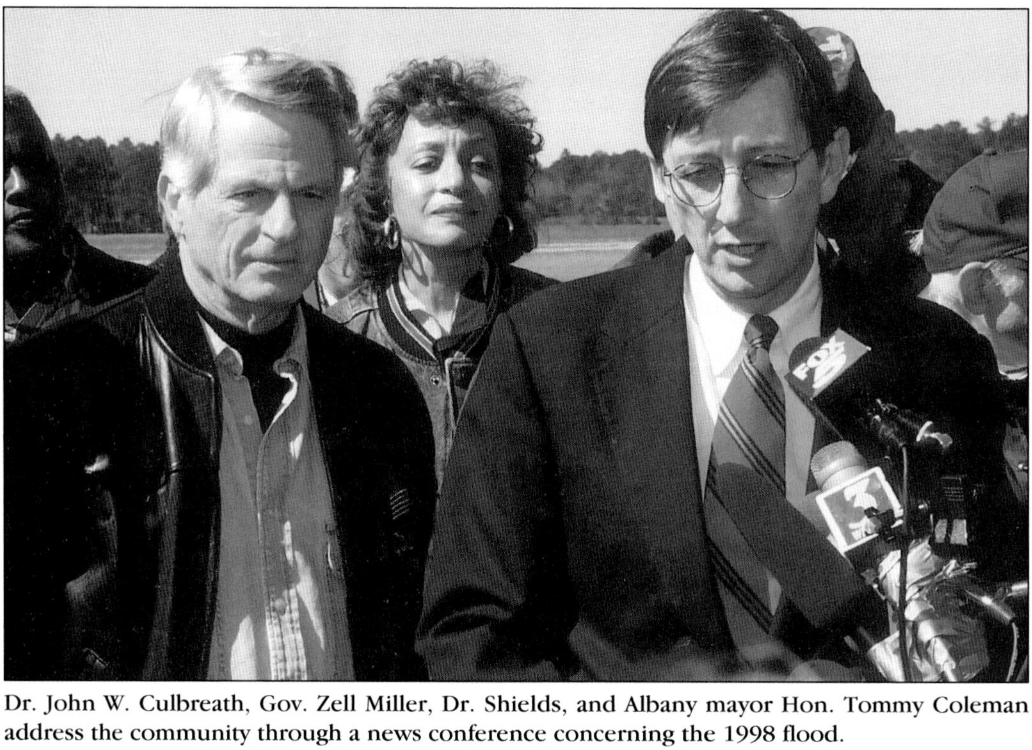

Dr. John W. Culbreath, Gov. Zell Miller, Dr. Shields, and Albany mayor Hon. Tommy Coleman address the community through a news conference concerning the 1998 flood.

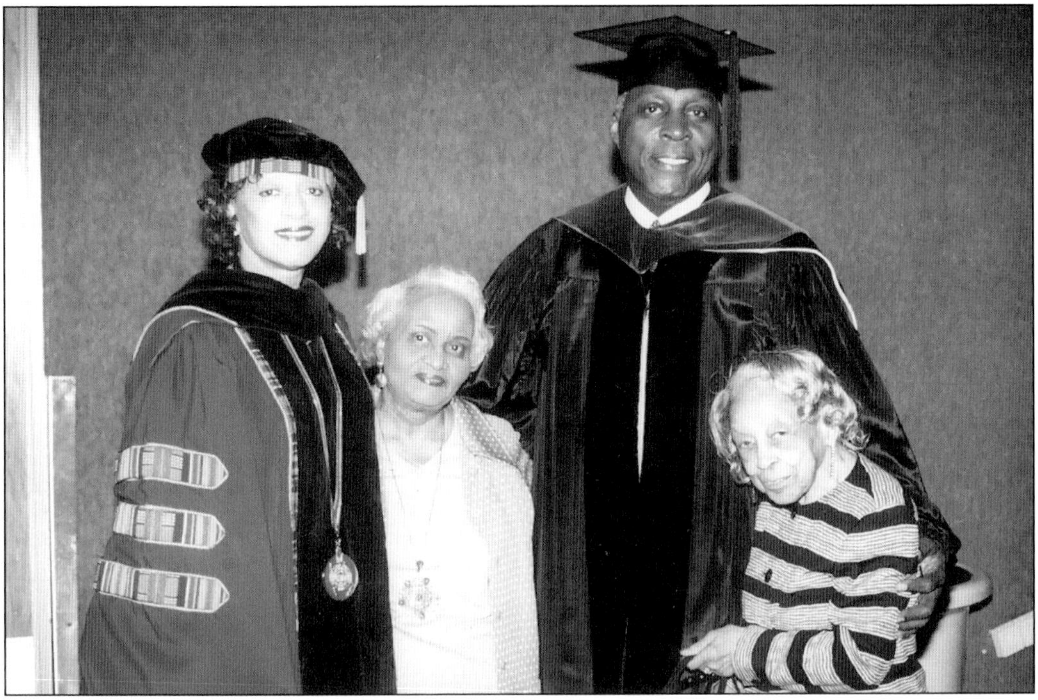

Dr. Portia Holmes Shields, Zenobia Cheevers, Vernon Jordan, and Odessa Hamilton are pictured here. Jordan served as the 82nd commencement speaker in the spring of 2001.

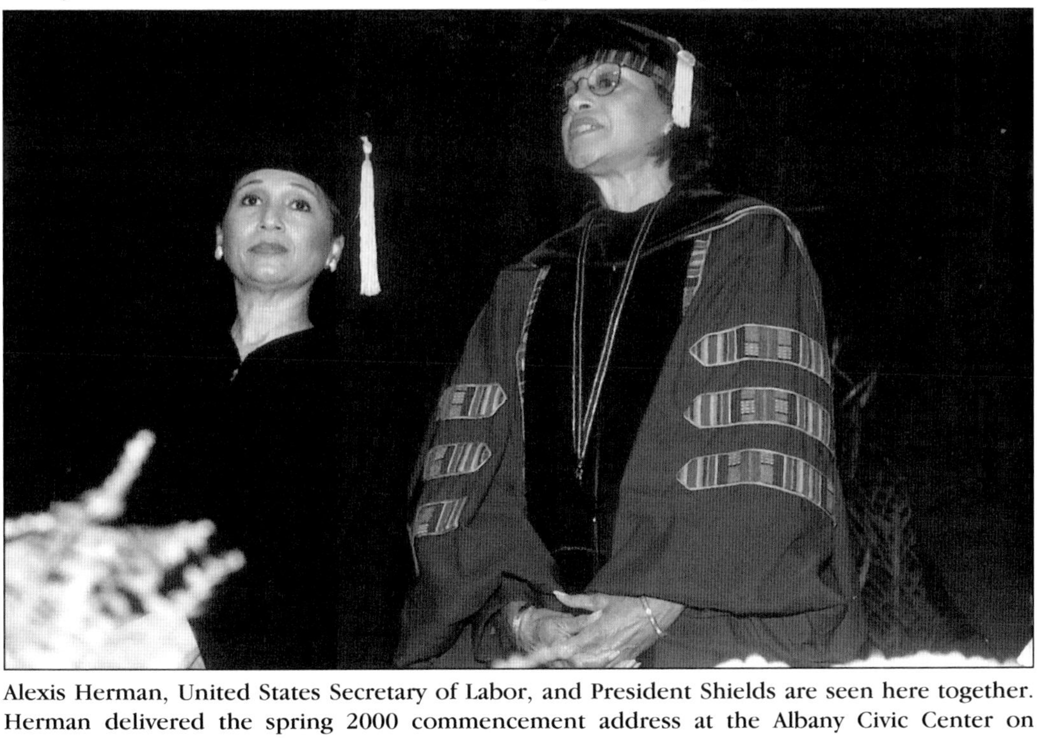

Alexis Herman, United States Secretary of Labor, and President Shields are seen here together. Herman delivered the spring 2000 commencement address at the Albany Civic Center on May 6 and became the first recipient to be conferred the Honorary Doctor of Philosophy degree in ASU history.

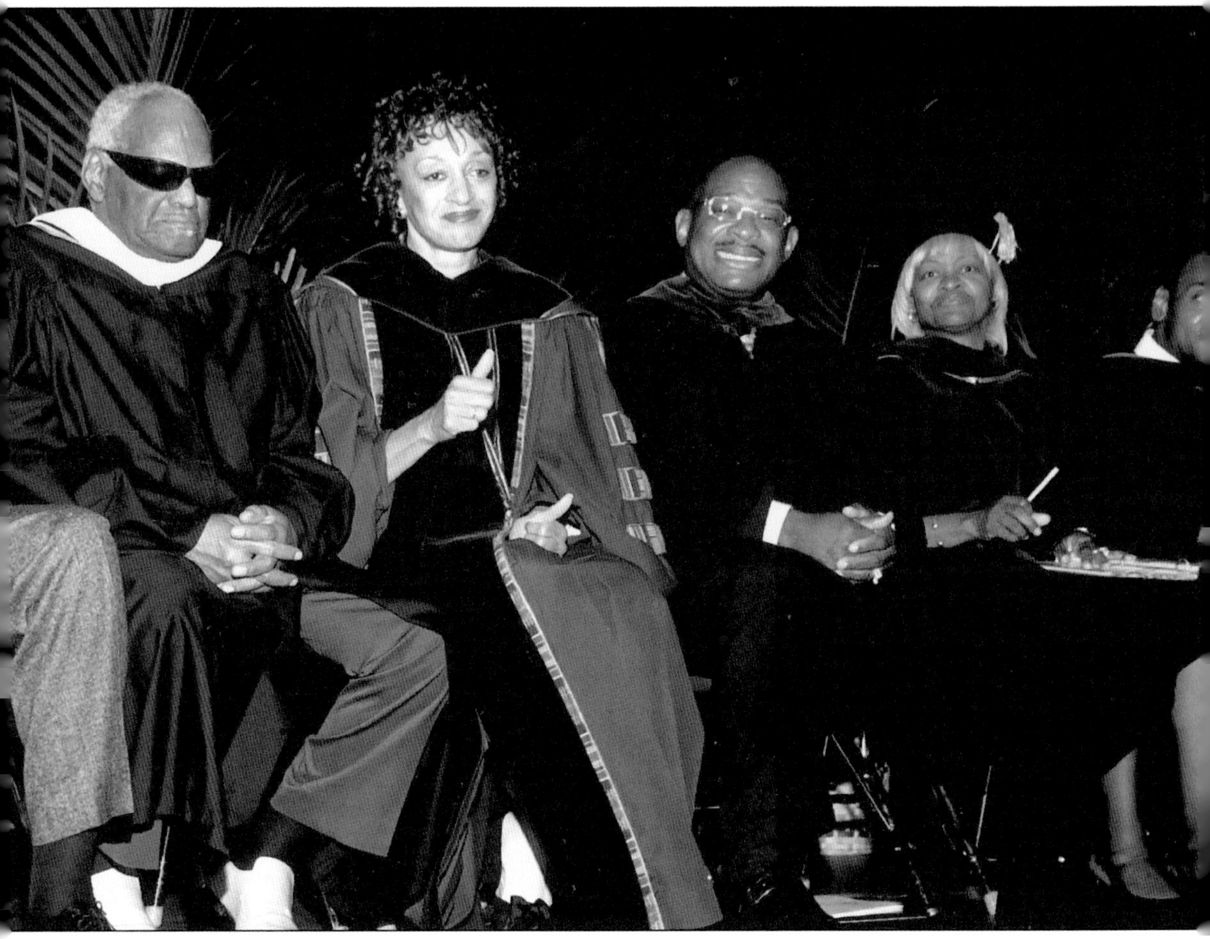

President Shields and famed musician Ray Charles, commencement speaker for Spring 2002, are pictured here. Ray Charles, an Albany native, donated $3 million to ASU to assist students with scholarships and a new fine arts building, which will include a theater named for Aretha Robinson, Charles's mother. Also pictured are Willie Gary, Esq.; Molly Brown, interim vice president for academic affairs, and Dr. Ellis E. Sykes, dean of the College of Arts and Sciences.

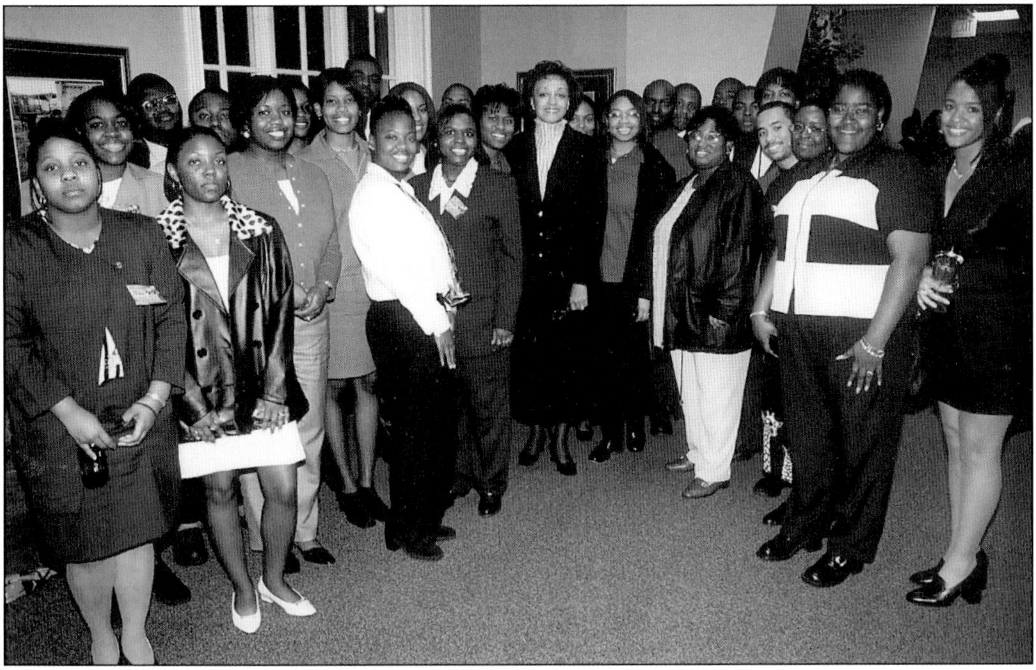

Dr. Shields is pictured with Presidential Scholars enrolled at ASU. Currently, Albany State University has over 80 scholars enrolled.

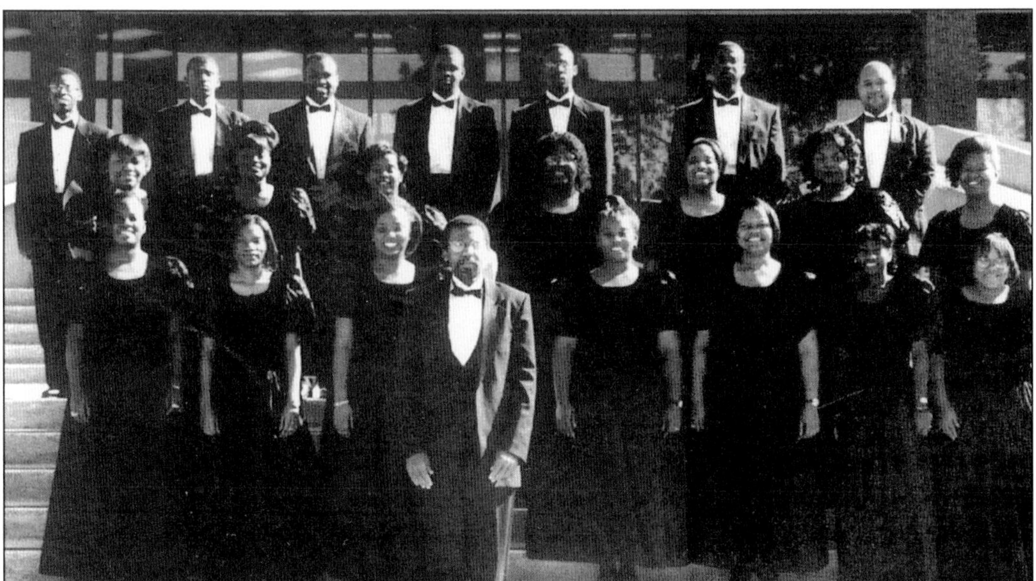

The ASU Concert Chorale, under the direction of Dr. Leroy E. Bynum Jr., toured Europe during the summer of 1997, including the Czech Republic and the former East Germany.

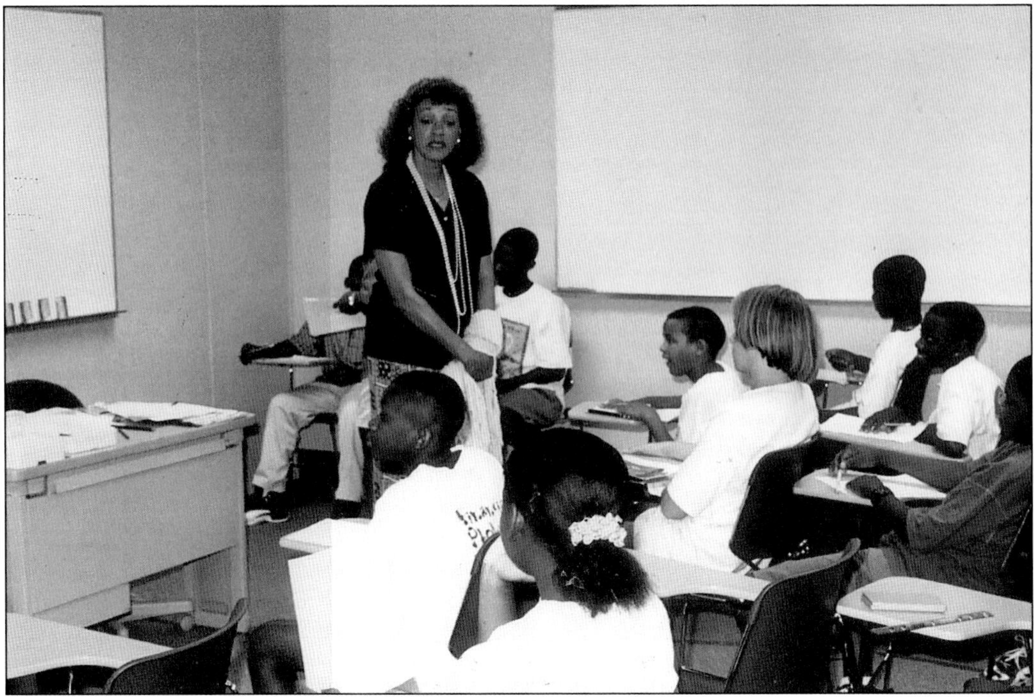

Dr. Shields is seen above with prep students. Below, "Madame President" recruits students from Columbus, Georgia for admission to ASU.

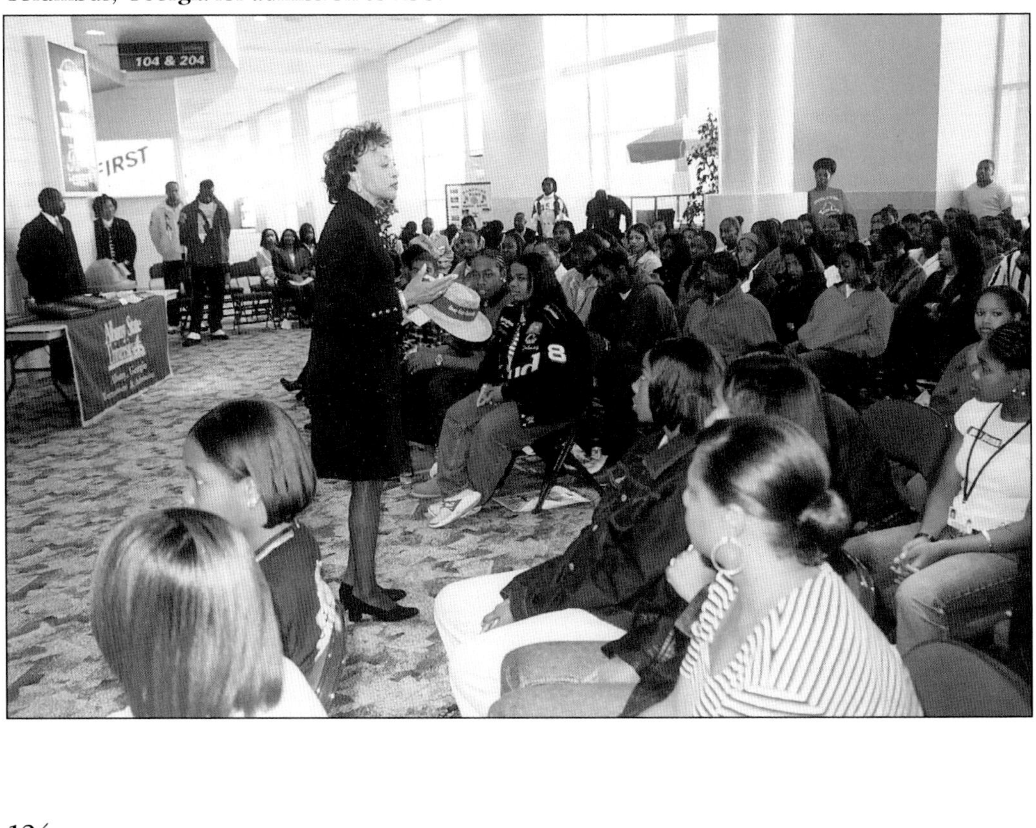

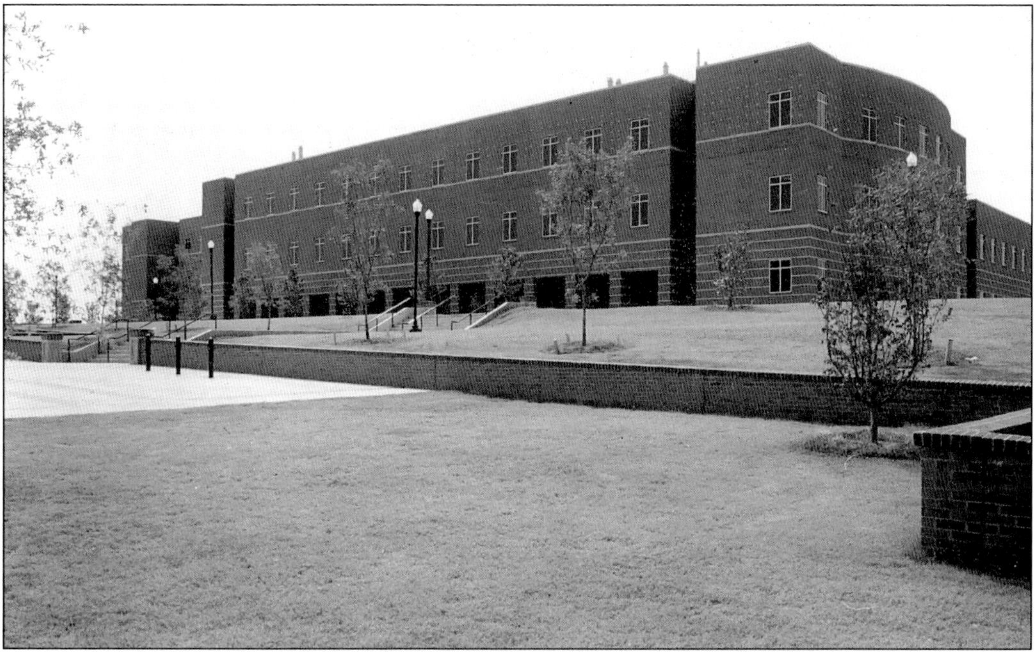

This academic facility currently houses administrative units, the School of Education, general classrooms, military science, the Department of Nursing and Allied Health, and the International Trade Center.

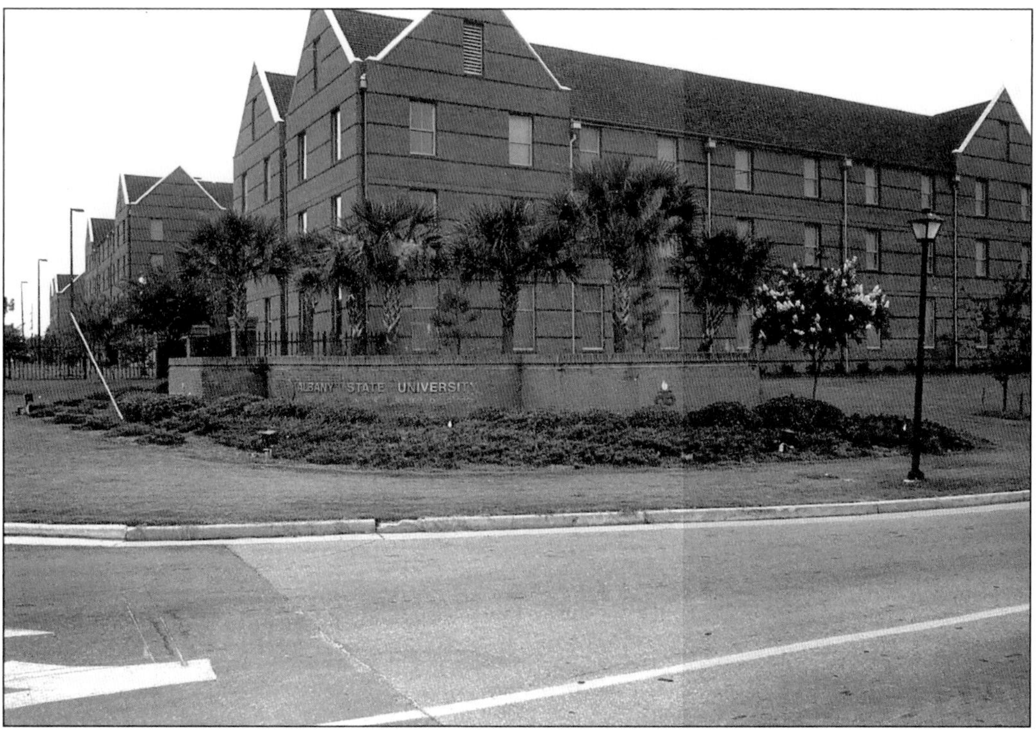

Here are North, South, and East Residence Halls.

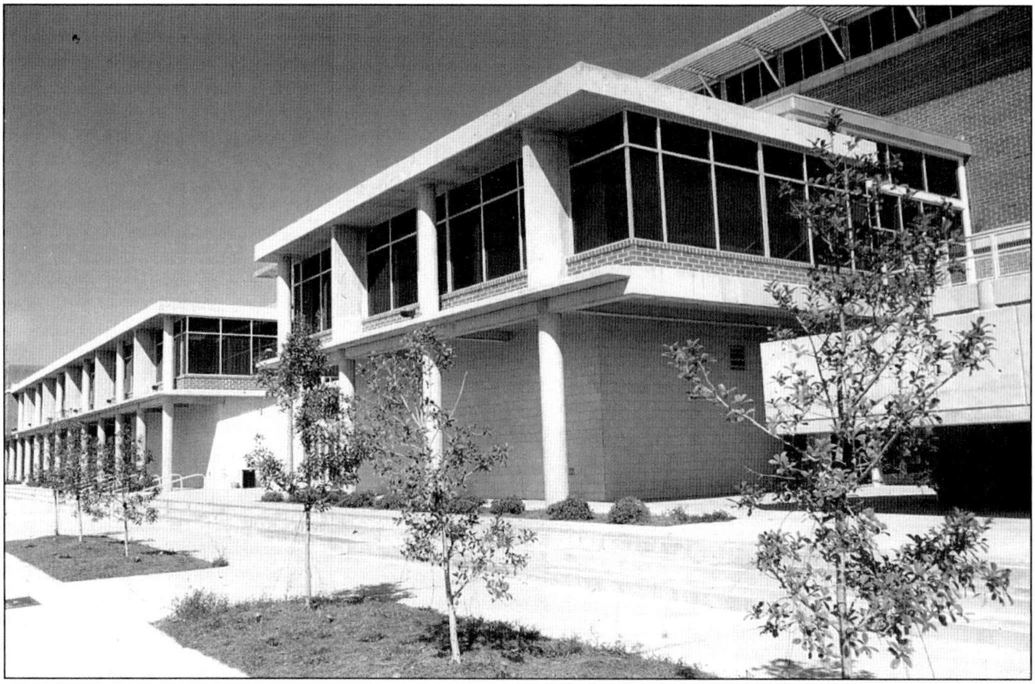

The Health, Physical Education, and Recreation Complex serves as a multi-purpose facility and includes an olympic-size swimming pool, basketball courts, classrooms, and fitness rooms with aerobic areas.

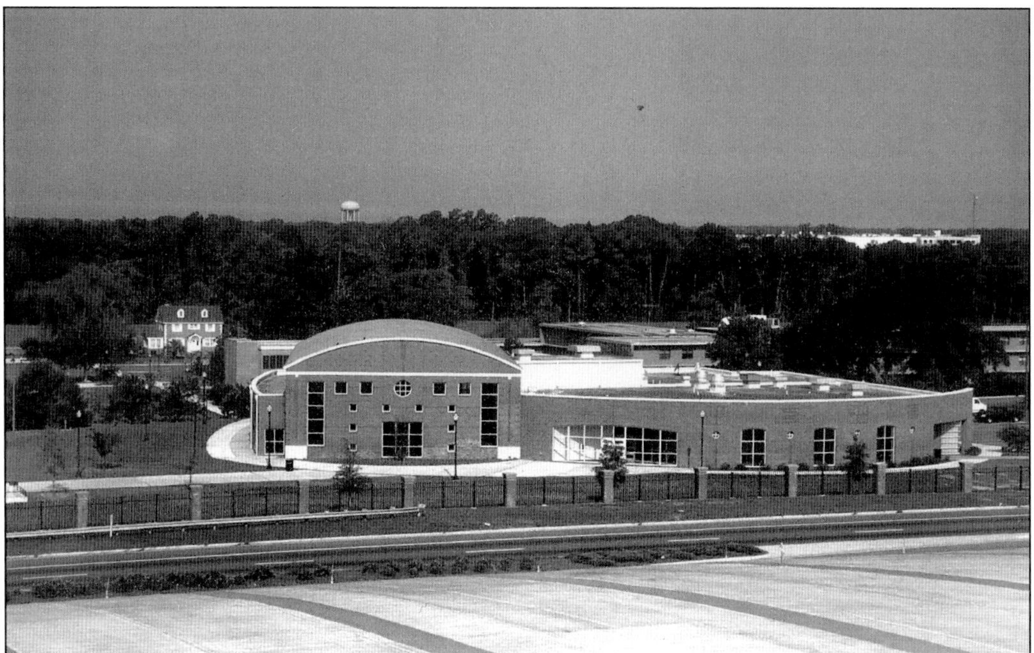

This photograph is of the Dining Hall.

Bibliography

Albany State College. *The Ram*. 1949–1998.

Branch, Taylor. *Parting the Waters: America in King Years, 1954–63*. New York: Simon and Schuster, 1989.

Brown, Aaron. *Retrospects: Briefs from the History of Albany State College*. Albany: 1947.

Brown, Titus. *Faithful, Firm, and True: African American Education in the South*. Macon: Mercer University Press: 2002.

Drinker, Frederick E. *Booker T. Washington: The Master Mind of a Child of Slavery*, Memorial Edition, 1915.

DuBois, W.E.B. *Souls of Black Folk*. New York: New American Library Edition, 1969.

Holley, Joseph W. *Education and the Segregation Issue*. New York: William-Frederick Press, 1955.

——. *What if the Shoe Were on the Other Foot?* New York: William-Frederick Press, 1953.

——. *You Can't Build a Chimney from the Top.* New York: William-Frederick Press, 1949.

Oliver Wendell Holmes Library, Phillips Academy, Andover, Massachusetts.

Orr, Dorothy. *A History of Education in Georgia*. Chapel Hill: University of North Carolina Press, 1950.

Ramsey, B. Carlyle. "The Public Black College in Georgia: A History of Albany State College, 1903–1965." Ph.D. dissertation, Florida State University, 1973.

Zinn, Howard. SNCC *The New Abolitionist*. Boston: Beacon Press, 1965.

Newspapers

The Student's Voice. 1946–2003.
Albany Daily Herald. 1904–1911.
Albany Herald. 1911–2003.
Atlanta Daily World. 1934–1990.
The Southwest Georgian. 1946–2003.